Successful ICT Projects

in

FrontPage 2000

R.S.U. Heathcote

B.Sc.(Hons)

Published by

Payne-Gallway Publishers Ltd
76-78 Christchurch Street
Ipswich IP4 2DE
Tel 01473 251097
Fax 01473 232758
E-mail info@payne-gallway.co.uk
Web site www.payne-gallway.co.uk

2000

Acknowledgements

I am very grateful to Paul Stokes of LightSpeed On-Line Ltd for his help and support in sorting out problems in publishing this web. I would also like to thank Pat and Oliver Heathcote for their help and advice.

Cover picture © "Canisp across Lochan Fada" reproduced with kind permission from James Hawkins
Cover photography © Mike Kwasniak, 160 Sidegate Lane, Ipswich
Cover design © by Tony Burton

First edition 2000

10 9 8 7 6 5 4 3 2 1

A catalogue entry for this book is available from the British Library.

ISBN 1 903112 28 1

Printed in Great Britain by
W M Print Ltd, Walsall, West Midlands

Preface

Projects in FrontPage 2000

Web site designers are in huge demand as the demand for corporate Web sites grows exponentially. Experience in the use of web authoring software, such as FrontPage, could be regarded as almost essential for anyone studying a Computing or ICT course.

FrontPage is a suitable software package for the project component in 'AS' level and Advanced VCE courses. Parts 1 to 2 of the book take the reader through the steps in creating and publishing a Web site both with and without the use of a wizard. Part 3 gives advice on all stages of project work from the definition of a suitable problem through to documentation.

The intended audience

The book was written primarily for 'AS' and 'A' Level Information and Communications Technology students and contains in Appendix B the AQA mark scheme for 'AS' Module 3: Coursework. It will also be suitable for students on many other courses at different levels since the mark scheme, with minor variations, is one which applies to projects in many ICT courses.

For a second year project in an 'A' Level course, data collected from a Web site can be exported and used in an Access database. This aspect could be developed further to fulfill the requirements of, for example, Module 6 of the AQA ICT specification.

The sample project

A sample project is included to show students how a complete project report may be laid out. Students should not assume that this is the only way to write a project report, and above all should use their own ideas and originality and check the mark scheme for their particular course. Moderators will not take kindly to seeing barely-disguised versions of the sample project turning up on their desks!

Contents

Table of Contents

APPENDIX A

Sample Project

APPENDIX B

AQA Project Guidelines

INDEX

Part 1
Using a FrontPage Wizard

Chapter 1 – Planning a Web Site

Objectives

By the end of this chapter you will have learned how to:

➢ plan a Web site

➢ start FrontPage

➢ use a standard FrontPage template

➢ explore different FrontPage views

Web pages and Web sites

By the time you come to read this book you have probably browsed dozens, if not hundreds, of Web sites. Virtually every organization of any size, including businesses, schools and colleges, government organizations and charities all have their own Web site. Thousands of individuals – some famous and others not – also have their own Web sites.

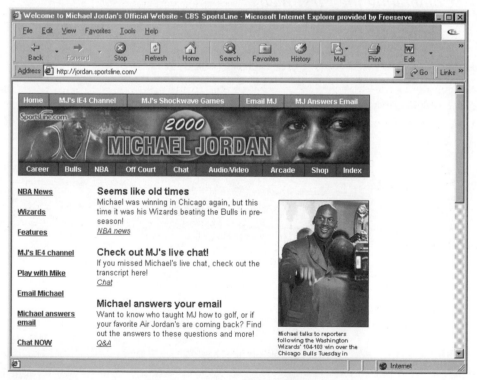

Figure 1.1: A personal Web site

All the millions of web pages around the world are basically similar in construction – they are simply pages of text, graphics and other objects with coded messages telling a browser how to interpret and display them. Some web pages can be opened in a word processor, and in fact many pages were created using word processors, with programmers writing the extra code.

The code is written in HTML ("HyperText Markup Language"), and web pages are HTML files. Using web-authoring software such as FrontPage, you don't have to know HTML since FrontPage writes the code for you. You just have to tell it what you want on the page and how it is to be formatted, in much the same way as you prepare a word-processed document.

Selecting your project

If you have decided to create a Web site for your project work, you may already have an organization or individual in mind for whom you are going to build the site. If not, then you should look for a real user who would like you to build one for them.

There are several important questions you need to ask before you embark on building a Web site. The most important ones are:

1. Who is the target audience?
2. What is the site designed to accomplish?

The more clearly you focus your site on the answers to these two questions, the more successful your site is likely to be.

Planning the Web site structure

Once you have settled on a project, the next step is to use paper and pencil and perhaps Post-it notes to design an outline of each page in the Web site and how they all link to each other (see Figure 4.1). You will have a better idea how to set about this once you have been through the steps of creating a practice Web site using FrontPage, so we'll come back to that after you have worked through the first sample FrontPage project.

Downloading the graphics you need

The next three chapters cover the design and implementation of a new Web site. Before you start, you may want to download all the photographs that are used in the web and store them in your own folder. You can download them from www.payne-gallway.co.uk/frontpage. In this book, all the pictures for both sample projects are stored in a folder called **Photos**.

The sample project

The Highland Holiday Company has approached you to ask you to design a Web site for them. This small independent company rents a charming cottage called Holly Cottage in the Scottish Highlands with more cottages to be on offer soon.

The target audience for the Web site consists of:

- Families and groups looking for a relaxing holiday break;
- Ramblers and country-lovers.

The Holiday Company hopes that the Web site will achieve the following objectives:

- increase the number of weeks that the cottage is rented out in a year;
- help them to establish a reputation for this type of holiday break;
- help them to gather feedback from past customers.

A rough outline of the proposed Web site is shown below.

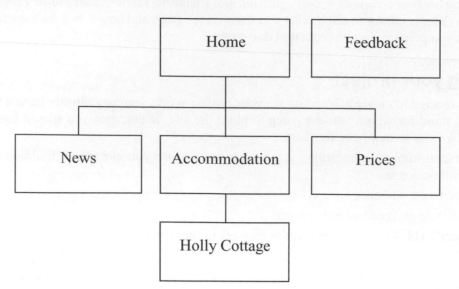

Figure 1.2: Outline of the HHC Web site

Loading FrontPage

Time to get started! You need to have Microsoft Windows 95 or a later version and Microsoft FrontPage 2000 on your computer.

- Click the **Start** button and choose **Programs, Microsoft FrontPage**.

Your screen should appear as shown below:

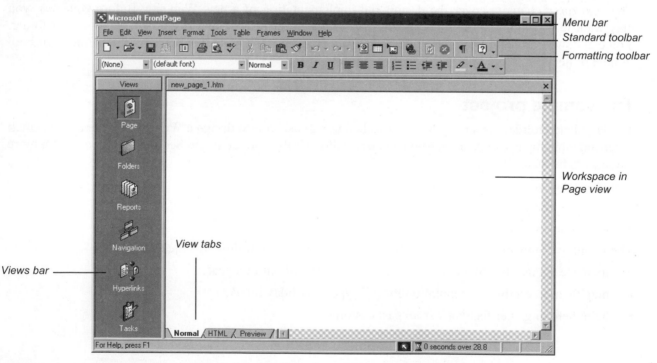

Figure 1.3: The FrontPage 2000 opening screen

The Views bar to the left of the workspace contains a set of icons which you can click to change the view of your work. (If your screen looks different from the one shown above, click the **Page** icon on the Views bar to switch to Page view.)

FrontPage terminology

In FrontPage terminology, the set of pages that make up your Web site are known as a **web**. It does not become a **Web site** with a capital W until it is stored on a Web server ready to be viewed by other people.

Every web has a **Home page**, which is the page that viewers will normally find first. Generally this serves as a 'Welcome to this Web site' page, gives a name, address and phone number and has links to the other pages in the web. Each and every page on the World Wide Web is a separate file containing a mixture of text, graphics, sound, animations and other objects. The pages in a web usually contain **hyperlinks** to other pages in the web or to pages on someone else's Web site.

Using a wizard

FrontPage has a number of built-in wizards to help you create various common types of Web site. Using a wizard takes a lot of the hard work out of creating a web but you may find there isn't one that creates just the layout you had in mind. However, you can always customize the basic layout that the wizard gives you. You should check out the various wizards and templates to see what is on offer. For this sample project, we'll use the **Corporate Presence** wizard.

- From the **File** menu select **New**, **Web**.
- A dialogue box will appear. Click the **Corporate Presence wizard** icon.
- In the **Specify the location of the new web** box, enter the name of the drive and folder where you would like your new web to be stored. By default all the webs that you create will be stored in a folder called **My Webs**. Each web will be saved in a subfolder – for example in the screenshot below, all the files making up the pages of the new web will be saved in a folder called **HHC**, which is a subfolder of **My Webs** on the C: drive. The folder that you specify will be created automatically by FrontPage.

Your screen should appear as shown in Figure 1.4:

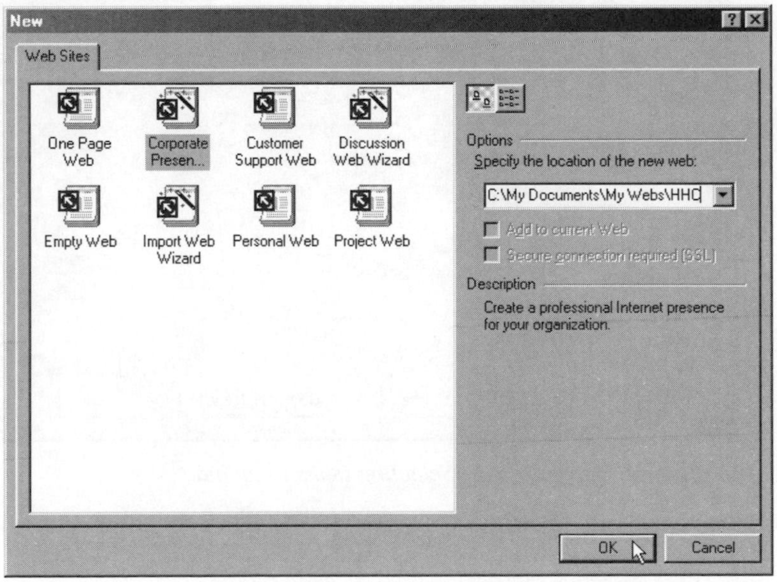

Figure 1.4: Choosing a wizard and specifying the web's location

- Click **OK**. FrontPage displays the first dialogue box for the Corporate Presence Web wizard.
- Click **Next**. The following dialogue box is displayed:

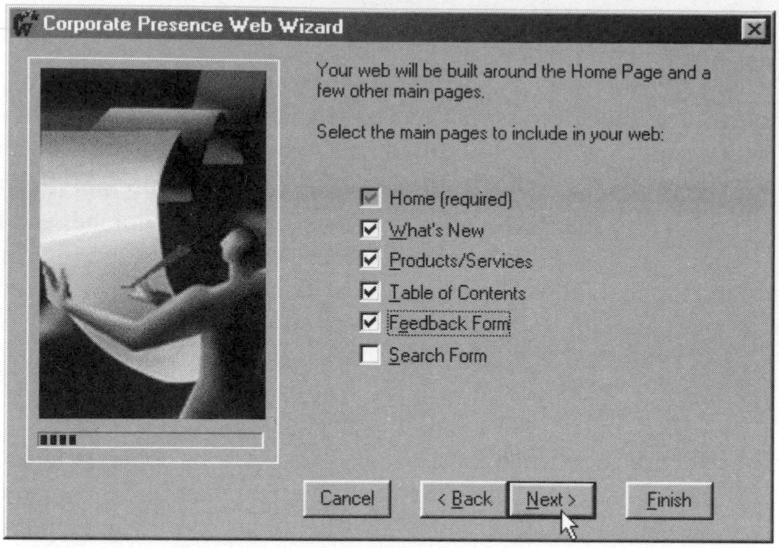

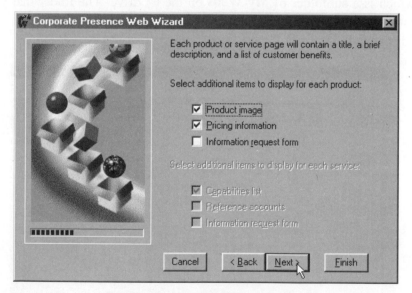

Figure 1.5: Selecting pages for the web

- Deselect **Search Form** and leave all the other options selected. Click **Next**.
- Select **Introduction**, **Company Profile** and **Contact Information**, and deselect **Mission Statement**. Click **Next**.
- Select **Articles and Reviews** and deselect **Web Changes** and **Press Releases**. Click **Next**.
- Enter *1* for the number of products and *0* for the number of services. Click **Next**.
- In the next dialogue box, select the options as shown in Figure 1.6, and then click **Next**.

Figure 1.6: Selecting items to include

- Select all the options except **Job Title** and **Company Affiliation** for the Feedback form. Click **Next**.

- Select **Yes, use tab-delimited format**. This will enable you to store the names and addresses in a database so that you can mail them using a mail-merge. Click **Next**.
- Select **Use bullets for top-level pages** and click **Next**.
- Fill in the next dialogue box as shown below:

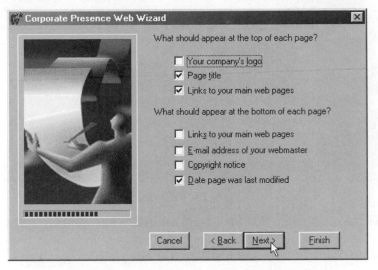

Figure 1.7: Selecting information to appear on every page

- Click **Next**.
- Select **Yes** to see the **Under Construction** icon on unfinished pages. Click **Next**.
- Type *Highland Holiday Company* as the name of the company, *HHC* as the one-word version and *Inverness* as the address. Click **Next**.
- Enter information as shown below in the next dialogue box – or make up your own, if you prefer. Click **Next**.

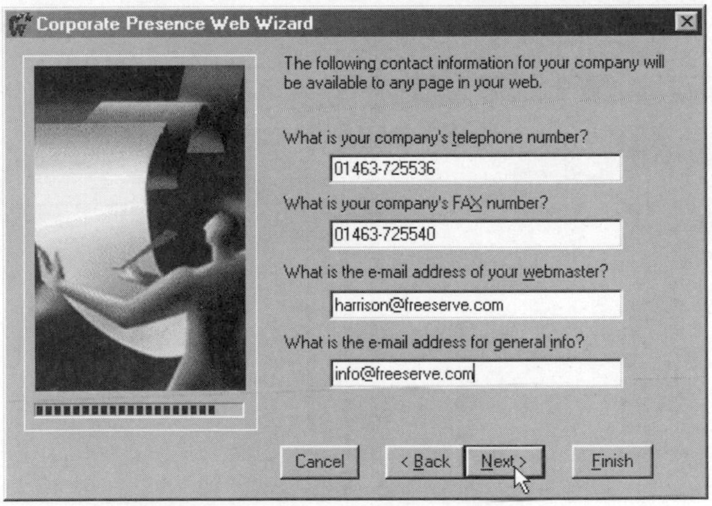

Figure 1.8: Specifying contact information

- Click **Next** without choosing a web theme. We will apply a theme later – in the meantime the default Corporate Presence theme will be applied to the web.
- Click **Finish** in the wizard's final dialogue box. FrontPage switches to Tasks view as shown below:

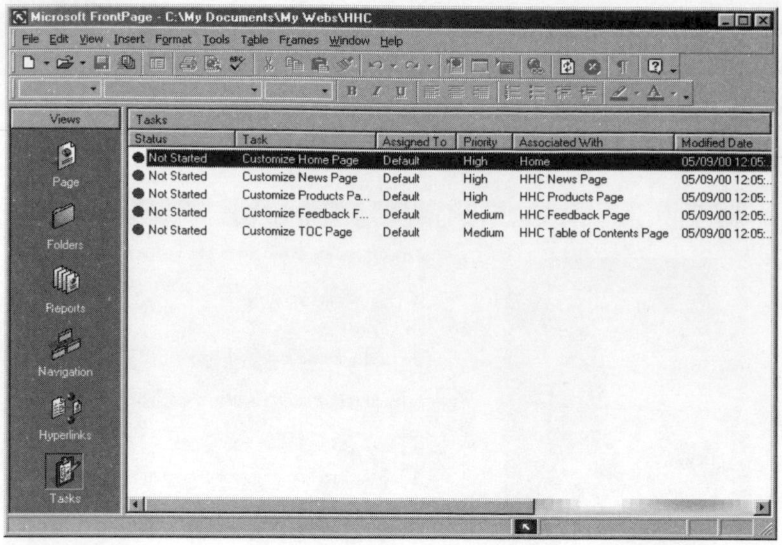

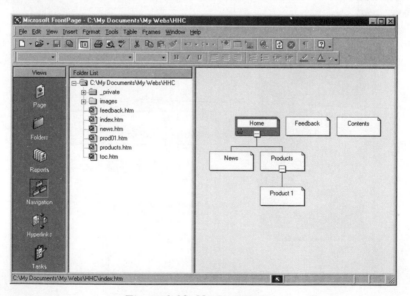

Figure 1.9: Tasks view

The Tasks view shows the main pages that the wizard created, with a priority and a status for each task to help you keep track of what has and hasn't been done. To help with the management of a project, you can add tasks to the list as you think of them and mark them as completed when done.

Navigation view

- On the Views bar, click the **Navigation** button.

You should now see the structure of the Web site so far. You need to have some sort of plan of how you want your Web site to look. It is unlikely that the wizard will have created exactly the layout that you want so in the next chapter you will see how to change things about.

Figure 1.10: Navigation view

- Close the web by clicking **File**, **Close Web** on the main menu.
- **Save** your web when prompted.
- Exit FrontPage by click **File**, **Exit** on the menu.

Chapter 2 – Organising a Web

Objectives

By the end of this chapter you will have learned how to:

➢ add and delete pages to and from a web

➢ move and rename pages in a web

➢ edit web pages

➢ apply a theme to a web page

➢ use navigation bars

➢ preview web pages in FrontPage or in a web browser

Creating the web structure

The quickest way to create the basic structure of a web is by using a wizard as described in Chapter 1. However, you may have to add, delete or move pages to suit your specific needs. The best way to do this is in Navigation view.

• Load FrontPage if it is not already loaded and open the **HHC** web by clicking **File, Open Web** on the main menu.

• Select the **HHC** web folder and click **Open**.

• Make sure that you are in **Navigation** view as shown in figure 2.1. If necessary, click the **Navigation** button in the Views bar.

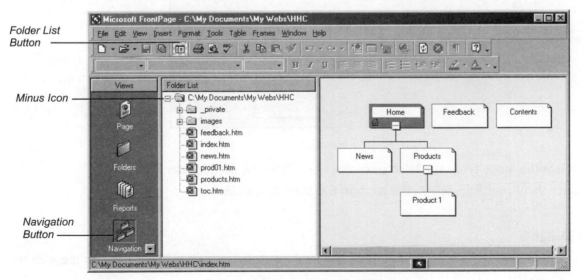

Figure 2.1: Navigation view

FrontPage displays your web as a hierarchical structure. This makes it easy for you to see the links between pages.

Each page in the structure represents a corresponding file that has automatically been created by FrontPage. These can be seen in the Folder List on the left of the screen. If you cannot see this, click on the **Folder List** button on the Standard toolbar.

> **Note:** You may find that some of the titles on the pages in Navigation view vary from the filenames given to these pages in the Folder List. E.g. the filename of the Home page is **index.htm**.

You will notice a minus icon on every parent page, i.e. a page that has links below it in the hierarchy. This icon will collapse all of its child pages when clicked and a plus icon will appear.

* Click the minus icon on the Products page and you will see its child page disappear.

Notice that the News page remains because it is a peer page. (This means it is on the same level in the hierarchy; check Figure 1.10.)

* Click the plus icon to expand the Products page again.

Deleting pages

Now that you know the basics of the navigation view, you can delete one of the pages that you don't need. This web is really too small to need a Contents page so it can be deleted.

* Click on the page labelled **Contents**.
* Press the **Delete** key.

You will see a dialogue box asking if you want to remove the page from the navigation bars or from the entire web. Removing the page from the navigation bars will keep the original page for later use but remove links to it so it is in effect deleted from the web, as it is inaccessible from the remaining pages.

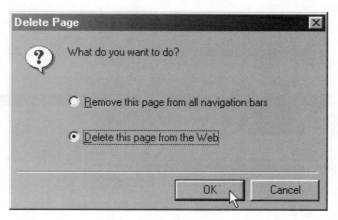

Figure 2.2

* Select **Delete this page from the Web** since this file will not be needed later.

You will notice that FrontPage deletes the **toc.htm** file from the Folder List.

Adding pages

Although a Contents page is not really necessary it would be useful to have a Prices page on the web so that people can check the prices of the cottages.

* Click the Products page to select it.
* Select **File**, **New**, **Page**.

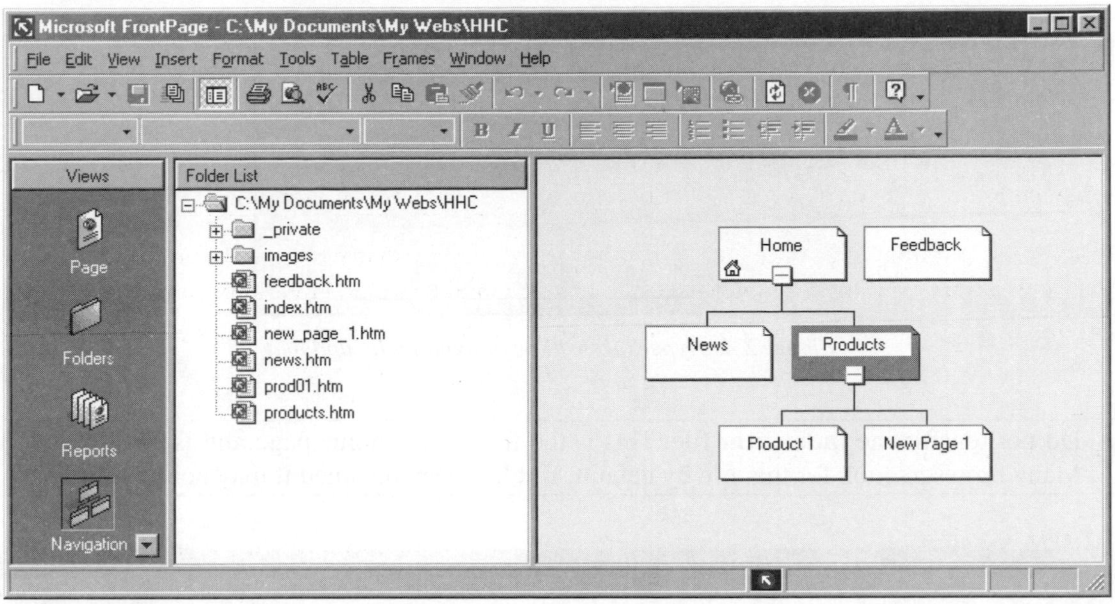

Figure 2.3: Adding a new page

A new page called **New Page 1** will appear as a child of the Products page and its associated file (**new_page_1.htm**) will appear in the Folder List. If it does not appear instantly, try clicking the **Refresh** button on the Standard toolbar.

New pages will always appear as children of the selected page. If no pages are selected, the new page will appear as a child of the Home page by default.

Renaming pages

Pages have a Name and a Title. The name of the page is the filename. The title is the name that appears on the page in Navigation view. It is also the title that users of the page will see at the top of the Web page in a browser.

The Name and Title of the new page are not very meaningful so they need to be changed.

- Right click on **New Page 1** and select **Rename** from the shortcut menu. (Although this menu option is called re*name* it will actually just change the title!)

- Type in *Prices* and press **Enter**.

- Repeat the steps renaming the **Products** page *Accommodation* and the **Product 1** page *Holly Cottage*.

The next step is to change the actual file names. It is best to give each file a name that closely matches the page title in order to keep track of what the file contains.

- Right-click the **new_page_1.htm** file and click **Rename**.

- Rename the file *Prices.htm* and press **Enter**.

- Repeat the steps renaming the **prod01.htm** file *Holly.htm*. The **Products** file can stay as it is.

- You will get a dialogue box appear asking you if you want to update the hyperlinks to the page. Click **Yes**.

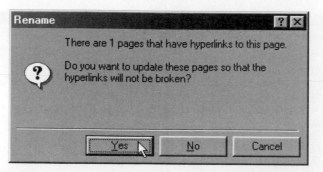

Figure 2.4: Hyperlinks will be automatically updated

Note: Do not rename the **index.htm** file. This is the file for the home page and is must be left as it is. Many browsers look for this file by default. If it has been renamed it may not be found.

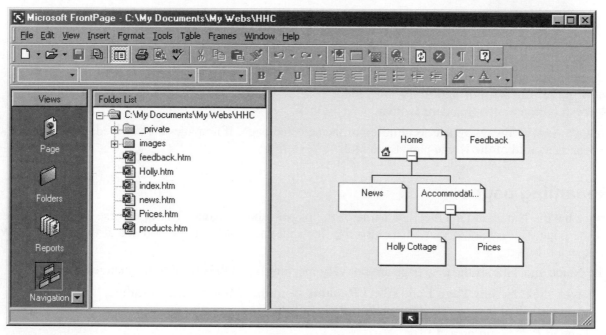

Figure 2.5: Renamed Accommodation page

Moving pages

Ideally you want the Prices page on the same level as the Accommodation page since it will eventually contain prices of all the cottages available for rent.

- With the mouse, click and drag the Prices page over towards the right of the Accommodation page. A faint link will appear in different places as you drag the page across the hierarchy (see Figure 2.6).

- Position the page below the Home page on the same level as the Accommodation page and let go of the mouse button to hold it there.

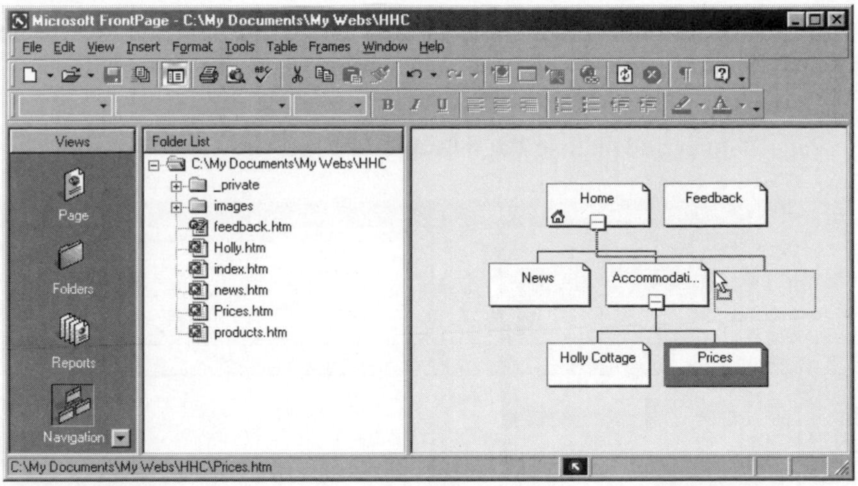

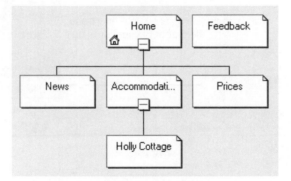

Figure 2.6: Moving pages

Your new web structure should now resemble Figure 2.7:

Figure 2.7: The edited web structure

Page view

In Page view, you can look at what the wizard has actually created on each of the web pages.

- Double-click the Home page and this will take you straight to Page view and display the page contents.

The Normal tab

There are 3 tabs at the bottom of the page labelled **Normal**, **HTML** and **Preview**. You will learn about the others later in this chapter but for now all you really need to use is the **Normal** tab which lets you add, delete and edit items on the page.

Editing the Page Banner

The Page Banner is the text and graphic that goes across the top of each page. This usually contains the page title.

You may want to rename the Page Banner currently saying '**Home**' because your viewers are going to know it is the home page and they will need something more specific, like the name of the company.

- To see more of the page on the screen, you can close the Folder List by clicking the **Folder List** button on the toolbar.

The page below is shown without the Folder List.

- Right-click the Page Banner and choose **Page Banner Properties...**

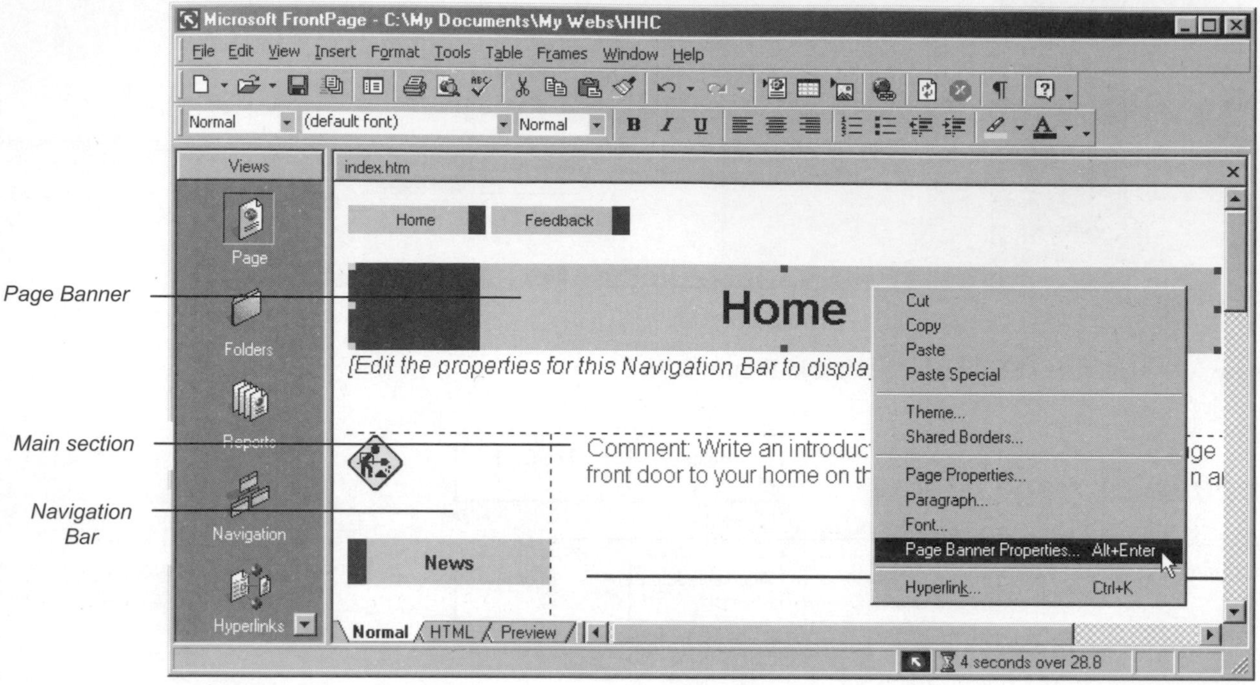

Figure 2.8

- You will see a small dialogue box in which to rename the Banner. Type in **Highland Holiday Company** and click **OK**.

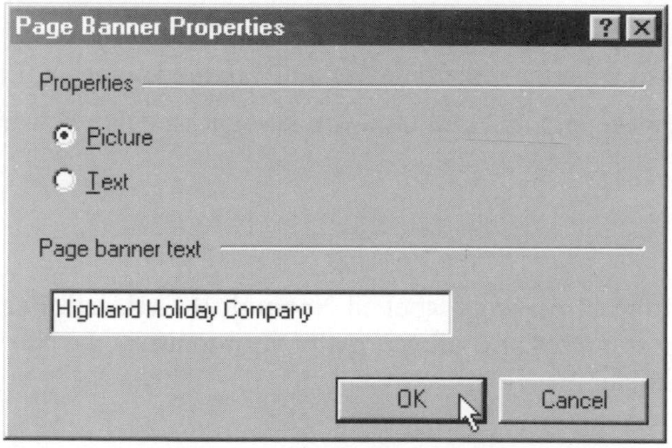

Figure 2.9: Changing Banner text

The new title will be displayed at the top of the page.

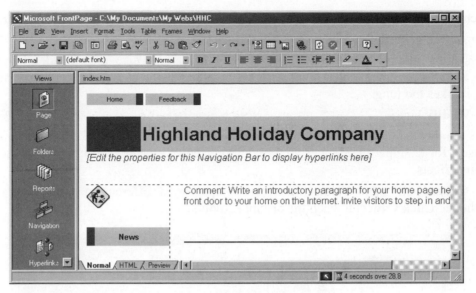

Figure 2.10

Changing the page theme

Changing the page theme will give it a new look. Themes apply a set of colours and styles to each object on the page, and you can either change the theme for the entire web or for individual pages. However, it is not always a good idea to change the theme on individual pages because it detracts from the unified look which tells viewers that they are still looking at the same site.

- Click **Format**, **Theme** on the main menu.

- The theme is currently set to **Straight Edge**. Change it to **Sumi Painting**.

Notice that as you scroll down the list of available themes, an example appears in the window.

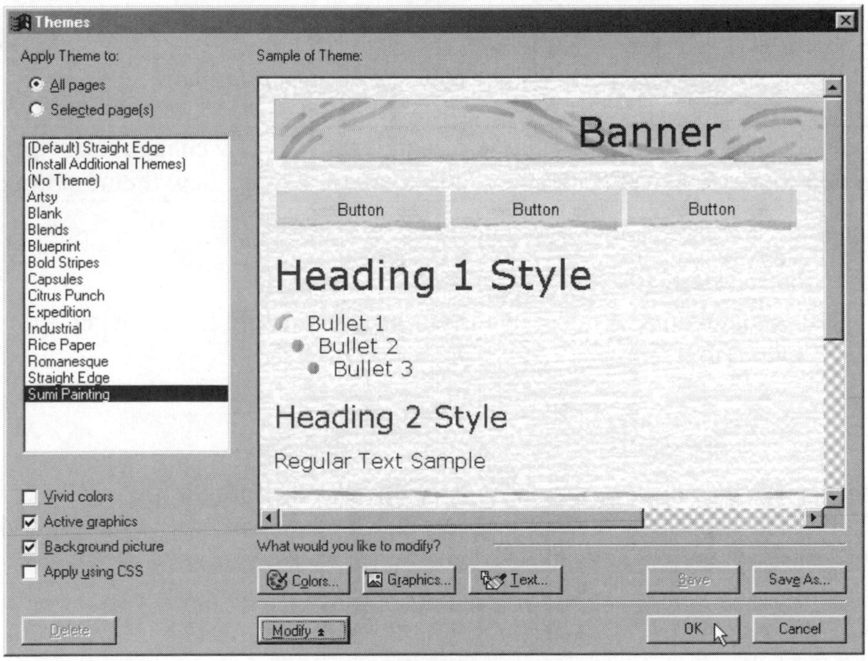

Figure 2.11: Changing a theme

There are 4 check boxes under the list of themes. These apply different effects to the themes.

- Select the **Active graphics** and **Background picture** boxes.

These settings add a little more colour and life to a web but you must take into consideration that the more graphics you add to a page, the longer it will take to download on the viewer's computer. This can be very frustrating if it takes too long.

- Click the **Modify** button.

This displays another 3 buttons that allow you to change the theme's colour scheme, text styles and the graphics it uses, for example the Banner picture, buttons, etc. You can experiment with these options to see the various effects.

- Click the **Colors** button and try out the effects of applying a different colour scheme to the selected theme. Click **Cancel** to keep the original colours.

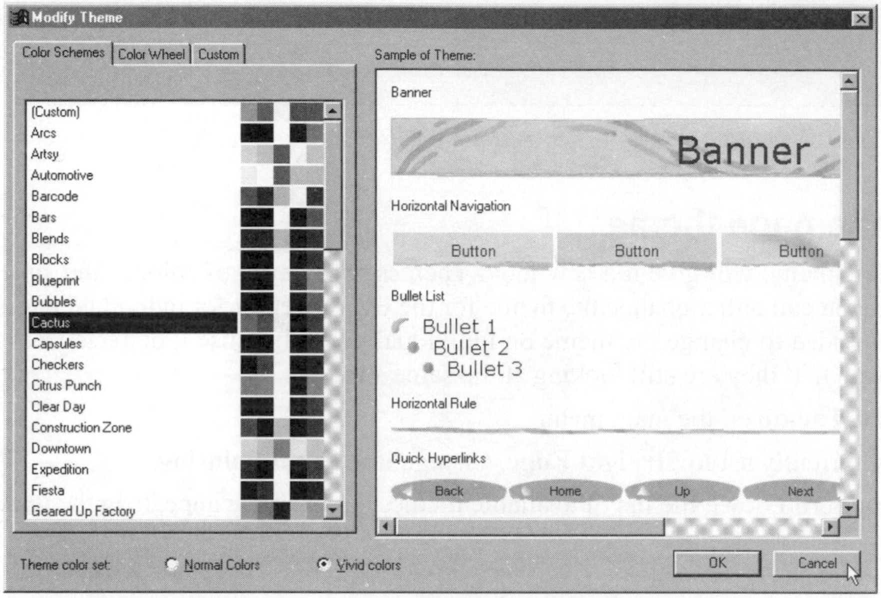

Figure 2.12: Changing the theme colour scheme

> **Note:** Themes are read-only. This means that you cannot permanently change the settings of a theme, so if you do make any changes FrontPage will ask you to save the new theme settings to a new file.

- Click **OK** and then click **Save** on the **File** menu to save your changes.

This will now apply the selected look to the entire web.

If you wanted to change the theme on just the current page you could have clicked the **Selected page(s)** option at the top of **Themes** dialogue box.

Saving

It is important that you save your work regularly. As with any other program this helps prevent accidental loss of work but an added importance in FrontPage is that some features that you can add to a page won't work properly until they are saved.

It is a good idea to get into the habit of making a quick save after you have made any major modifications.

> **Note:** The **Save** command only applies to the current page you are editing. If you want to save all the pages in your web, you have to save each one individually.

Navigation bars

You will notice that there are several buttons already on the page. These are placed on what FrontPage refers to as **Navigation Bars**. These enable the viewer to go to a different page when the appropriate button is clicked.

Navigation bars

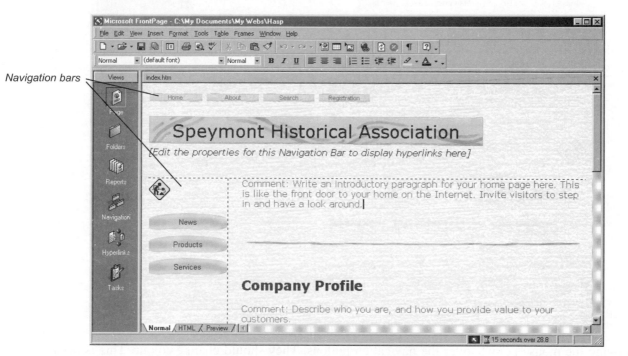

Figure 2.13: Navigation bars

While you are building a web you go to other pages by holding down the **Control** (**Ctrl** on some keyboards) key and clicking a button on a Navigation bar. The mouse pointer will change to a pointing finger. This is only applicable when you are in Normal view.

- Try holding down **Ctrl** and clicking on the **News** button. You should be taken to the News page.
- To go back to the Home page, hold **Ctrl** and click on the **Home** button in the top left of the page.

The Preview tab

- To see the web page as viewers will see it, click the **Preview** tab at the bottom left of the page near the **Normal** tab.

You will now find that you don't need to hold down **Ctrl** any more when you click a navigation button. This is because the Preview view is trying to simulate what people will see when they log on to your site. Several of the comments visible in the Normal view, and the dotted boundary lines around the borders, will have disappeared.

Preview in Browser

This option lets you view the web exactly as your viewers will see it. It will only work if you have a browser already installed on your computer.

- Click the **Preview in Browser** button on the toolbar.

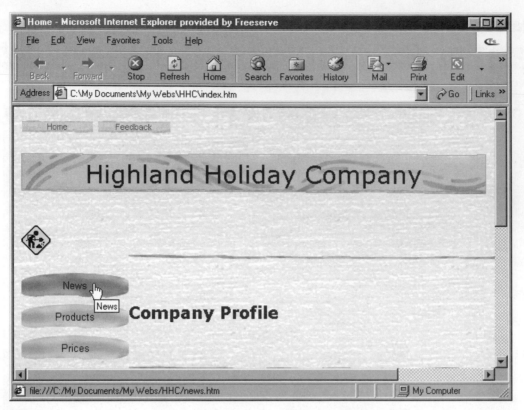

Figure 2.14: Preview in Browser mode

Try moving the mouse pointer over the navigation buttons. They should change colour. This is because the Active Graphics option was selected when the new theme was applied.

- Close the browser window to return to FrontPage.

> **Note:** If you use Internet Explorer 5 or a later version, you will usually see the same as in Preview mode. Some other browsers may give you a slightly different view.

The HTML tab

The other tab at the bottom of the page is the HTML tab. This shows all the underlying code that is automatically generated by FrontPage as you work. You can click on the tab to have a look but you should never change anything unless you know exactly what the outcome of your changes will be!

- **Save** and **Close** your web.

Chapter 3 – Completing the First Web

Objectives

By the end of this chapter you will have learned how to:

➢ import picture files into your web

➢ add thumbnail images

➢ insert tables into a web page

➢ create hyperlinks between pages

Editing content

Now we can look at adding some proper content into the web.

● Make sure that the **HHC** web is open by selecting **File**, **Open Web** from the main menu.

● Select the **HHC** web folder and click **Open**.

● Open the **Home** page (called **index.htm**) in **Page** view.

● Scroll down the page until you can see where it says **Company Profile**.

This is one of the headings that you asked FrontPage to add to the Home page in the wizard in chapter 1. Beneath the heading are some comments on what to include on the page. These comments are placeholders and should be deleted and replaced with your own text.

● Highlight the first comment by clicking on it and replace it with the text shown below:

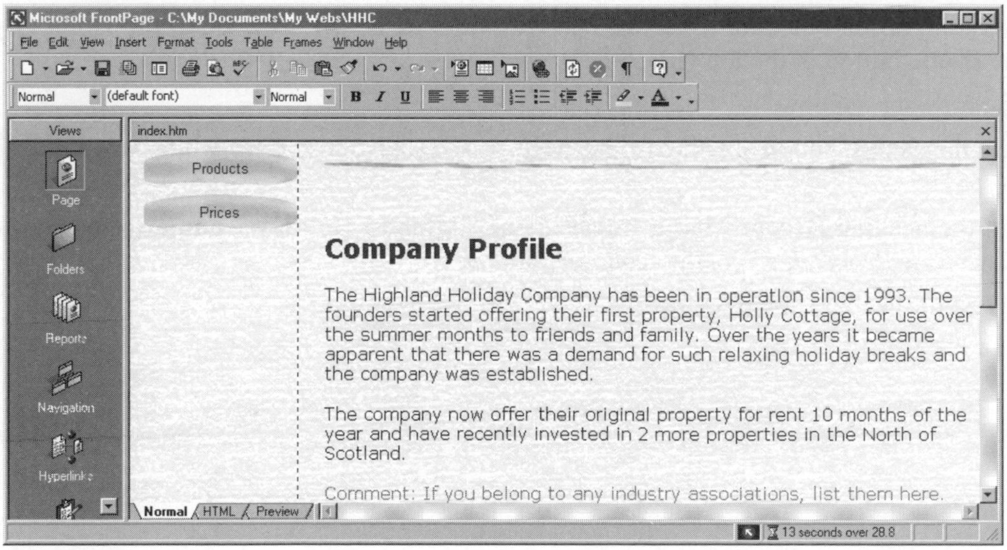

Figure 3.1

- Highlight and delete the remaining comments on the page using the **Delete** key. You may want to remove some of the extra lines as well.
- Highlight the yellow and black **Under Construction** icon and delete this too.
- **Save** the web.
- Preview the page using the **Preview in Browser** button.

Figure 3.2

- Try navigating around the site using the **Navigation** buttons. To get back to the Home page press the **Home** button in the top left of the pages.
- **Close** the browser window.
- Ctrl-click the **News** button on the Home page. (i.e. Hold down **Ctrl** while you click the button.)
- Highlight the heading **Recent Media Coverage of Highland Holiday Company** and replace it with *Two New Properties Shortly Available to Rent*.
- Add the rest of the text shown below:

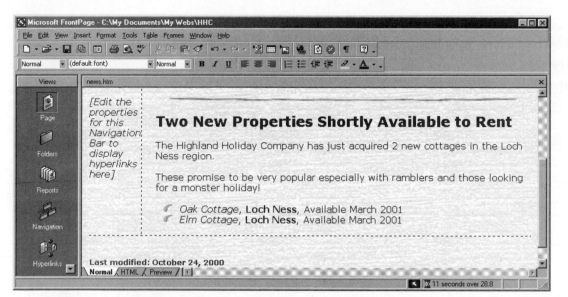

Figure 3.3

- Ctrl-click the **Accommodation** button and enter the following content:

Figure 3.4

Now Ctrl-click the **Holly Cottage** name or button. They are both links to the Holly Cottage page.

Importing files

This page would really be brightened up if it had a picture on it. Before we insert a graphic, it is important to know that FrontPage assumes that all the files to be inserted are already part of the site and would show up in the Folder List. If you cannot see the Folder List press the **Folder List** button now.

Note:	Pictures for this exercise are available on the Payne-Gallway Web site at www.payne-gallway.co.uk/frontpage.

You will notice that there is a folder called **Images** already in the list. This is automatically created by FrontPage for every Web site. It is here that all the graphic files should be stored.

- To add a file to this list, click the **Images** folder.

- Select **File**, **Import** from the main menu.

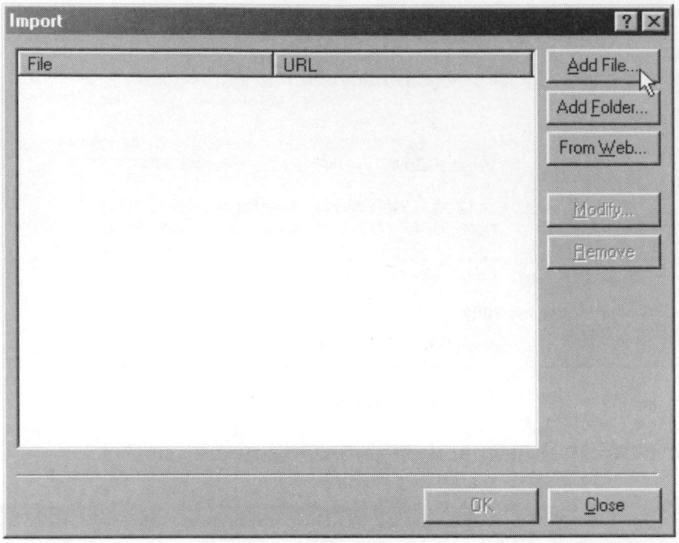

Figure 3.5: Importing a file

- Click the **Add File** button and you will be able to browse through the file directory on your computer for the correct graphic.

Figure 3.6: Selecting a file to import

- Move to the folder where your files are saved.

- Select **Farley.jpg**, hold down **Ctrl** and click **Ullapool.jpg**.

- Click **Open** to add them to the **Import** List.

- Click **OK** on the Import window. Your files should appear in the **Images** folder in the **Folder List**.

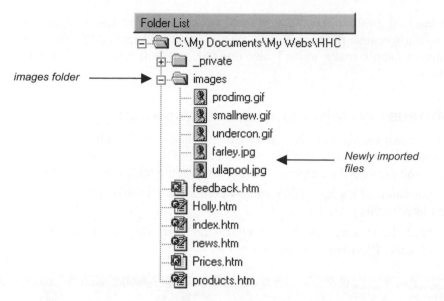

images folder ──────────▶

Newly imported
files ◀──────

Figure 3.7: The Folder List

Now that the images we need are contained in the site, they can be inserted.

Inserting photographs

In this page you can add a picture of the cottage.

- Making sure that you have the **Holly Cottage** page open, click the **Product Image** graphic and press **Delete**.

- Delete the comment too.

- The mouse cursor should be just under the dotted line near the top of the page. Select **Insert**, **Picture**, **From File**.

- Double-click the **Images** folder to open it and select the **Farley.jpg** file. Click **OK**.

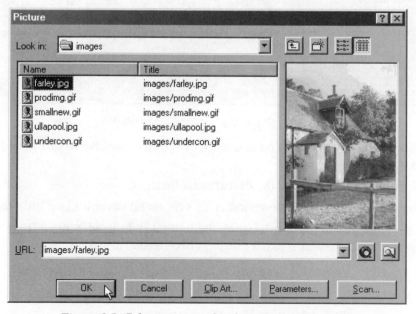

*Figure 3.8: Selecting a graphic from the **Images** folder*

The picture will be inserted into the page. It is probably going to appear much bigger than you actually want it. The photo will also cause the page to take much longer to download to the viewer's computer. Since making it smaller won't make it load any quicker, we will solve this problem by adding a Thumbnail of the photo.

Adding thumbnails

Thumbnails are scaled-down versions of a photo which will load very quickly and provide enough of the image for the viewer to tell what it is. If they choose to see more they can click on it and it will expand to its full size. This gives the viewers the flexibility to look only at the things they are interested in.

You cannot make a thumbnail of a graphic that already contains hyperlinks, hotspots or animation. All of these will be covered later in this book.

- Firstly you will need the Pictures toolbar on your screen. If you cannot see it, right-click another toolbar and select **Pictures** from the list.

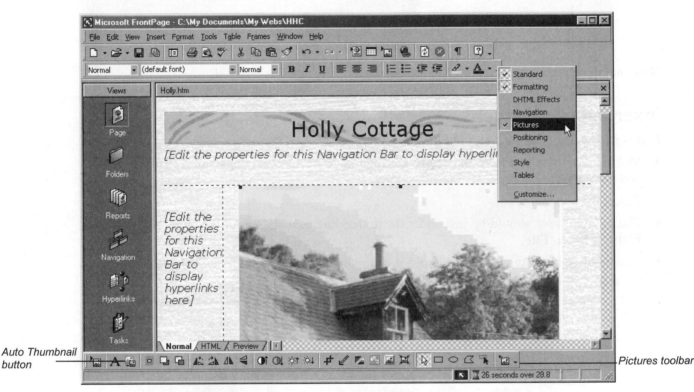

Figure 3.9: Displaying the Pictures toolbar

- Select the picture by clicking on it. You can tell it is selected because it will have little black handles around it.
- Click the **Auto Thumbnail** button on the **Pictures** toolbar.

The picture will shrink to a much smaller version. This version however looks a little *too* small.

- Increase the size of the Thumbnail by dragging the bottom-right handle away from the picture slightly. The mouse cursor will turn into a diagonal two-headed arrow.

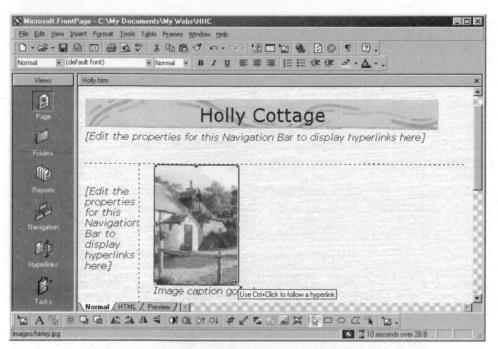

Figure 3.10: The graphic reduced to a Thumbnail

- Replace the text **Image caption goes here** with *Click photo to see more*.

Now you can add some or all of the following text about the cottage. There is no need for you to type out all the text unless you want to finish the web properly.

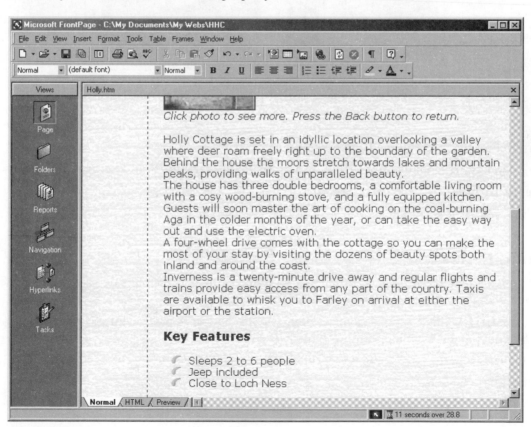

Figure 3.11

- Highlight the **Pricing** header and the table at the bottom of the page and delete them.
- **Save** the page. You may see a window pop up asking if you want to save embedded images. Click **OK**.
- Press the **Preview in Browser** button.
- Try clicking on the thumbnail image. What happens? How do you get back to the Web site?

The only way back to the HHC site from the expanded picture is by clicking the **Back** button on the Browser toolbar. This information should be included in the page text. Details like this are extremely useful to the inexperienced user.

Figure 3.12

- Return to FrontPage to edit the Holly Cottage page.
- Where you have entered the photo caption, add **Press the Back button to return**.
- **Close** the **Browser**.
- **Save** the web page.

Inserting tables

The pricing table that was deleted from the bottom of the Holly Cottage page needs to be recreated on the Prices page with the prices of the new properties.

- Using the **Ctrl + Click** action, navigate your way to the Prices page from the Holly Cottage page by clicking the **Up** button followed by the **Prices** button.
- With the cursor in the page content area, click the **Insert Table** button.
- Select a **4 by 4** table by dragging the mouse over the cells in the option box.

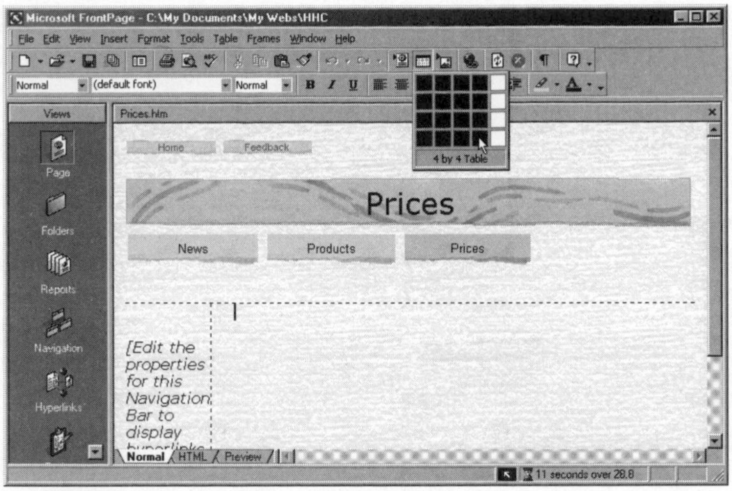

Figure 3.13: Inserting a table

This will create a table of 4 rows and columns. Complete the table as shown below:

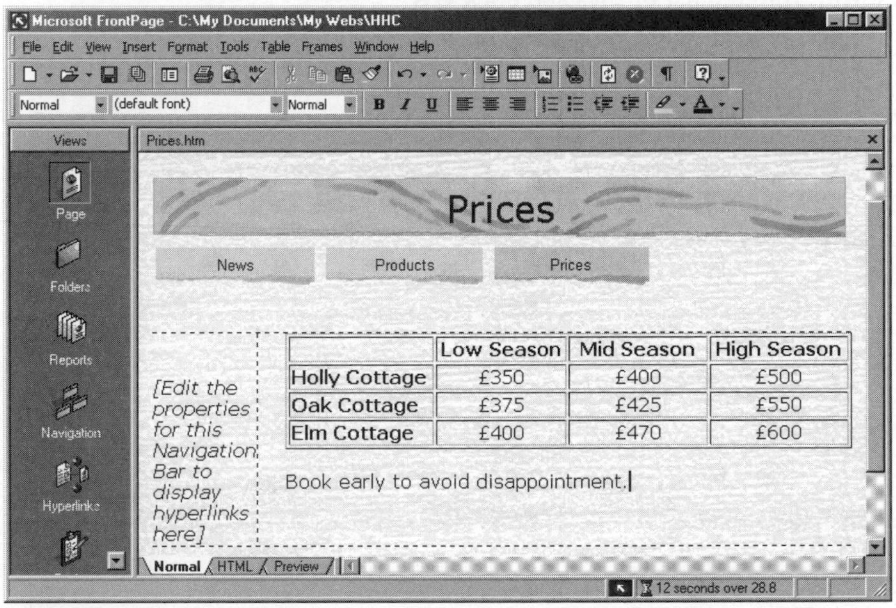

Figure 3.14

- **Bold** the headings and **Center** the prices.
- **Save** the page.

Creating a hyperlink

When you navigated your way from the Holly Cottage page to the Prices page you had to go via another page. Ideally the site needs a link directly from the product to the price.

- Go back to the Holly Cottage page.
- Scroll down to the bottom of the page and type **Check Prices** underneath the Key Features.
- Highlight **Check Prices** and click the **Hyperlink** button on the Standard toolbar.

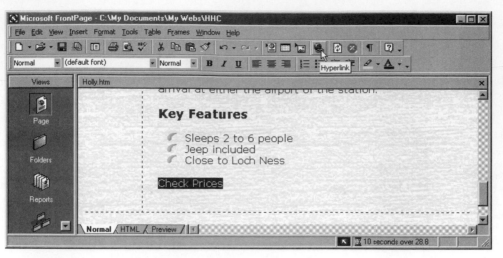

Figure 3.15

The **Create Hyperlink** window will appear.

- Select **Prices.htm** from the list of files and click **OK**.

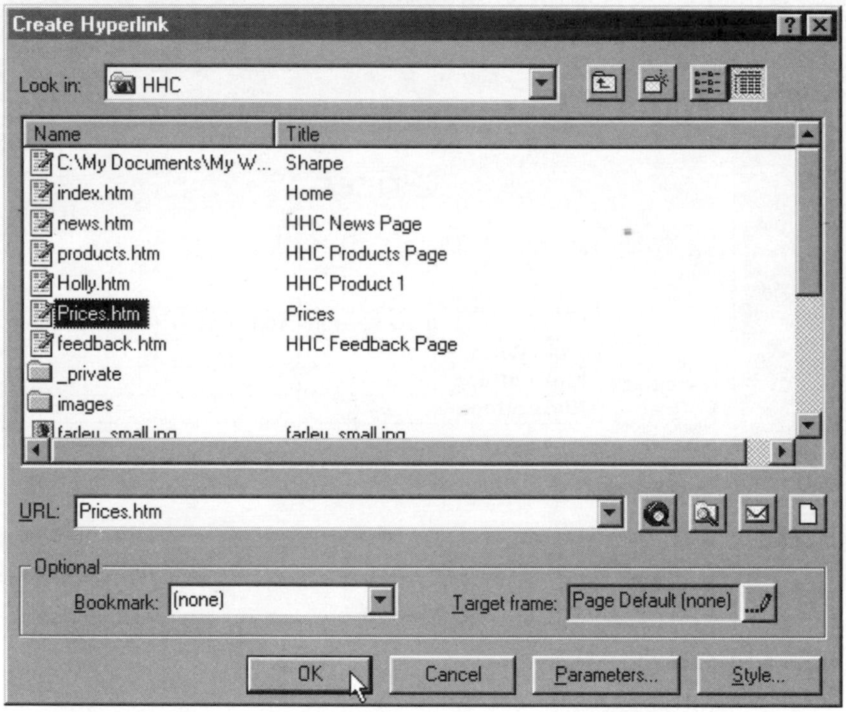

Figure 3.16: Creating a hyperlink

The **Check Prices** text will change to blue underlined text. This is a standard style on many Web sites for hyperlinked text.

- **Save** the current page. (Without saving, the new hyperlink will not work.)

- Click the **Preview in Browser** button to test your new hyperlink and view your web.

The only page that has not been edited is the **Feedback** page. This page is used to collect comments from viewers which are then submitted to you by e-mail. The **Submit** function won't actually work unless you have published your web with a Web Presence Provider that has got FrontPage Server Extensions. If you try it without you will see the following message:

The best way to plan a Web site is to use Post-it notes to represent different pages so that you can move them around as you alter the structure.

A rough outline of the proposed Web site is shown below.

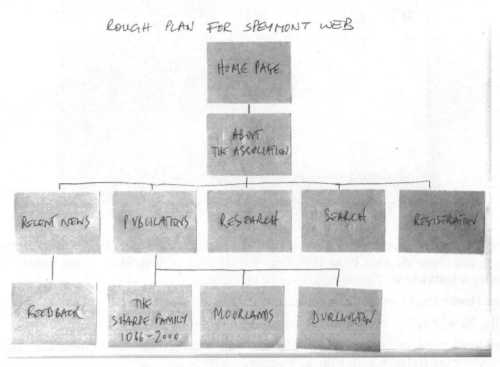

Figure 4.1: Outline of the HASP Web site

Getting started

There is no particular order in which you should build a web. You can either build it page by page or make all of the pages and build them up from there. This book will take the second option by creating the structure of the web as designed in the figure above.

- Click **File**, **New**, **Web** on the main menu.

- Select the **One Page Web**. In the box labelled **Specify the location of the new web:** type *C:\My Documents\My Webs\Hasp* (or select the folder where you intend to store your new web. **My Webs** need not be a subfolder of **My Documents**).

- Click **OK**.

Figure 4.2

> • Click the **Navigation** view button. You will see that FrontPage has already given you a Home page since you chose the **One Page Web** from the selection of Web Sites. In the **Folder List**, its filename is **index.htm**. This should *never* be changed.

- Select the **Home Page** icon in the right hand pane.

- Click **File**, **New**, **Page**. A new page will appear called **New Page 1**.

- In the left hand pane, you should see the filename **new_page_1.htm** in the Folder List. (If it is not there, click the **Refresh** button on the Standard toolbar.

- In the right hand pane, right-click the new page and **Rename** it **About**. Press **Enter**.

- **New_page_1.htm** in the Folder List should automatically be renamed **About.htm**. (If it is not, right-click the file name and **Rename** it *About.htm*.)

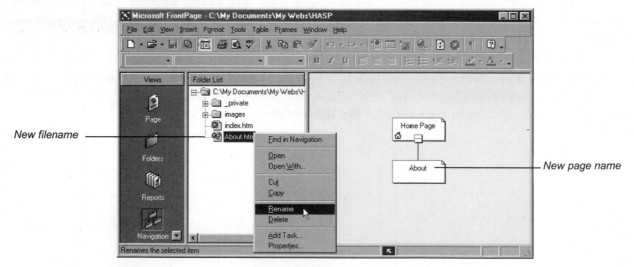

Figure 4.3: Renaming files

You need to create more pages to add to the structure.

- Click the About page in the right hand pane to select it.

- Add 5 new pages, the details of which are given below. Make sure that you remember which files correspond to which pages. You don't want the page titled 'News' to be given the filename **search.htm**, which can easily happen if you are not methodical.

  The pages are to be renamed: News

                                         Products

                                         Research

                                         Search

                                         Registration

- Rename the filenames with the following names:

                                         News.htm

                                         Products.htm

                                         Research.htm

                                         Search.htm

                                         Registration.htm

  Make sure that you remember to add the extension **.htm** to each file.

- Click the Products page in the right hand pane to select it.

- Create 3 new pages by clicking the **New Page** button 3 times.

  These will be renamed: Sharpe

                                         Moorlands

                                         Durlington

- Click the **Refresh** button. You should see that the files automatically appear with the following names: if not, then rename them manually.

                                         Sharpe.htm

                                         Moorlands.htm

                                         Durlington.htm

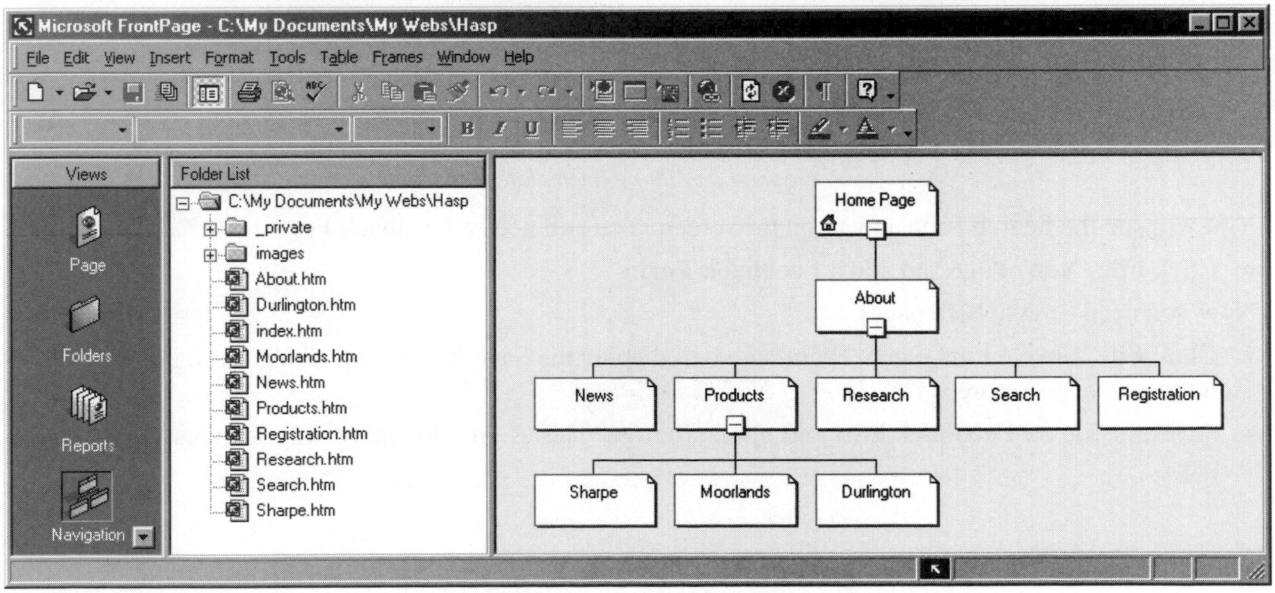

Figure 4.4: The web structure

Editing the structure

If you make a mistake in the positioning of the pages, you can drag them to the correct position.

If you want to delete a page, delete it from the Folder List and it will automatically remove the page from the right hand pane. We will delete the Search page because it will be created below in another way.

- Click the **Search.htm** file in the Folder List to select it.
- Press the **Delete** key.
- Click **Yes** in the Confirm Delete window.

Using a template to create a page

FrontPage can give a helping hand in setting up the remaining pages (the Search and Feedback pages). It has several types of web page that already have the right page layout for what we need to do, so we can borrow a layout for each of these pages.

- Double-click on the **Home** page. You will go to Page view.
- Click **File**, **New**, **Page** from the menu.
- Select **Search Page** and click **OK**.

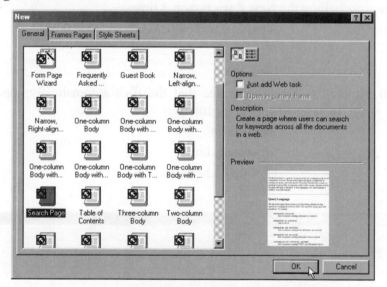

Figure 4.5: Adding a template page

You will see the Search Page appear on the screen. You still need a Feedback Form.

- Click **File**, **New**, **Page** and add a **Feedback Form**.

Now you need to save both pages.

- Click **File**, **Save** on the menu. FrontPage will display the Save As window since this page has not been saved before.
- Save the file as **Feedback.htm** and click **Change**. This is an alternative way to rename the page.

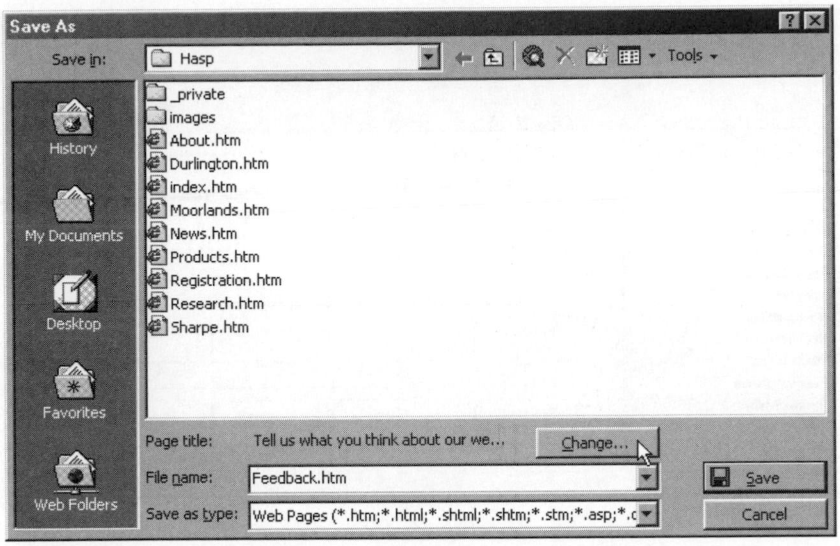

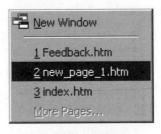

Figure 4.6

- Type **Feedback** and click **OK**.

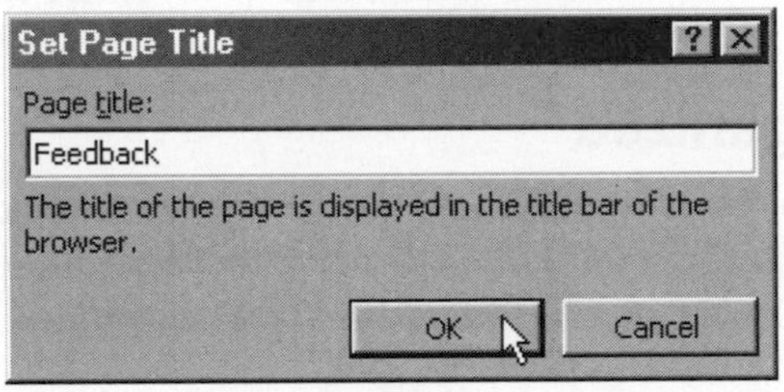

Figure 4.7

- Click **Save** in the **Save As** window.

Now you can save the Search form.

- Click on **Window** on the main menu and select **new_page_1.htm**. New Page 1 will appear in the window.

Figure 4.8

- Click **File**, **Save** and save this page as **Search.htm**. Click **Change** to change the page title to **Search**.
- Go back to **Navigation** view.
- Click and drag the **Feedback.htm** filename onto the page hierarchy and make it a child of the News page. (Move it about until its connection line goes to **News**.)
- Drag the **Search** page in the same way to the page hierarchy between the Research page and the Registration page.

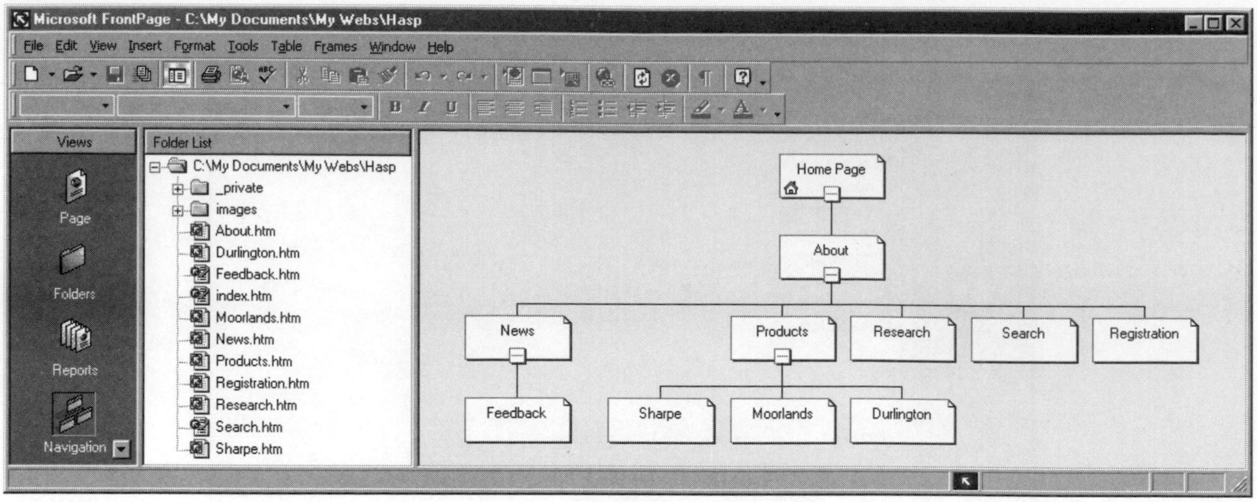

Figure 4.9

You should now have completed the hierarchy as shown in figure 4.9. The next stage is to add content to the pages.

- If you are finishing here for the day, choose **File**, **Close Web**. Exit FrontPage.

Keeping your files organized

As you develop what may be a fairly sophisticated Web site with pages containing text, photographic images, Java applets, database forms etc., you will need to keep things tidy. In the same way as you organize different types of document in subfolders of **My Documents**, you need to work out a logical folder structure.

When you install FrontPage 2000, it automatically creates a folder called **My Webs**, in which any webs that you create will be stored by default. Each separate web that you create will be stored in a subfolder of **My Webs**.

At least 3 different folders will be automatically created in which FrontPage saves web pages and files. Understanding these folders and knowing when you should create new ones will help you to keep your work organized.

Here are the folders that you will see in the Folder List:

Folder name	Purpose
Main Folder	Default folder for all web files
_private	FrontPage stores files of its own in here. Do not mess with this folder!
Images	Save all your graphic images in here.

You can create new folders to hold, for example, Java applets. We will be doing this in Chapter 10. The main thing to remember is that if you want to move files between folders, you *must* do this in FrontPage and not Windows Explorer, because FrontPage will then automatically update the links to the pages you have moved.

Chapter 5 – Working with Frames

Objectives

By the end of this chapter you will have learned how to:

➢ create a frames page

➢ add a background graphic

➢ change the Frame colours

➢ remove borders and scroll bars

Frames

You need to decide whether there are going to be any common elements on all the pages making up your site, such as a border, colour scheme, header etc. These can then be designed and displayed on all pages.

There are two ways of achieving this – one, through the use of frames, and two, through the use of shared borders, which will be covered in Chapter 13. The decision of whether or not to use frames is an important one and one which you should be prepared to justify. Turn to Chapter 13 for a further discussion of the pros and cons of frames and shared borders. The **Hasp** web will be built using frames.

A Frames page is a page that can contain two or more web pages and display them simultaneously. Within the frames page are your pages of content and any other sections of a page (such as a heading and navigation bar) that you may want displayed.

• Load FrontPage 2000 and open the web **Hasp** created in the last chapter.

Creating a Frames page

• Click the **Page** view icon.

• Select **File**, **New**, **Page** and click the **Frames Pages** tab.

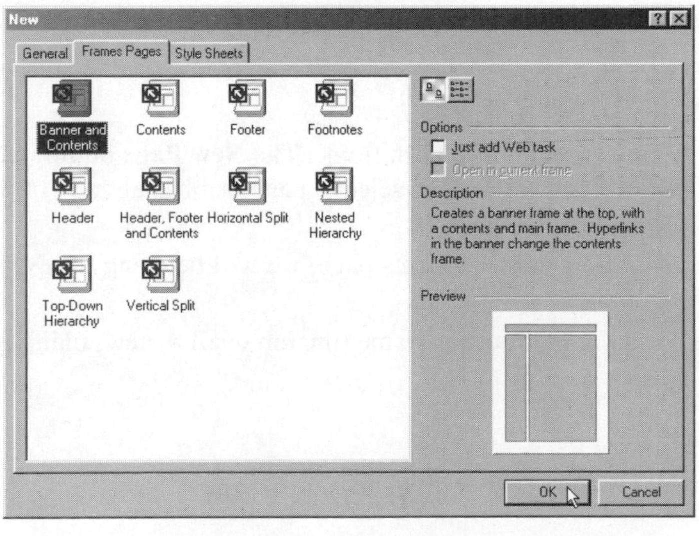

Figure 5.1: Creating a Frames page

- Select the **Banner and Contents** page and click **OK**.

A new page will appear which is divided up into three sections. The top frame, the Banner, will be where the organisation's name will appear. This frame will always be visible. The left frame, Contents frame, will also be constantly visible and contain the contents of the web and links to other pages. The main section will change according to which page the viewer has selected to look at.

In total, FrontPage will have four pages open at the same time - the Frames page, Banner page, Contents page and the Main page. It is usually best to minimize the number of pages you use in a Frames page. Frames increase the download time of each page and this can get frustrating for the viewer if it takes too long.

Understanding Frames

Frames pages can often get confusing. To help you understand the Frames page used in this web, the diagram below illustrates it:

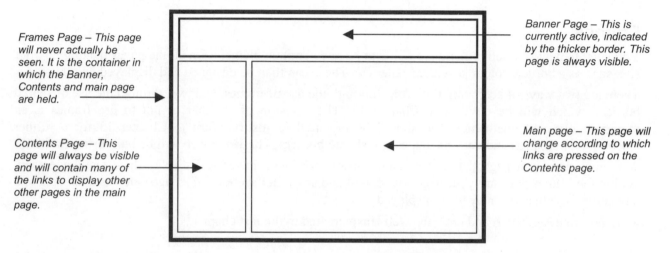

Figure 5.2: Understanding frames pages

Any of the pages in a Frames page can be scrolled separately. Thus if the user scrolls down the main page, the other pages (e.g. Banner and Contents) will remain stationary. This is one of the major differences, from the site visitor's point of view, between frames and shared borders. With shared borders which are part of the page, when you scroll down, everything scrolls.

Customising the Frames page

You will notice that there are two buttons in each frame. The **New Page** button will create a new page for that frame, and the **Set Initial Page** button will select a page that has already been created to show in the frame when the Frames page is first opened.

As we have not yet created a Banner or Contents page, we will be using the **New Page** option for these two frames.

- Click the **New Page** button in the **Banner** frame (the top one.) A new, blank page will appear in the frame.

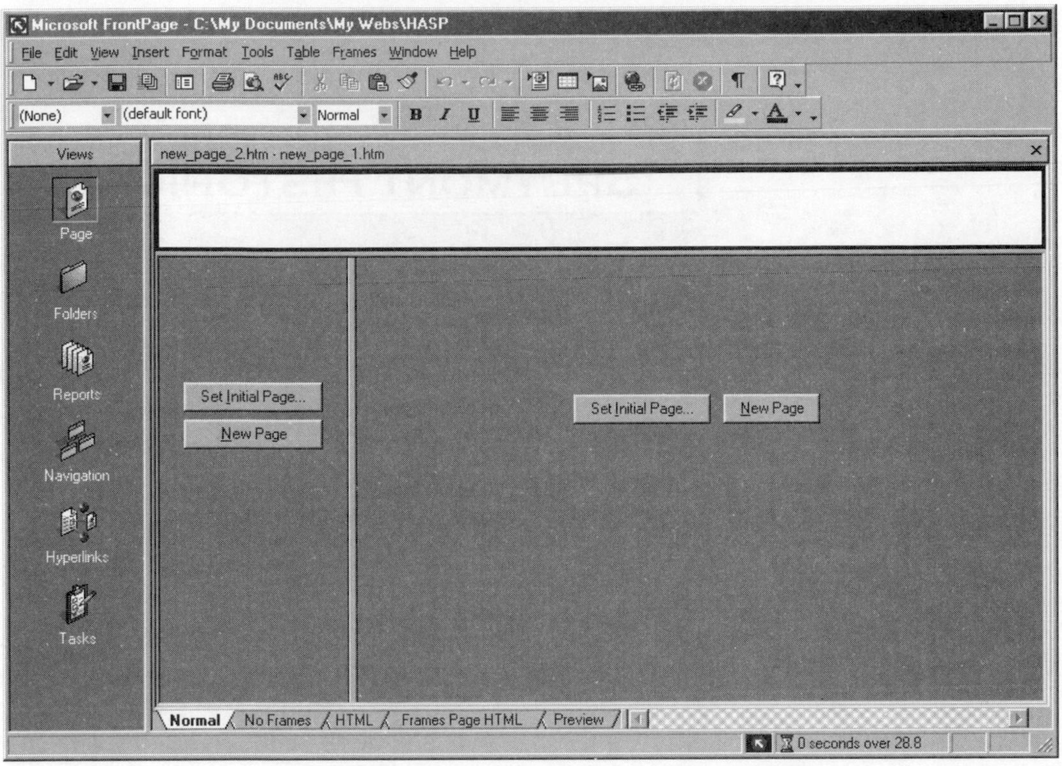

Figure 5.3

Now you can design a title bar for the web. This will always be visible while someone is logged on to the site.

- Type *Speymont Historical Association.*

- Highlight the text and format it as **Copperplate Gothic Bold** Font, size **36pt**, and **Centered**. (Use an alternative font if you don't have this one.)

- Hold the mouse pointer over the lower frame border and when the pointer changes into a vertical two-headed arrow, drag it down slightly to leave a little white space underneath the name. (You will only be able to see the first two words of the heading, until you view it in a browser, which we will do later. Depending on the resolution and size of your computer screen, you may want to make the title smaller. Only experimentation can tell you this – and do not forget that you may need to cater for other viewers of your Web site using low-specification monitors.)

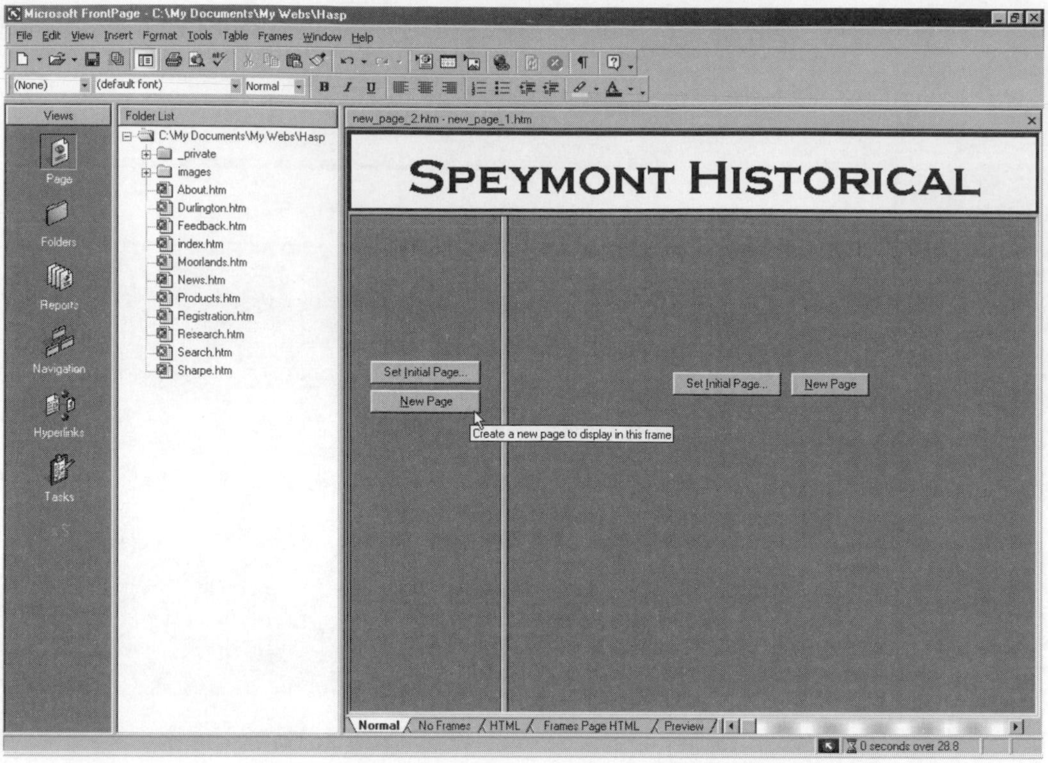

Figure 5.4

- Next, click **New Page** on the Contents frame (the one on the left).

Adding a background graphic

In this frame you are going to add a background graphic which will appear on each page in the site.

- Right-click the page and select **Page Properties** from the pop-up menu.
- Select the **Background** tab.
- Check **Background Picture**.

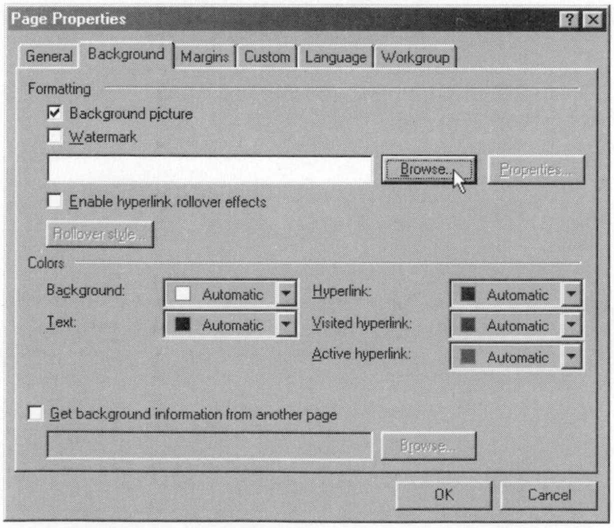

Figure 5.5: Inserting a background graphic

The graphic used for this is available to download on the Payne-Gallway Web site at www.payne-gallway.co.uk/frontpage or you may want to use a graphic of your own. The graphics used in this book have all been saved in a folder called **Photos**.

- Select **Browse** to find the picture file.

- You will only be able to look in the files within your web here. To see other files, click the **Select a file on your computer** button near the bottom right of this window. The **Select File** window will appear as shown in Figure 5.6.

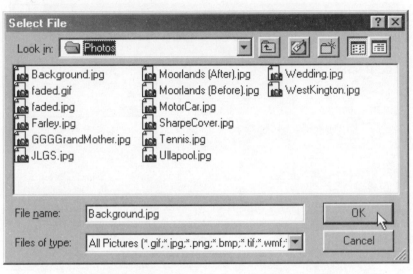

Figure 5.6: Selecting a file from the Photos folder

- Select the **Background.jpg** file and click **OK**.

- Click **OK** on the **Page Properties** window.

- Drag the frame border over to the right to display the picture properly. There should be just a trace of pure white down the right-hand side of the picture.

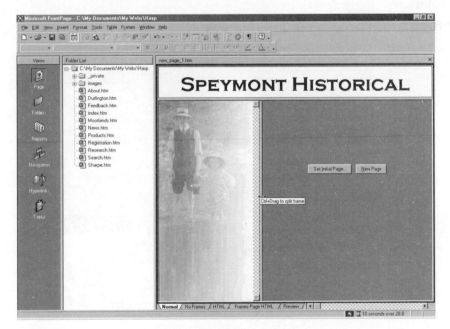

Figure 5.7

Changing frame colours

To give the Banner frame and the graphic in the Contents frame a little more harmony, you can change the colours of the text and background.

- Select the **Banner** frame and right-click the mouse. Choose **Page Properties** from the menu.
- Click the **Background** tab. In the **Colours** section, and click the down arrow by the **Text** colour box.

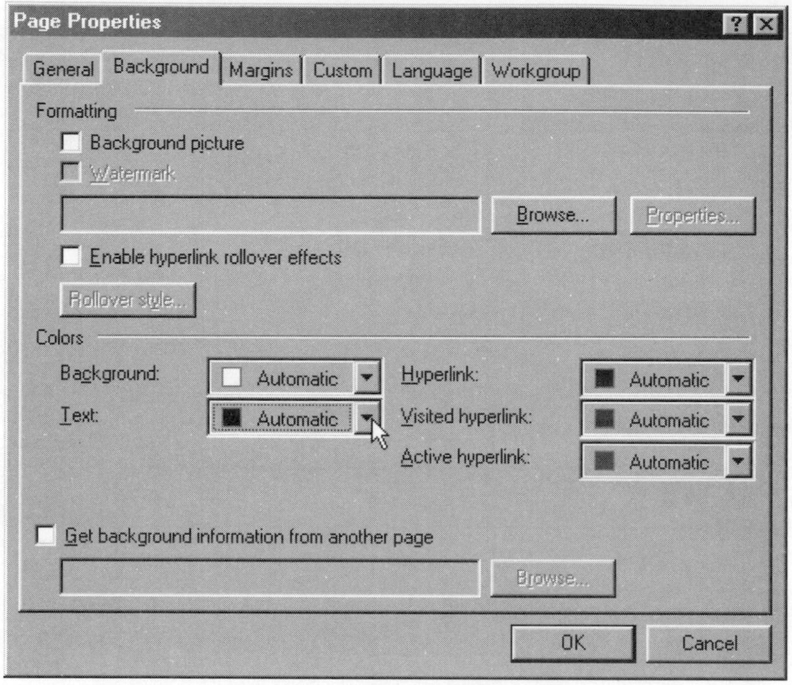

Figure 5.8

- Click **More colors**.
- Select **Dark Brown** from the selection and click **OK**.

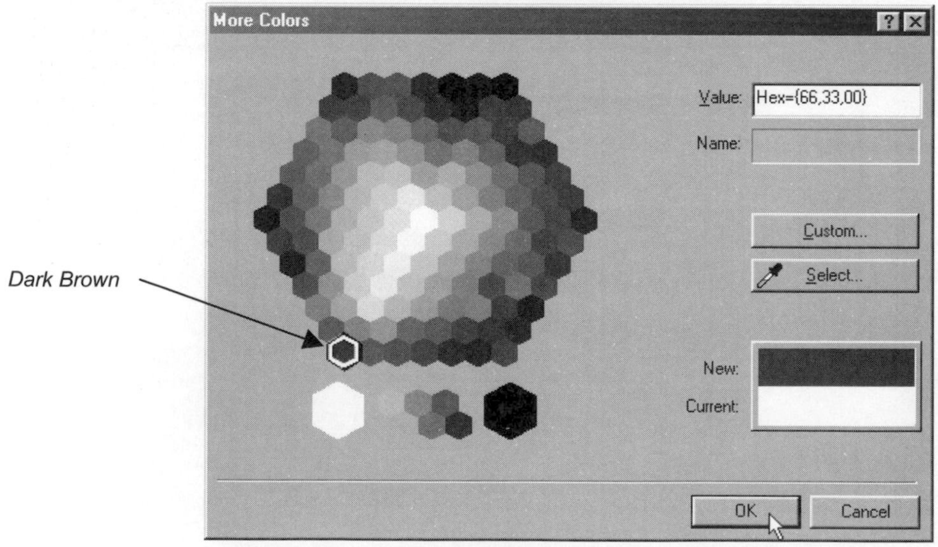

Figure 5.9: Selecting a colour

- You will be returned to the **Page Properties** window. Move this window by dragging its title bar out of the way of the **Contents** frame, which you will need to be able to see for the next step.

- Click the down arrow by the **Background** option in the **Colors** section, and select the **More Colors** option.

- Click the **Select** button. This will change the mouse pointer into a pipette in which you can use to select any colour you can see on the screen and 'suck it up' for use on your page.

- Select a colour from around the man's hat in the picture. This will make the Banner match the picture. Click **OK**.

- Click **OK** again on the **Page Properties** window to see your results. If you are unhappy with the colour selection, try again!

Note:	The colours you choose here may display slightly blurred or dithered on a computer if the monitor is set to only 256 colours. To be sure that the user will be able to see the exact colour you choose, you should use the palette that FrontPage provides, shown in figure 5.9.

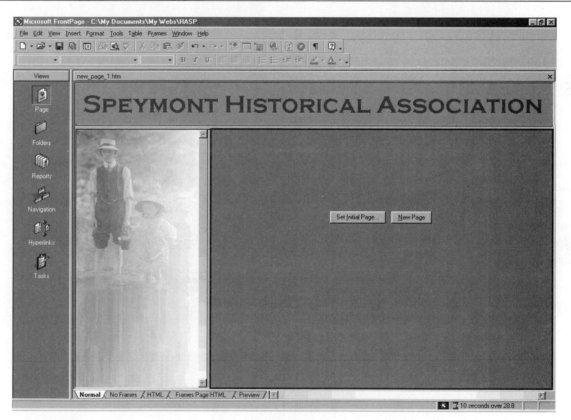

Figure 5.10

Saving Frames

- Click **File**, **Save** to save the pages so far.

You will be shown the Save As window. Since there are four different files to be saved you need to be careful when naming them. The blue section on the right of the window indicates which frame is currently being referred to. The Banner frame is highlighted below.

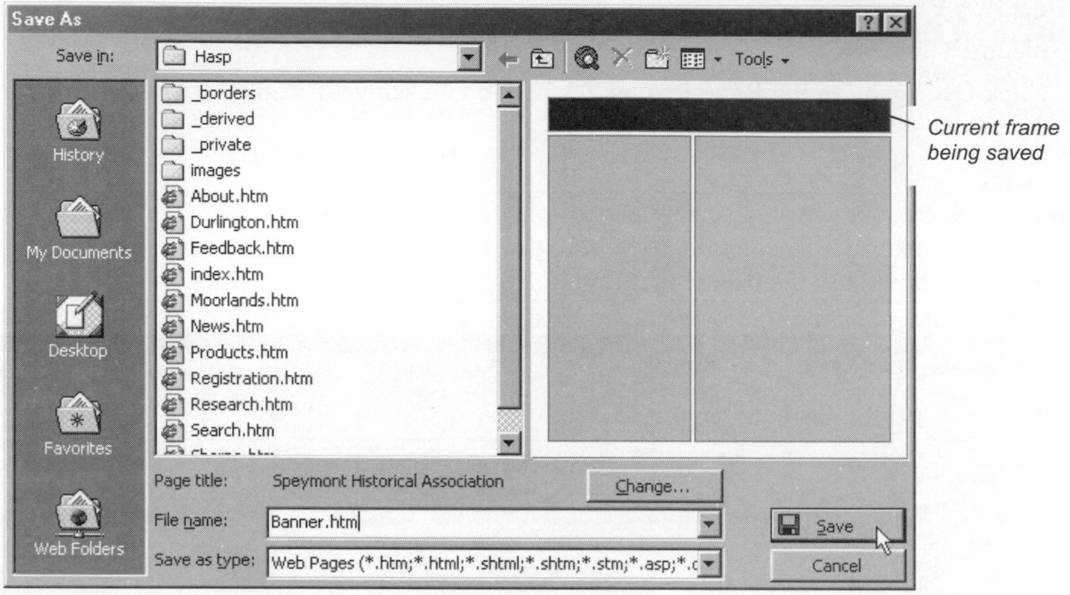

Figure 5.11

- Name the Banner frame **Banner.htm**. Click **Save**.

- The window will reappear asking you to save another frame. **Save** the Contents frame as **Contents.htm**. Another window will appear prompting you to **Save Embedded Files**. Although the picture may already have been saved on your computer somewhere, FrontPage needs to save it in its own directory. Just click **OK**.

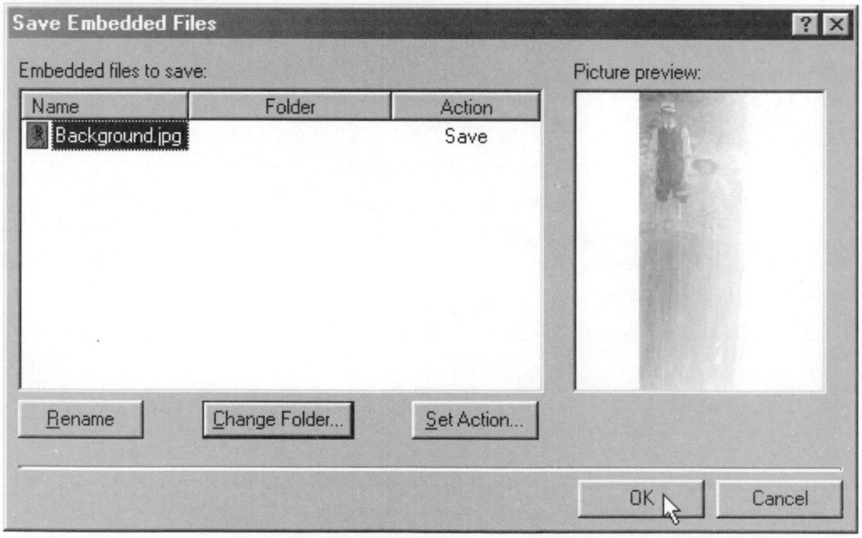

Figure 5.12: Saving an embedded image

- Save the actual Frame page, containing all of the other frames, as **FramesPage.htm**. FrontPage will not ask you to save the Main page at the moment since you have not made any changes to it.

Moving files between folders

Notice that **Background.jpg** has been saved in the **Hasp** main folder. Logically, all pictures should be saved in the **Images** folder, so we will move it.

- In the **Folder List**, click and drag the file name **Background.jpg** and drop it on the **Images** folder.

FrontPage will automatically update the path. *You must not do this in Windows Explorer as the paths will not be correctly updated in your web.*

Removing scrollbars

Inactive scrollbars clutter up the page and divide it unnecessarily. You can remove them as follows:

- Right-click the Contents frame and select **Frame Properties**.
- Select the arrow by the **Show scrollbars** options and click **Never**. Click **OK**.

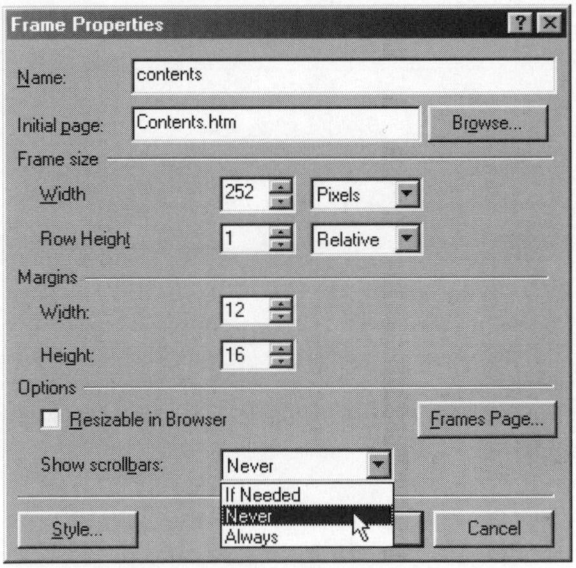

Figure 5.13: Scrollbar options

Removing frame borders

Removing the borders also helps to improve the look of a page. It makes the page look a little neater and more cohesive.

- Open the **Frame Properties** window again by right-clicking the Contents frame and click the **Frames Page** button.
- This will open the **Page Properties** window. Click the **Frames** tab and uncheck the **Show Borders** option.
- Click **OK** and **OK** again.

Preview in Browser

- Click the **Preview in Browser** button to see what your Web site looks like so far. The elements that you can see will appear on every page. In the next chapter we will add hyperlinks to the **Contents** page so you can link to the other pages in the web.

If you are viewing the page on a lower resolution screen than the one shown here, you will not be able to see all the title. You can change the font size if you wish.

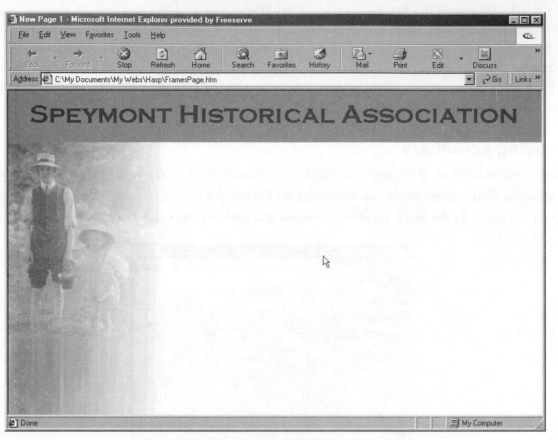

Figure 5.14: Previewing the web page in a Browser

- Return to FrontPage.
- **Save** and **Close** the web.

Chapter 6 – Creating Hyperlinks

Objectives

By the end of this chapter you will have learned how to:

➢ assign web pages to frames

➢ create text and image hyperlinks

➢ add colours and effects to hyperlinks

➢ create a front door page

➢ use a bookmark

Setting the initial page

- Load **FrontPage** and open the **HASP** web.

- Double-click on **FramesPage.htm** in the Folder List to open the Frames page.

In the last chapter, you created the Frames page and clicked on the **New Page** button in two of the frames to create new pages called **Contents** and **Banner**. The main frame still remains empty, and this time, instead of creating a new page to be displayed here, we will tell FrontPage to display the **About** page which we created and named in Chapter 4. Of course this page has no content as yet, but we can add that later.

- Click the **Set Initial Page** button in the middle of the frame. This will create a hyperlink to the page that the frame will display initially when the Frames page (**FramesPage.htm**) is opened.

- Select the **About.htm** file from the **Create Hyperlink** window and click **OK**.

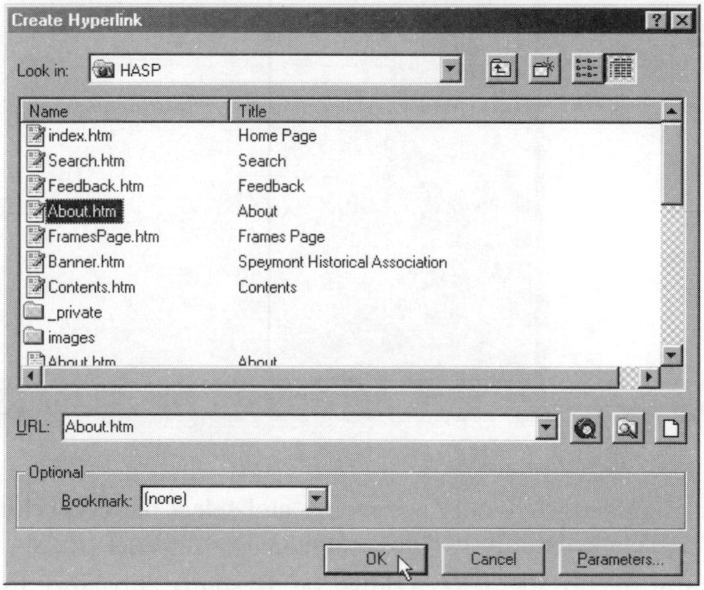

Figure 6.1: Setting the initial page

The About page will now be displayed as the Main page although nothing will appear since it has no content yet.

Hyperlinks

Hyperlinks are links to other pages or Web sites. They are used for navigating around a Web site, or to provide helpful links to other sites of relevant interest. When the mouse pointer moves over a hyperlink, it changes into a pointing hand. This tells the user that it is a link they can click.

Hyperlinks can be added to text, buttons or graphics. When clicked on, the hyperlink will be activated and the target page will be displayed.

Adding text hyperlinks

We will begin by adding several hyperlinks to the Contents frame.

- Make sure that the Frames page is visible in Page view.

- Click in the Contents frame and type *About*.

- Select the text and change it to **Copperplate Gothic Bold** text, size **18pt**. (If you don't have this font installed, select a different one.)

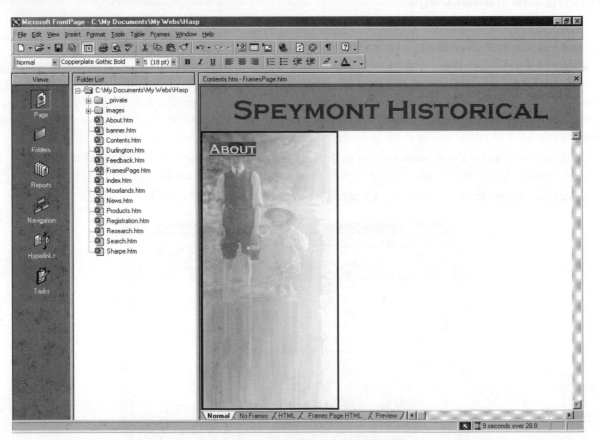

Figure 6.2: Creating a hyperlink in the Contents frame

- With the text still highlighted, right-click the mouse and select the **Hyperlink** option. (You could alternatively have clicked the **Hyperlink** button on the toolbar.)

- Select the **About.htm** file as the **URL** (**U**niversal **R**esource **L**ocator) from the **Create Hyperlink** window.

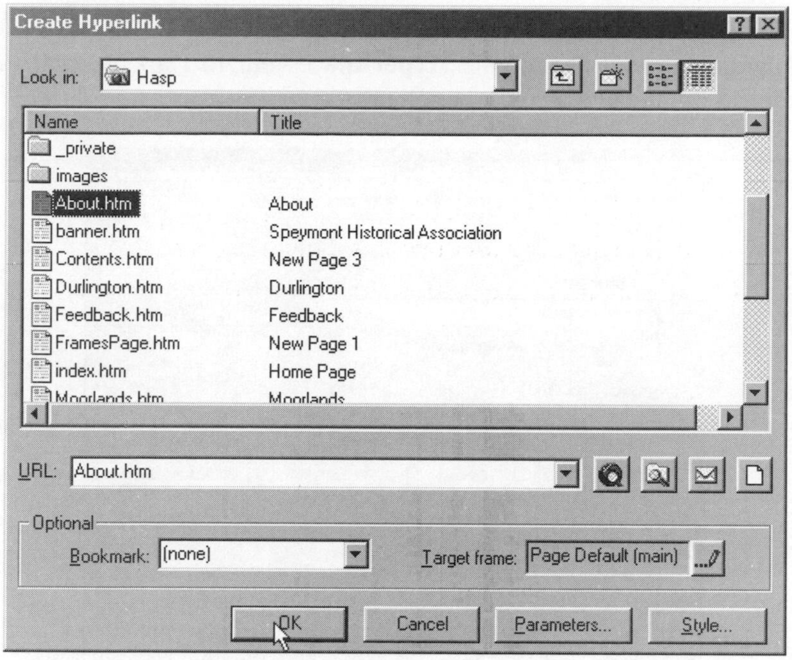

Figure 6.3

Make sure that the Target frame is set to **Page Default (main)**. This means that only the main section of the Frames page will change when the hyperlink is clicked on by the user. The Banner and Contents frames will remain on the screen. The page will also load slightly more quickly because the computer has already got the other two frames in memory.

- Click **OK**.

- Position the mouse cursor on the line below the **About** hyperlink.

- Enter the following 5 page titles, pressing **Enter** between each one:

    News

    Products

    Research (Press **Enter** twice here.)

    Search

    Registration

- Highlight the **News** title and click the **Hyperlink** button.

- Select the **News.htm** file and click **OK**.

- Repeat the steps for the remaining titles, linking each title with its corresponding page file.

- **Save** the file.

Changing the hyperlink colours

By default a hyperlink is shown in blue and underlined, and text in this style is instantly recognised by experienced users as a hyperlink. However, if it is clear enough on your site that a hyperlink exists, it is fine to change its colours.

A hyperlink can be in any one of four states: unvisited, visited, currently active and 'being hovered over' (this means that the mouse pointer is directly over the hyperlink but hasn't clicked on it). Each of these states can be given a different colour to help the regular user recognise which pages they have or haven't looked at, for example.

- Right-click the Contents frame and select **Page Properties** from the menu.
- Click the **Background** tab and change the **Hyperlink** colour to Dark Brown, matching the colour of the organisation name heading in the Banner.

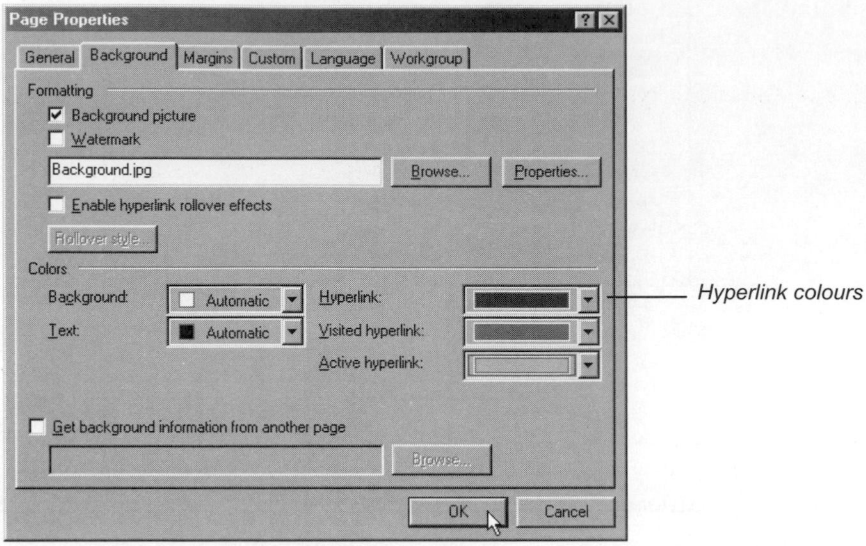

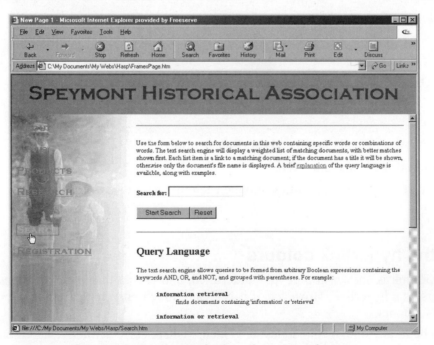

Figure 6.4: Changing hyperlink colours

- Change the **Visited hyperlink** colour to a light brown and the **Active hyperlink** colour to a light orange. Click **OK**.
- **Save** the **Contents** page and click the **Preview in Browser** button. Test the hyperlinks. Try the **Search** page since this is the only page containing any content. If the page is not saved, the new hyperlink colours will not show up.

Figure 6.5: Previewing the Search page in a browser

- Close the Browser window to return to **FrontPage**.

Rollover effects

The last hyperlink 'state' that was mentioned was when it is hovered over by the mouse cursor. This can also have its own colour, and you can also change several other text properties for this state.

- Right-click the **Contents** frame once more, selecting **Page Properties** from the menu.
- Click the **Background** tab and check the **Enable hyperlink rollover effects** option box.
- Click the **Rollover Style** button.

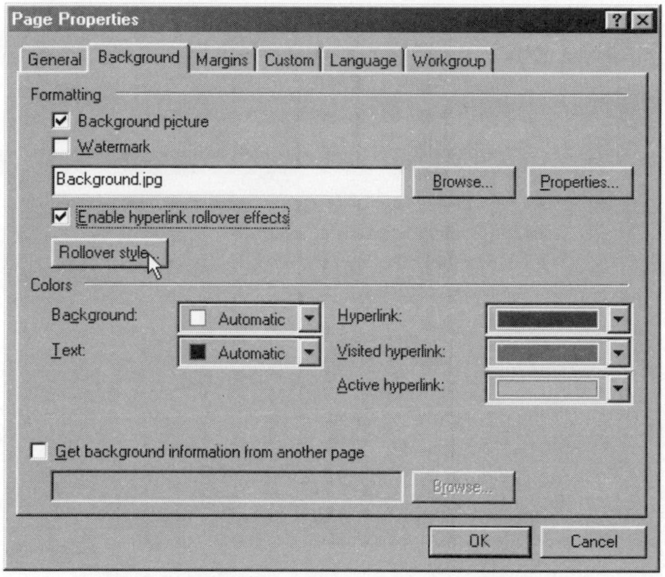

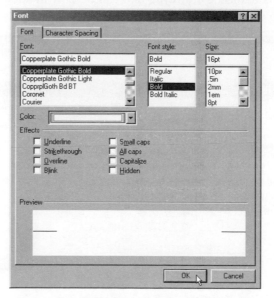

Figure 6.6: Selecting a Rollover effect

- Select **Copperplate Gothic Bold** from the **Font** box, and **18pt** in the **Size** box.
- Select **Cream** as the **Color** by selecting **More Colors** in the Color box.

Figure 6.7: Selecting a font for the hyperlink

- Click **OK** three times.
- **Save** your changes.

Creating a front door page

A front door page acts as an entrance to your site. It has no links to anywhere except the first page in your web. Often a front door page is used to give the user the chance to select whether they want to view the site with or without frames since some of the early browsers cannot handle them properly. This will be covered in more detail in Chapter 13.

- In the **Folder List**, double-click on the **index.htm** file. This is the file that will automatically be loaded first by a browser.

- Click the **Center** button.

- Click the **Insert Picture from File** button.

- Click the **Select a file on your computer** button.

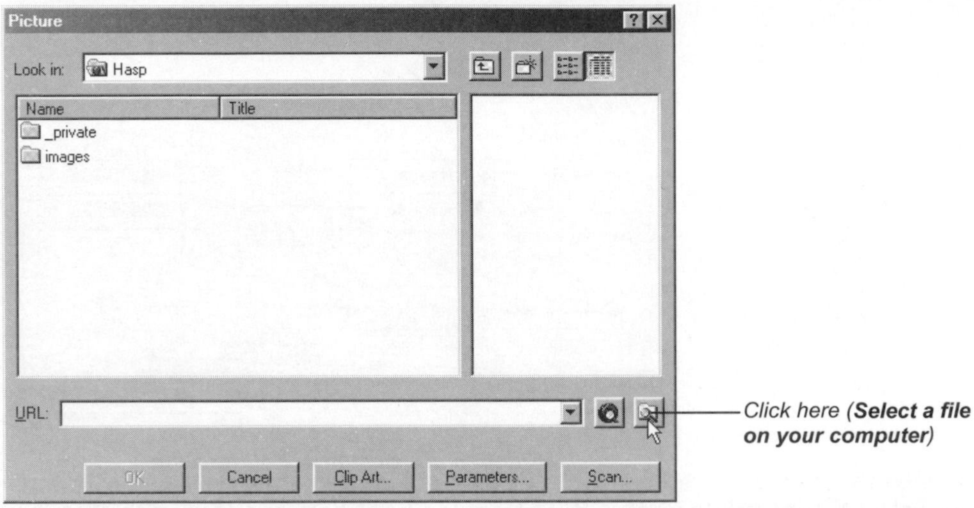

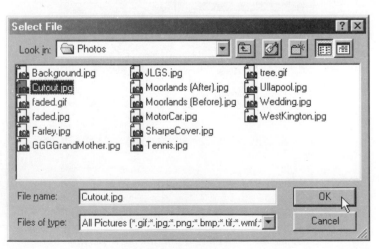

Figure 6.8: Inserting an image

The image used on this page is named **Cutout.jpg** and can be downloaded from the Payne-Gallway Web site at www.payne-gallway.co.uk/frontpage.

- Find the location on your computer where the image is stored, select the **Cutout.jpg** file and click **OK**.

Figure 6.9

The image will appear in the centre of the page. You may need to size it to fit the screen.

- Press **Enter** to go to the next line. Type in **Welcome to the Speymont Historical Association**.

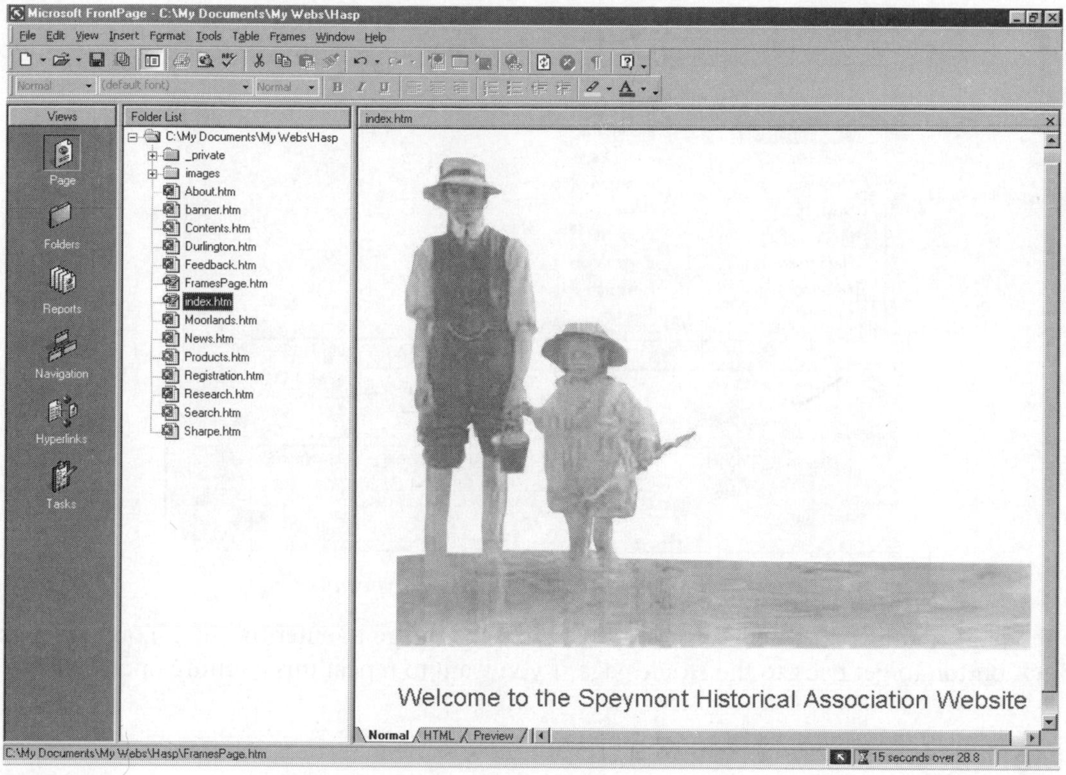

Figure 6.10

- Highlight the text and make it **Arial** size **18pt**. (Because the graphic has some white space on its left hand side, you may need to put in a few spaces before the text to centre it under the graphic.)
- Click the **Font Color** button on the Formatting toolbar and colour the text **Dark Brown**. 
- **Save** the page. You will be asked to **Save Embedded File**, **Cutout.jpg**. Click **OK**. This will move the file into the web folder.
- Move **Cutout.jpg** into the **Images** folder.

Images as hyperlinks

You can make almost anything on a web page into a hyperlink in the same way as you would text.

- Right-click the image and select **Hyperlink**.
- Select **FramesPage.htm** and click **OK**.

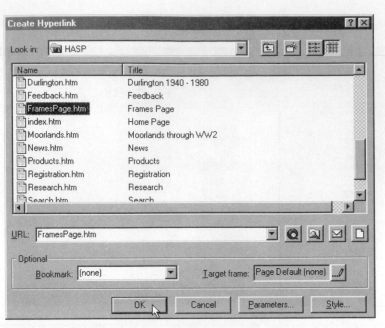

Figure 6.11: Creating an image hyperlink

- **Save** the page and test it in your Browser. Just click the image to enter the site. You can click the **Back** button to get back to the Home page if you want to repeat this exciting operation!

Bookmarks

Bookmarks are hyperlinks that go to another location on the same page or to a specified location on a different page in the web. For example, you will often see a **Back to Top** hyperlink at the bottom of a page. An example of this is shown on the Search page.

- Click the **Search** page hyperlink and scroll down to the bottom.
- Click the **Back to top** hyperlink. You are returned to the beginning of the text.
- Close the Browser to return to **FrontPage**.

Download time

You may have noticed an hourglass symbol in the bottom right-hand corner of the screen. This indicates the **Estimated Time to Download** that particular page. This will increase every time you add more graphics or effects to a page.

Figure 6.12: Estimated Time to Download

It is important to keep this as low as possible. If it becomes too high, users can get very impatient and exit the site before they have even finished loading it up. A friend of mine adopts a 10 second rule – 10 seconds before he gets frustrated and looks somewhere else!

The figure **28.8** represents the modem speed in kilobits/second. Most modems these days are 56kbps.

- Save and close your Web site.

Chapter 7 – Creating Tables

Objectives

By the end of this chapter you will have learned how to:

- ➤ create a page using tables
- ➤ move and hide cell borders
- ➤ merge cells
- ➤ add buttons to a page
- ➤ create picture hotspots

Using tables

Perhaps surprisingly to a novice, the majority of web pages are created using tables, with text, graphics, hyperlinks and other objects occupying cells in the table. Borders may be hidden, cells merged, column widths and row heights altered so that the table structure is completely invisible, but it is still there. The advantage of placing an object in the cell of a table is that it anchors it in place, and the various objects on the screen can be neatly lined up.

You may have already learned techniques for formatting tables in Word, and they are exactly the same in FrontPage. If the techniques are new to you, you will also find them useful in Word!

Page outline plan

You will need to plan the design of a page before you come to putting it all together on the screen. We'll be starting with the Products page, and the plan looks something like Figure 7.1:

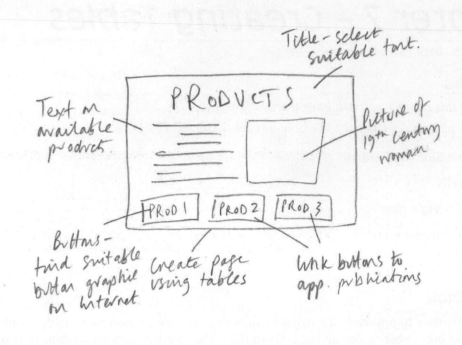

Figure 7.1: Outline for Products page

- **Open** the **HASP** web to start work on this chapter.

- **Double-click** the **FramesPage.htm** file to open it. It will open with the About page as the main page.

- **Ctrl-click** the **Products** hyperlink in the contents. The main page will change to the Products page. Although there is no content on either of these pages, it is evident that it has changed to the Products page because the filename shown at the top of the page (when the page is selected) has changed to **Products.htm – FramesPage.htm**.

Creating a page using tables

- Click the **Insert Table** button. This will give you a grid in which to select and drag the number of rows and columns you need.

- Select a **3 by 4** table.

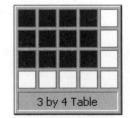

Figure 7.2: Inserting a table 3 rows by 4 columns

The table will be inserted into the Products page.

Moving borders

In order to display more of the page, you can close the **Folder List** and if necessary, drag the right-hand border of the **Views** pane to the left.

- Click the **Folder List** button to close it.

Next you will need to move the cell borders to create the right shape for your page components to fit in.

- Hold the mouse over the cell borders and when it becomes a two-headed arrow, click and drag them to the positions shown below. (The first and last columns are each roughly one third of the total width, and the two middle columns are the same width.)

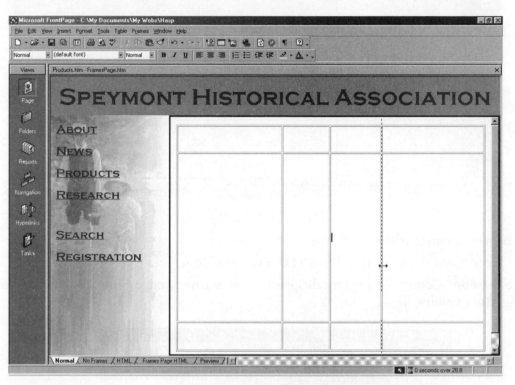

Figure 7.3: Moving cell borders

Merging cells

Ideally you want the page heading to be in the center of the top cell. To do this, the best way is to merge the 4 cells on in the top row.

- Select the top row by clicking and dragging the mouse over the cells.

- Select **Table**, **Merge Cells** from the menu. Alternatively, you can click the right mouse button and select **Merge Cells** from the shortcut menu.

- Repeat this operation with the two cells in the middle row, left of center, the two cells right of center and the middle bottom two cells.

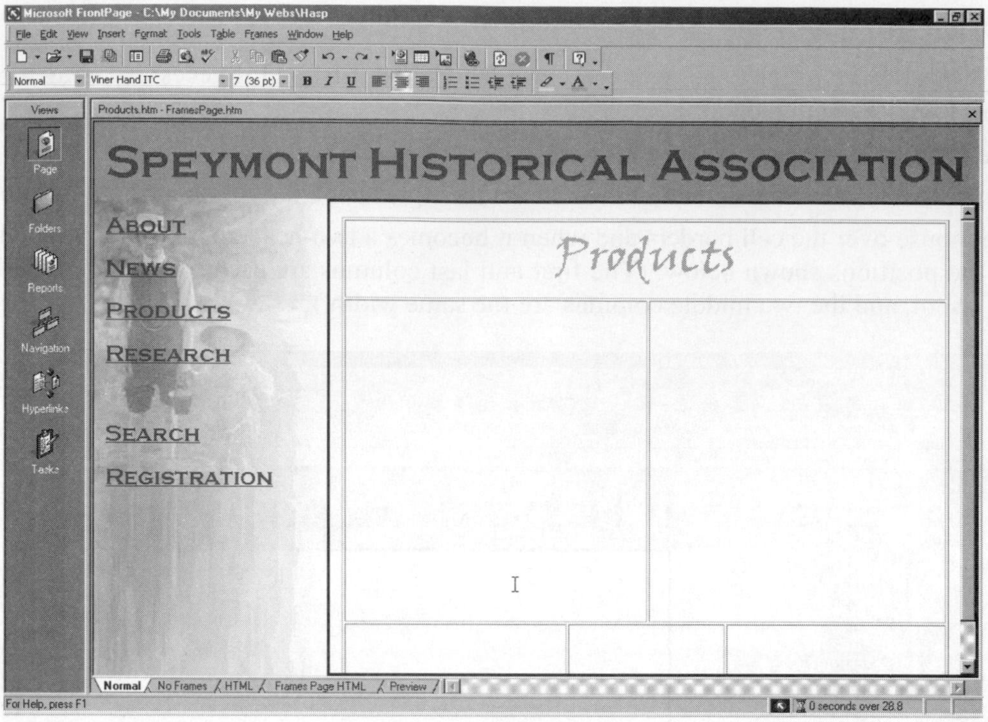

Figure 7.4: Merging cells

- Click the mouse cursor in the top cell and type *Products*.

- **Center** the text and make it **Viner Hand ITC**, **Font Size 36pt**.

- Change the **Font Color** to orange by clicking the down-arrow on the **Font Color** button and clicking **More Colors**.

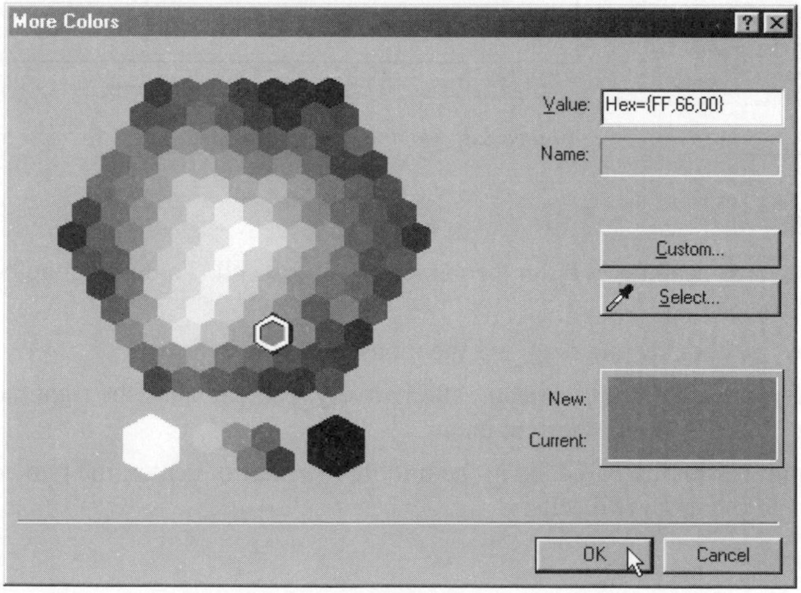

Figure 7.5: Changing the text colour

Hiding cell borders

The page will look better without all the cell borders showing.

- Right-click the table and select **Table Properties** from the shortcut menu.
- Reduce the **Border Size** to **0** and click **OK**.

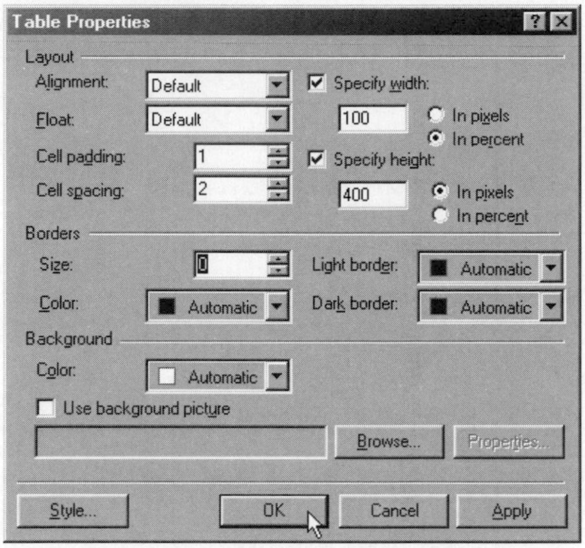

Figure 7.6: Changing the border size

Adding background colour

- Select the 2 large cells in the middle row.
- Right-click on them and select **Cell Properties** from the pop-up menu.
- Change the **Background Color** to off-white or cream from the **More Colors** palette.
- Click **OK**.
- Add text to the left hand cell as shown in Figure 7.7.

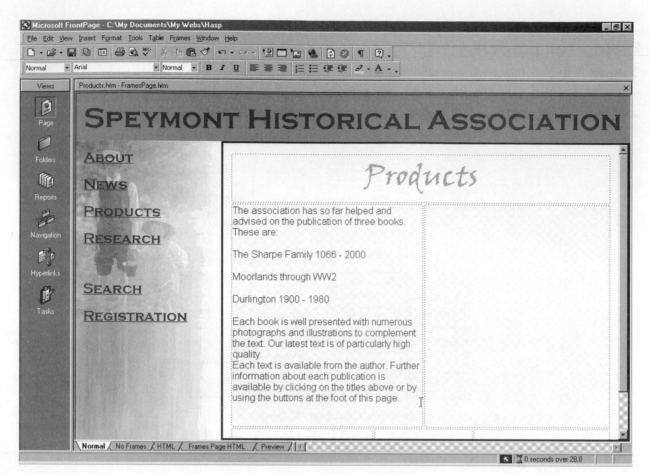

Figure 7.7: Text on the Products page

> **Note:** To start a new line with no spacing underneath the previous line, hold down the **Shift** key when you press **Enter**.

- Select the text and change the **Font** to **Arial**. If necessary, size it so that the text fits on the screen.

Inserting an image

By this time you should be getting to know how to insert pictures into a web page but here is another chance to practise. Pictures are very important to Web sites and many rely on them to provide the necessary interest to keep viewers reading the information on the site.

- Click the large right-hand cell. The cursor will move to it.
- Click the **Centre** button and the cursor will jump to the middle of it.
- Select **Insert**, **Picture**, **From File** from the main menu.

> **Note:** If you wanted to insert a piece of Clip Art, you would select **Insert**, **Picture**, **Clip Art** from the menu.

- Click the **Select a file on your computer** button and find the file **GGGGrandmother.jpg**.

A picture of a 19th century woman will appear.

- Click **OK**. Size the picture if necessary.

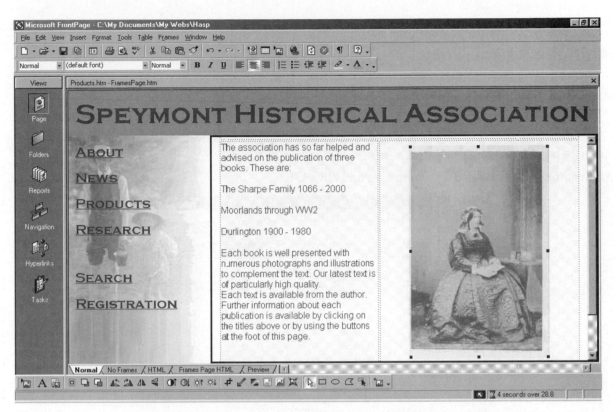

Figure 7.8

- **Save** the page and click **OK** to save the embedded image.
- Click the **Folder List** button to redisplay the Folder List.
- Move the new picture into the **Images** folder.
- Hide the Folder List again.

Adding text hyperlinks

This page will have buttons which the viewer can press in order to get information on each of the publications listed. You can add hyperlinks to the book titles in the text as well, as an alternative means of navigation.

- Highlight the first title (**The Sharpe Family 1066 – 2000**) and right-click the selected area.
- Click **Hyperlink** from the shortcut menu.
- Select the **Sharpe.htm** file from the list and click **OK**.

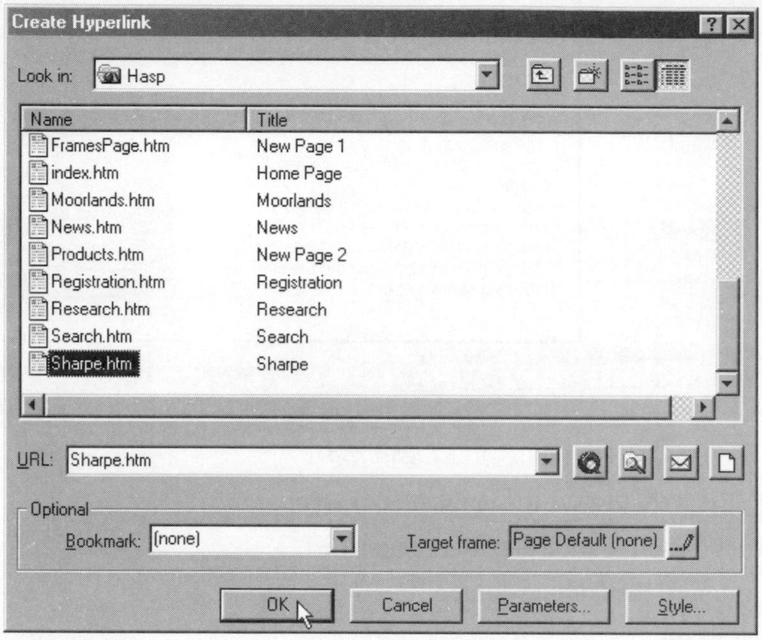

Figure 7.9: Adding text hyperlinks

The title will be appear underlined and blue, the default hyperlink style.

- Select the remaining two titles in turn and assign hyperlinks to the corresponding files for the Moorlands and Durlington pages.

Changing the hyperlink colour

The colour of the hyperlinks on this page can be changed in the same way that you used to change the colour of the hyperlinks in the Contents page earlier on in the book.

- Right-click the page and select **Page Properties**.
- Click the **Background** tab and change the **Hyperlink** colour to orange.
- Change the **Visited Hyperlink** colour to dark orange.
- Leave the **Active Hyperlink** colour as **Automatic** and click **OK**.

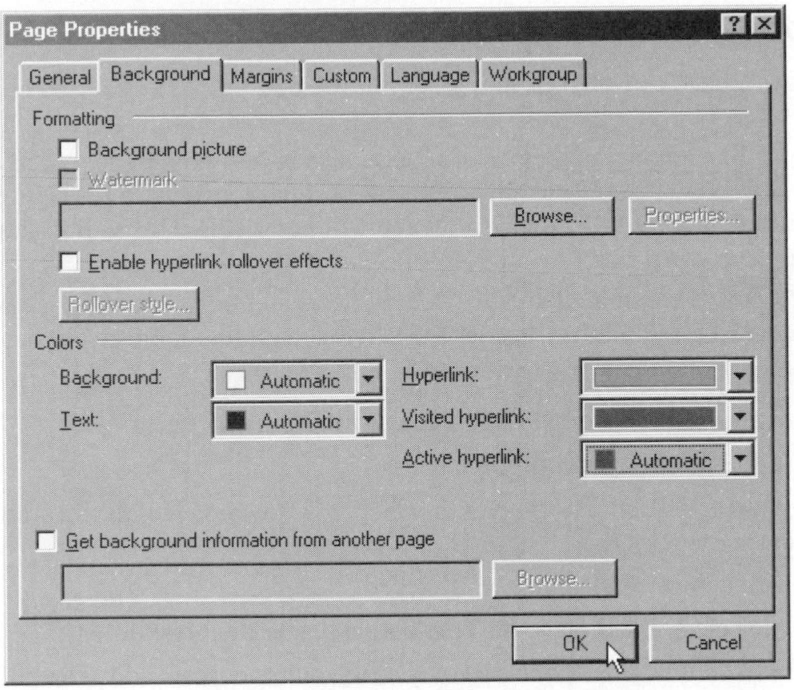

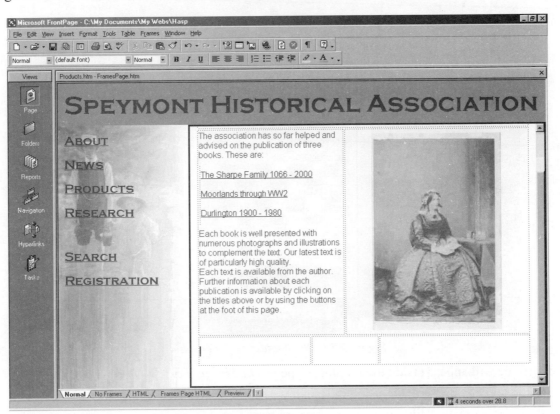

Figure 7.10: Changing hyperlink colours

The page should now show all three titles as orange hyperlinks.

Figure 7.11: Text hyperlinks

Adding buttons

Buttons can be added in each of the remaining cells at the bottom of the page as alternative links to the other product pages.

Adding buttons is just like adding a picture to the page. The button graphic is placed on the page and text is written over it. However, in order to place text on an image it must be a **GIF** file (with a **.gif** file extension). If the image is not a **GIF**, then FrontPage will convert it. This will usually make the file size bigger and the image less sharp.

If you have not got a suitable graphic that you wish to use as a button, you can try looking on the Internet – the Microsoft Online Clip Art Gallery has several suitable button graphics.

- Position the cursor in the bottom left cell.
- **Center** the cursor and select **Insert**, **Picture**, **From File** from the menu.
- Click the **Select a file from your computer** button.
- Select the **Button.gif** file from the folder into which you downloaded all the graphics for this book (e.g. **Photos**) and click **OK**.

The button graphic will appear in the cell.

- Click the graphic to select it and click the **Text** button on the Pictures toolbar.

(If the Pictures toolbar is not visible, right-click any of the other toolbars and select **Pictures** from the pop-up menu.)

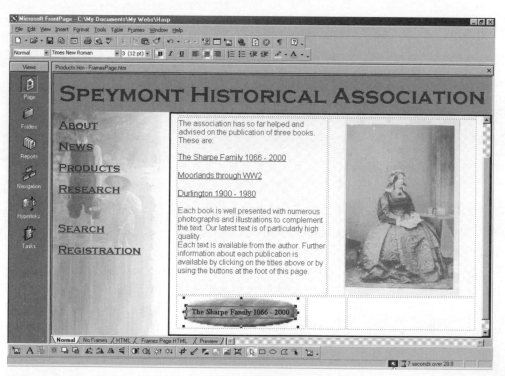

Figure 7.12: Placing text over a graphic

- A text frame will appear inside the graphic. Type in *The Sharpe Family 1066 – 2000*.
- Resize the text box and graphic using the handles as appropriate. (See figure 7.13.)

The text can be formatted like any other piece of text. For this project, leave the text as the default selection.

- Click in the middle cell to place the second button.

- Center the cursor.
- Insert the same graphic (**Button.gif**).
- Type *Moorlands through WW2* and resize the text box if necessary.
- Do the same again for the third cell calling this button *Durlington 1900 – 1980*.

(Don't worry if the cells aren't quite evenly spaced. They will be when you view the page in a browser.)

- **Save** the page and the embedded image.
- Move the **Button.gif** file into the **Images** folder.
- Click the **Preview in Browser** button to view the page.

Figure 7.13: Adding buttons

Creating picture hotspots

Hotspots are hyperlinks that cover a selected area, usually invisible to the user. In this case, the text box containing the book title will act as the boundary for a hotspot.

A hyperlink could be applied to the actual graphic instead of the text box but since the graphic boundary is rectangular, there would be corners hanging over the edge of the image that the user could still click on. This would look a bit funny.

- Right-click the button text and select **Hyperlink**.

Note: Selecting **Picture Hotspot Properties** from the shortcut menu will achieve the same end result and will be mentioned in further detail in Chapter 8.

- Select the **Sharpe.htm** file from the list and click **OK**.
- Do the same for the other text boxes, selecting **Moorlands.htm** and **Durlington.htm** respectively.
- **Save** the page and click the **Preview in Browser** button to test the new functions.
- **Close** the browser and web.

Chapter 8 – Adding Content, Bookmarks and Hotspots

Objectives

By the end of this chapter you will have learned how to:

➢ copy and paste pages

➢ create a bookmark

➢ create a hyperlink that sends e-mail

➢ reveal the location of hotspots

Taking different views of a web

We will start this chapter with a brief review of different ways of looking at the pages in your web. Remember that there are basically 3 ways to view your pages:

1. **Normal view**. This is the view used for editing.

2. **Preview**. This gives you some idea how the page will look when published, but many features will not actually work until the web is published. The hyperlinks behave as they will when published.

3. **Preview in Browser**. This gives you a more accurate picture of exactly how the Web site will look, but there are some features (such as a Hit Counter or online form) which will not actually work until the site is published.

If you are in Normal view, looking at a page which has not yet got any links in place, you can move to other pages that you have opened previously from the **Windows** menu. We will practise working in these views and navigating between the pages of a site in progress.

- **Open** the **HASP** web to start work on this chapter.

- **Double-click** the **FramesPage.htm** file to open it. It will open in Normal view with the **About** page as the main page.

- Close the **Folder List**.

- **Ctrl-click** the **Products** hyperlink in the contents.

- **Ctrl-click** the **Sharpe Family** button.

The **Sharpe.htm** page will open in full view. It is completely empty. However, if you were to get to this page from the Products page in Preview or via a browser, you would see that it actually has the frames in place.

- Try looking at the page in preview (click the **Preview** tab at the bottom of the screen.) The page still remains empty. Return to Normal view.

- From the **Windows** menu, select **Products.htm – FramesPage.htm**.

- Now click the **Preview** tab. Click the **Sharpe Family** button.

This time, the Sharpe page is shown with the Contents and Banner frames.

After this brief interlude, it is time to get to work on this page. The first step is to return to the Products page in Normal view.

- Click the Normal view tab. You will be returned to the Products page, where you were last in Normal view.

Copying pages

Suppose that you want the pages for the individual products (books in this case) to take on the same format as the main Products page. Rather than recreating the table and all the buttons, you can copy it. This will give you the main structure which you can then edit.

- Select the entire table by dragging across it.

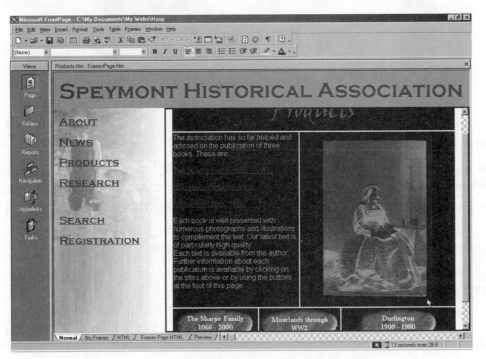

Figure 8.1: Copying page contents

- Right-click the highlighted area and select **Copy**.
- Deselect the area and Ctrl-click **The Sharpe Family 1066 – 2000** button. The Sharpe page will open on its own with the cursor flashing in the top left-hand corner.
- Right-click and select **Paste**.
- The content from the Products page will appear. Highlight the title **Products** and replace it with *The Sharpe Family 1066 – 2000*.

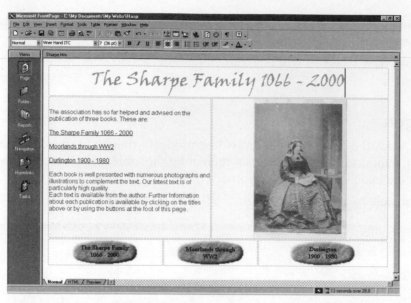

Figure 8.2: Editing a copied page

Replacing images

Replacing an image is done in almost exactly the same way as inserting one. If the image to be replaced is selected when the new one is inserted, the new image will erase the original one and take its place.

- Select the image to insert the new image over the top by clicking **Insert**, **Picture**, **From File**.
- Select the **SharpeCover.jpg** file to replace the picture of the nineteenth century lady. The original picture will disappear and the new one will be displayed.

Replacing existing text

Replace the existing text on the left hand side with the following:

Book Title: **The Sharpe Family 1066 - 2000**
Published: **September 2000**
Author: **J L Sharpe**
Pages: **200**
ISBN: **1-901398-23-X**
Price: **£16.00**

Click here for Ordering Information.

John Sharpe, our honorary life president has recently published this thoroughly well researched book on the history of his family over the past millennium, with evidence that traces back to William the Conqueror in 1066.

The book contains a detailed family tree in which all the known family members feature.

It provides interesting reading for anyone related and indeed non-relatives. It is a truly fascinating account of a family's history over such a long period of time.

Ordering Information

The publication is only available from the author himself.
Please send an e-mail request or written order with a cheque for £16.00 plus £3.00 P&P to:

**J L Sharpe
Hemmingford Way
Bournemouth
BH12 7PB**

e-mail: jlsharpe@payne-gallway.co.uk

Figure 8.3

Picture alignment (Top)

The page looks a little strange with the picture half way down the page so it needs to be aligned at the top.

- Right-click the cursor in the cell.
- Select **Cell Properties** from the menu.

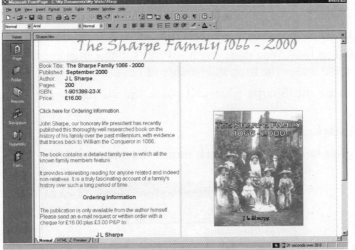

Figure 8.4: Changing the cell alignment

- Select the **Top** option from the drop-down **Vertical alignment** menu in the **Cell Properties** window.
- Click **OK**.

The picture will now move to the top of the cell. To move it down just a little:

- Place the cursor to the left of the picture so that the left picture border flashes and press **Enter**.

Creating a bookmark

A bookmark is a hyperlink that links to a specific location on a web page. In this case, the ordering information is at the bottom of the page and requires the user to scroll down to find it. If the user already knows that they want the book without reading the rest of the information they could click on a bookmark at the top to take them straight to the details they need.

This example will show you how to create a bookmark on the same page, but linking to a different page is done in exactly the same way.

Bookmarks are best used in long Web pages with several subheadings containing a lot of information. A bookmark is there to save the user the time and trouble of having to look for the information they require.

- Scroll to the bottom of the Sharpe page and place the cursor by the author's name, **J L Sharpe**.
- Select **Insert**, **Bookmark** from the menu.
- Type *Ordering Information* in the **Bookmark name** box and click **OK**.

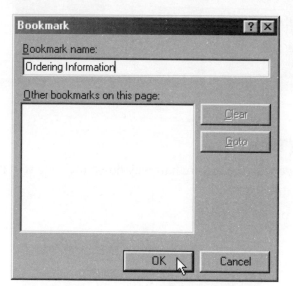

Figure 8.5: Creating a bookmark

This will add a flag icon next to the author's name indicating that there is a bookmark there. This is invisible in a browser.

- Scroll to the top of the page and highlight the words **Ordering Information** from the sentence **Click here for Ordering Information**.
- Right-click the selected words and click **Hyperlink** on the menu.

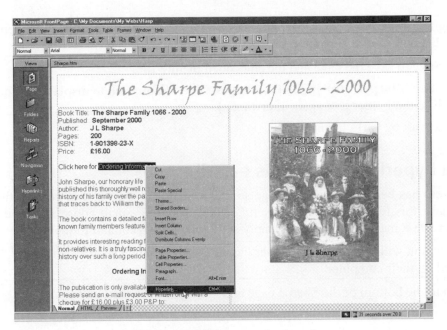

Figure 8.6: Linking to a bookmark

- Click the **Sharpe.htm** filename.
- Click the small downward-facing arrow next to the **Bookmark** box and select the **Ordering Information** bookmark.
- Click **OK**.

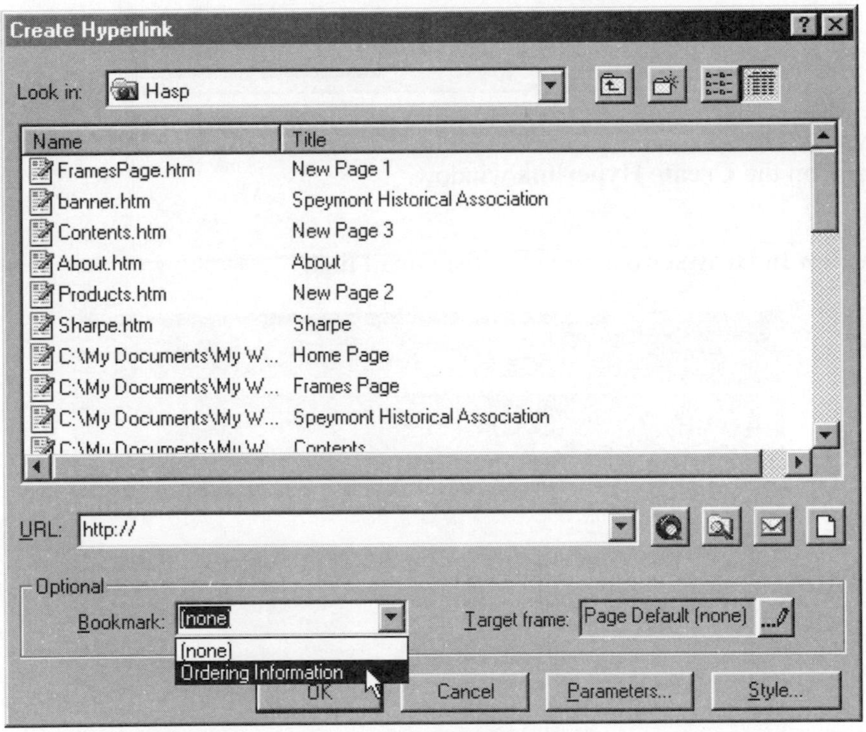

Figure 8.7: Creating a bookmark on the same page

The words **Ordering Information** will now show up in blue indicating that this is a link. You can change this colour if you wish.

> **Note:** Linking to a bookmark on a different page would require you to select a different page file from the file list before selecting the bookmark to link to.

- Select **File, Save** to save the page and the embedded picture file.
- Move the picture **SharpeCover.jpg** to the **Images** folder. (You need to display the Folder List to do this. Close the Folder List again afterwards.)
- Test the bookmark by Ctrl-clicking it.

Creating a hyperlink that sends e-mail

An e-mail address has been given on the page so that a visitor to the site can contact the author if they wish to. To make this feature even more useful, a link from the e-mail address can be set up that will allow them to create e-mail on the spot by simply adding their own content to the letter.

> **Note:** This function will only work if the user has an e-mail program such as Microsoft Outlook Express installed on their computer.

- Scroll down to the bottom of the Sharpe page and highlight the e-mail address.
- Right-click the selection and click **Hyperlink**.
- Click the **Make a hyperlink that sends E-mail** button.
- Type in the address *jlsharpe@payne-gallway.co.uk* and click **OK**.

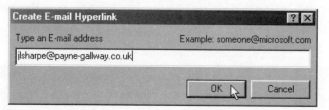

Figure 8.8: Creating a link that sends and E-mail

- Click **OK** again on the **Create Hyperlink** window.
- **Save** the page.
- Click the **Preview in Browser** button to test the e-mail link.

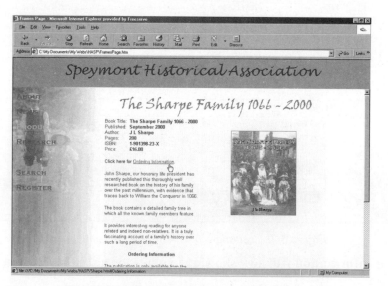

Figure 8.9: The web page as seen in a browser

Your computer should open your e-mail program and automatically add the address into the **To:** box. You can then type in the contents of your e-mail and send it.

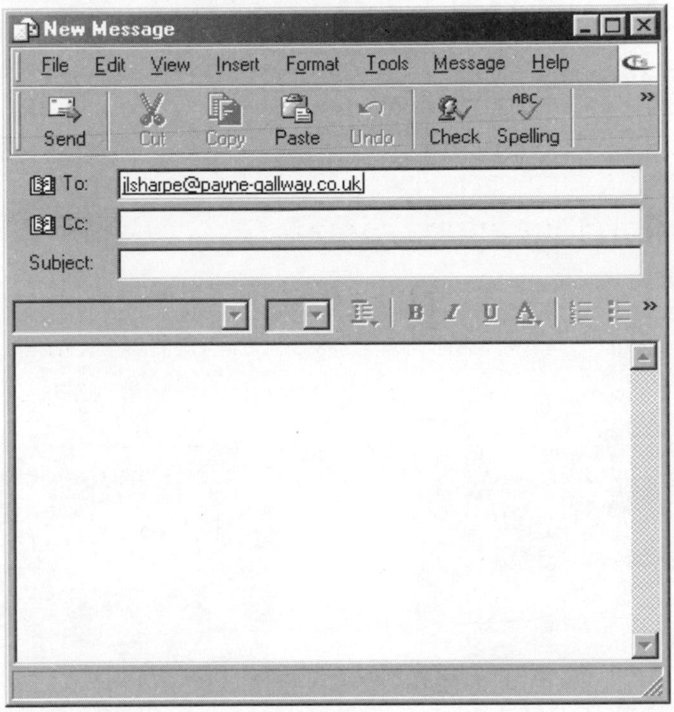

Figure 8.10: Sending an E-mail from a Web site

- Close the e-mail window and return to **FrontPage**.

You now need to link the buttons at the bottom of the Sharpe page to the other Product pages. The Sharpe button will link back to this page so in effect nothing will happen.

- Right-click the Sharpe button and select **Hyperlink** from the menu.
- Select the **Sharpe.htm** file and click **OK**.
- Repeat the operation with the other two buttons, selecting **Moorlands.htm** and **Durlington.htm** respectively.

This page is now complete. Hurrah!

Creating the Moorlands and Durlington pages

These pages are created in an identical way to the Sharpe page. Text and images are added, then hyperlinks and bookmarks can be set up.

If you wish to create these pages to help complete the Web site and give you more practice at some of the techniques covered in chapter 7 and 8, you can copy the information in the screenshots below.

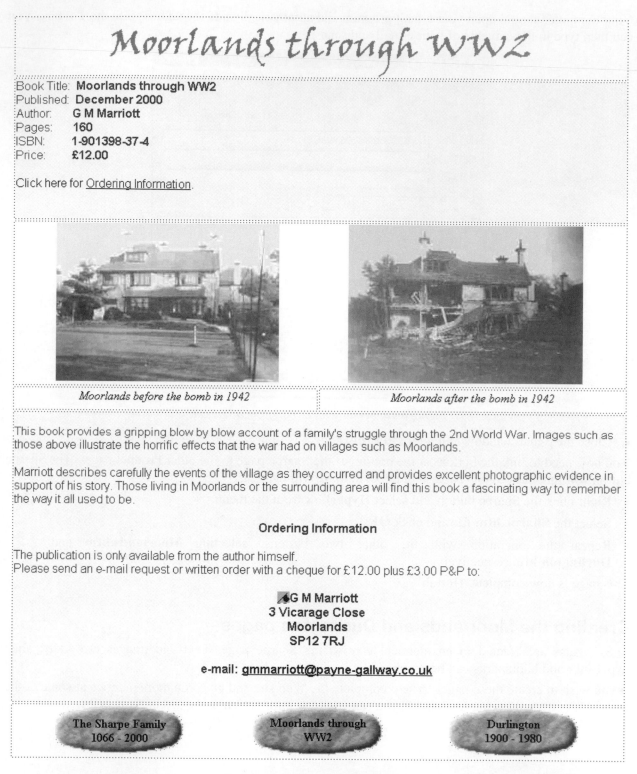

Figure 8.11: The Moorlands page

This Moorlands page includes the images **Moorlands_Before.jpg** and **Moorlands_After.jpg**. Once you have inserted these pictures, remember to move all images to the **Images** folder.

Book Title: **Durlington 1900 - 1980**
Published: **September 2000**
Author: **H M Pryce**
Pages: **120**
ISBN: **1-901398-68-6**
Price: **£9.95**

Click here for <u>Ordering Information</u>.

This book has been well written and provides some interesting history about the village of Durlington through this period of time.

Haylee Pryce has collected information from a variety of sources to compile the book and has clearly drawn on many of her own experiences.

Ordering Information

The publication is only available from the author.
Please send an e-mail request or written order with a cheque for £12.00 plus £3.00 P&P to:

H M Pryce
17 Lancaster Gate
Clapham
SW4 7PB

e-mail: <u>hmpryce@payne-gallway.co.uk</u>

Figure 8.12: The Durlington page

This page contains the **MotorCar.jpg** image. (Remember to move it to the **Images** folder.)

Research page design

The Research page will incorporate some of the basic features of design such as tables and colours that you have already used. Once the general layout of the page has been designed, some more advanced features can be added. First of all you need to return to the Products page.

- From the **Windows** menu select **Products.htm – FramesPage.htm**.

- Ctrl-click the Research page. You should see the blank page appear in the main area of the Frame page.

- Insert a **2 by 1** table (two rows and one column).

- Create the page layout as shown below.

- Type the text as shown in the figure below, and format it. Notice that there is a blank line under the words **Click on an area for more information:**. This should be centered because a map will go in here.

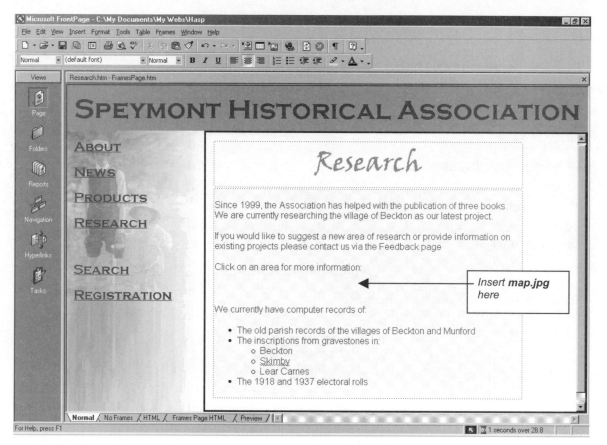

Figure 8.13: The page layout of the Research page

To insert the map into the picture:

- Insert the picture file **map.jpg** using the **Insert**, **Picture**, **From File** commands on the menu at the location indicated shown in figure 8.13.

- Now double-click the word **Feedback** in the second sentence to highlight it.

- Click the **Hyperlink** button and link it to the **Feedback.htm** file from the **File List**. Click **OK**.

- Change the colour of the hyperlink to **Olive** by right-clicking the page, selecting **Page Properties** from the pop-up menu and clicking the **Background** tab.

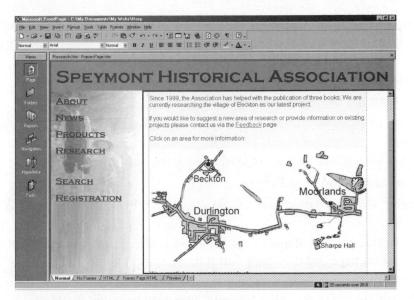

Figure 8.14

Creating an image map

An image map is a picture that has hidden links over it called *hotspots*. This allows the user to access different areas of the Web site depending on which areas of the map they click. In this case, they will be able to click on each village and be taken to the page containing the relevant information about that village. Clicking on **Beckton** will take them to the Feedback page where they can provide any information about the village since this is a new area of research.

Hotspots

- Click on the map and make sure that the **Pictures** toolbar is visible. If not, right-click a different toolbar and select **Pictures** from the list.

- Click the **Rectangular Hotspot** button and draw a rectangle over the village of Durlington.

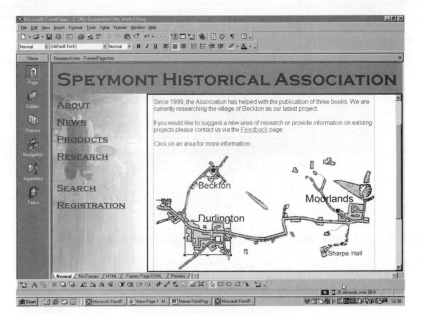

Figure 8.15: Adding Hotspots

- The Create Hyperlink window will appear. Click the **Durlington.htm** file and click **OK**. This will create a link to the Durlington page whenever the mouse hovers over the area inside the rectangle.

- **Save** the page and the image.

- Move the image **map.jpg** to the **Images** folder.

- Click the **Preview in Browser** button to test it. Click the **Research** link if necessary to go to the Research page.

- Test the hotspot. It should take you to the Durlington page.

- Close the browser to return to FrontPage.

- Click the **Circular Hotspot** button and draw a circle over **Beckton** village. Link this to the **Feedback.htm** file.

- Draw two more **Rectangular Hotspots** over **Moorlands** village and **Sharpe Hall**. Link these to the **Moorlands.htm** page and the **Sharpe.htm** pages respectively.

- Click the **Highlight Hotspots** button on the Picture toolbar to reveal their location clearly. This function is particularly useful when hotspots are added to darker images.

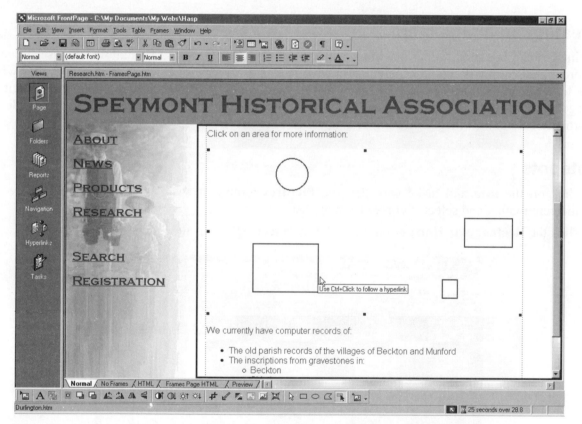

Figure 8.16: Revealing hotspots

- **Save** the page.

- **Close** the **Web** and exit **FrontPage. Save** any other pages if prompted.

Chapter 9 – Special Effects

Objectives

By the end of this chapter you will have learned how to:

➢ add special effects including a marquee, an animated GIF and a hover button

➢ use a dynamic HTML effect

➢ add a page transition effect

Using special effects

Special effects such as scrolling text, text that appears one letter at a time, animated graphics and page transition effects when moving between pages all help to make your Web site more interesting, and are not difficult to add. We will start by adding some special effects to the News page.

- **Open** the **HASP** web to start work on this chapter.
- In **Navigation** view, double-click the **Home Page**. Ctrl-click the image to go to the About page.
- Ctrl-click the **News** link.
- Position the cursor at the top of the **News** page and click the **Center** button.
- Type *News* and format it to **Viner Hand ITC**, **36pt** to match the other pages.
- Colour the text **Orange** and press **Enter** to insert a new line.

Adding a Marquee

A marquee is a line of text that scrolls across the screen repeatedly. This will serve you well as it is eye-catching and will get your message noticed, but bear in mind that too many animated components on a page can become annoying and make the page look too busy.

- With the cursor on the new line, select **Insert**, **Component**, **Marquee** from the main menu.
- Type *New research on village of Beckton – archeological trips planned for September* in the **Text** box.
- Make sure that the **Align with text** option is **Middle**.
- Change the **Background color** to light orange and click **OK**.

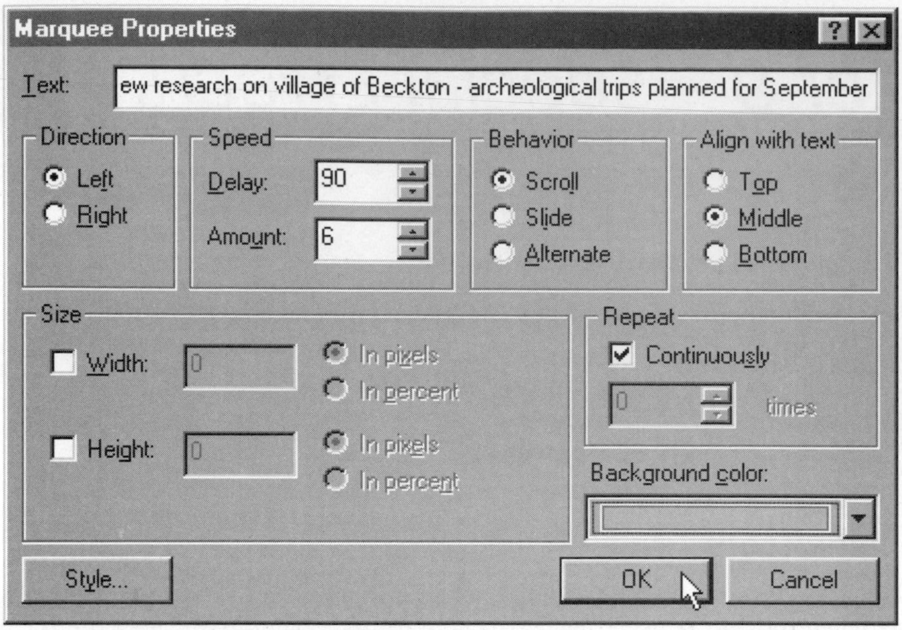

Figure 9.1: Adding a marquee

- Right-click the new marquee and select **Font**.
- Change the text to **Arial, Bold,** size **14pt** and click **OK**.

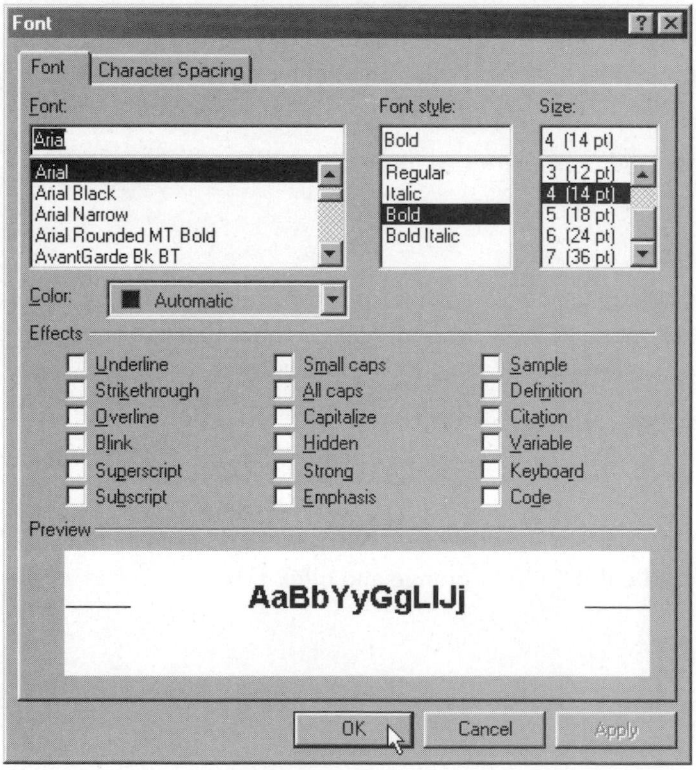

Figure 9.2: Changing the marquee font

You may want to increase the marquee's height slightly to accommodate the new, larger font size.

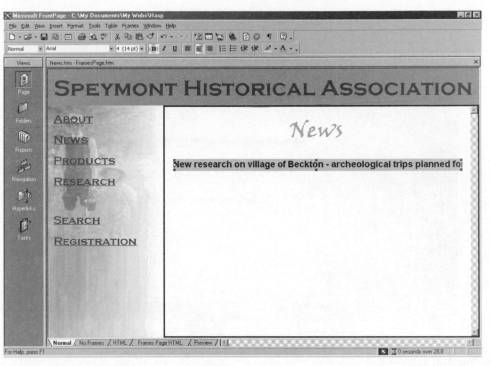

Figure 9.3: The marquee

- Click the **Preview** tab to see the effect of the marquee, then click the **Normal** tab to return to editing mode.

Adding an animated GIF

An animated GIF file is composed of many images that are displayed in rapid succession. This has the effect of animating the graphic. The best place to look for an animated GIF is Microsoft's Online Clip Art Gallery, which you can access by clicking the **Clips Online** button in the Clip Art Gallery window or by logging on to www.microsoft.com/clipgallerylive.

In this example we will use one that you should already have downloaded and stored in the **Photos** folder.

- Position the cursor centrally below the marquee you just created.
- Select **Insert**, **Picture**, **From File** from the main menu.
- Insert the **Qmark.gif** file and click **OK**.
- On the next line, insert the text *Do you know anything about Beckton?*
- Change the **Font** to **Arial** and make it size **24pt**.
- Click the **Preview** tab to see the effect.

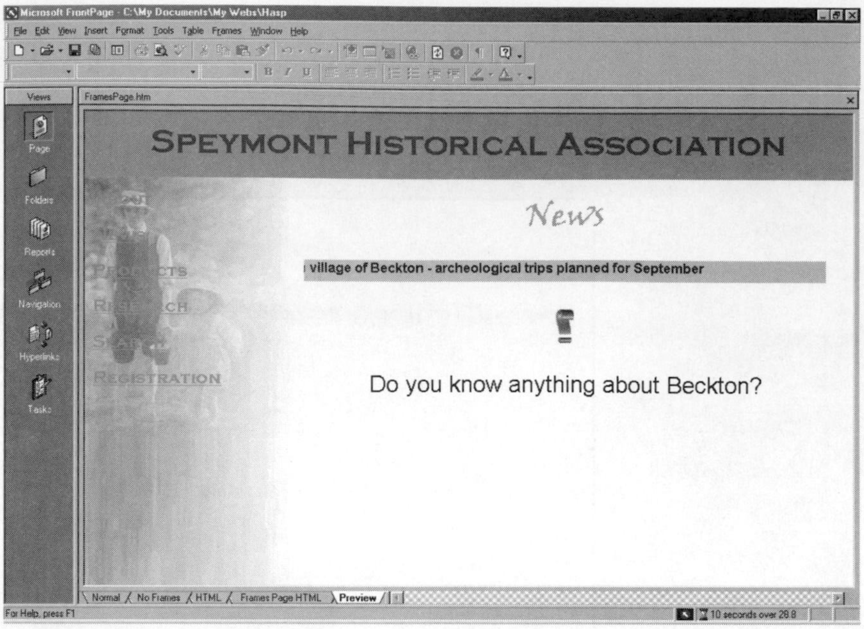

Figure 9.4: Inserting an animated GIF file

- Click the **Normal** tab.

Adding DHTML (Dynamic HTML)

Dynamic HTML is text that will perform various effects on different events, for example flying in from an edge of the screen or changing font when either the page loads or the mouse cursor hovers over the text. It is best to experiment thoroughly with all the different effects to get to know which to use when. Most of the effects are very similar to those you can apply to text in PowerPoint.

- Highlight the text **Do you know anything about Beckton?**
- Click **Format**, **Dynamic HTML Effects** from the main menu.
- From the first box, click the down-arrow and select **Page Load**. This will apply an effect to the text when the page is opened by the site visitor.
- Select **Wipe** from the second box.
- Select **Left to Right** from the third box.

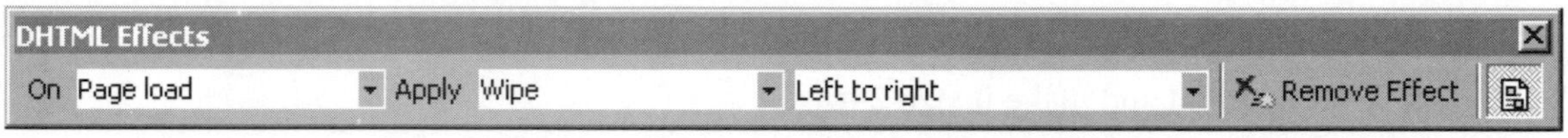

Figure 9.5: Applying a dynamic HTML effect

There should be a blue box around the highlighted text. This indicates the area in which this effect will be applied. You can move the blue box around or size it to the shape you want and the text inside will wrap. Unfortunately, there is no way to guarantee that it will be displayed in the center of the screen since browsers and screen sizes differ.

- Close the **DHTML Effects** window.
- **Save** the page and the **Qmark.gif** image. Remember to move it to the Images folder.
- Click the **Preview** tab to see the effect.

Add some more content

Add the following text underneath the Dynamic HTML text:

If you think that you can help us with our research on Beckton village as it was in the early 1900s, please send us your information. We would also welcome any suggestions for other areas of research. Just click the button below.

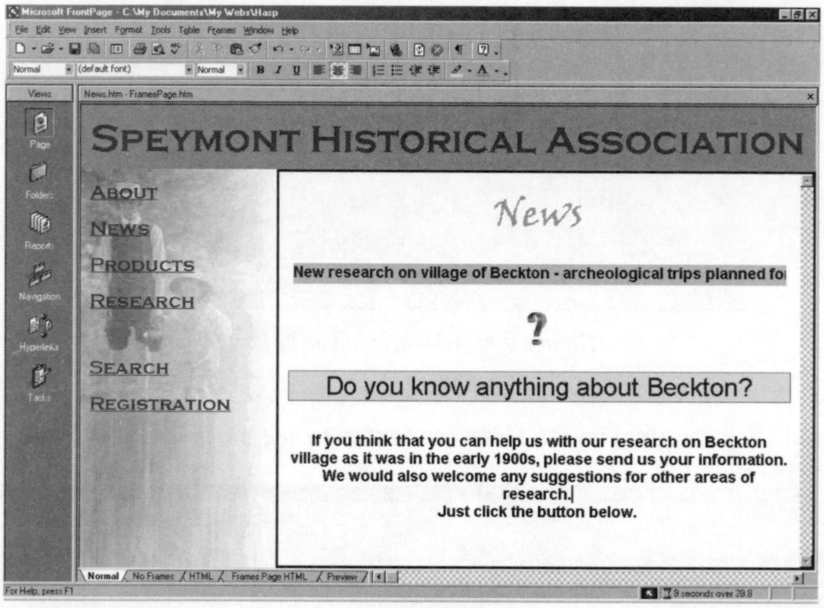

Figure 9.6

Adding a Hover Button

A hover button is another type of animation that you can add to a web page. In a similar way to DHTML text, a hover button will change colour, size or appearance as though it has been pressed like a button on a toolbar.

- Centre the cursor on a blank line underneath the text that you have just entered in Figure 9.6.
- Select **Insert**, **Component**, **Hover Button** from the menu.
- Enter *Click here to send us your comments* as the **Button text**.
- Click the **Font** button and change the text formatting to that shown in Figure 9.7. Click **OK**.

Figure 9.7: Formatting the hover button text

- Select **Bevel In** as the effect that you want to occur when the mouse cursor hovers over the button.

- Change the **Width** to **340** and the **Height** to **30**.

- You can change the colours to suit the ambience of the Web site.

- Now click the **Browse** button and select the **Feedback.htm** file. This is the page that will be displayed when the Hover button is clicked.

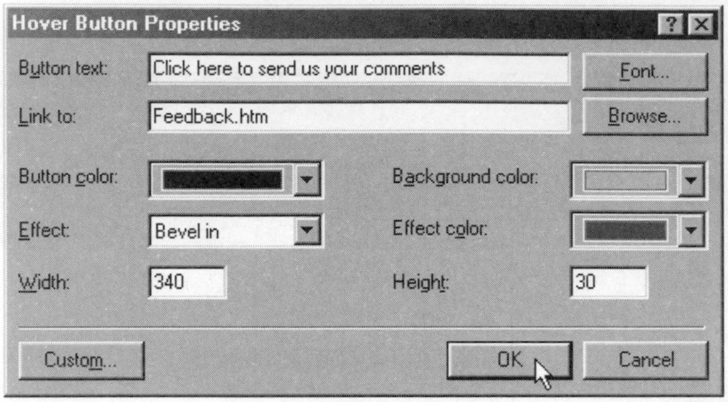

Figure 9.8: Adding a hover button

- Click **OK**.

- **Save** the page and click the **Preview in Browser** button to see the finished effects.

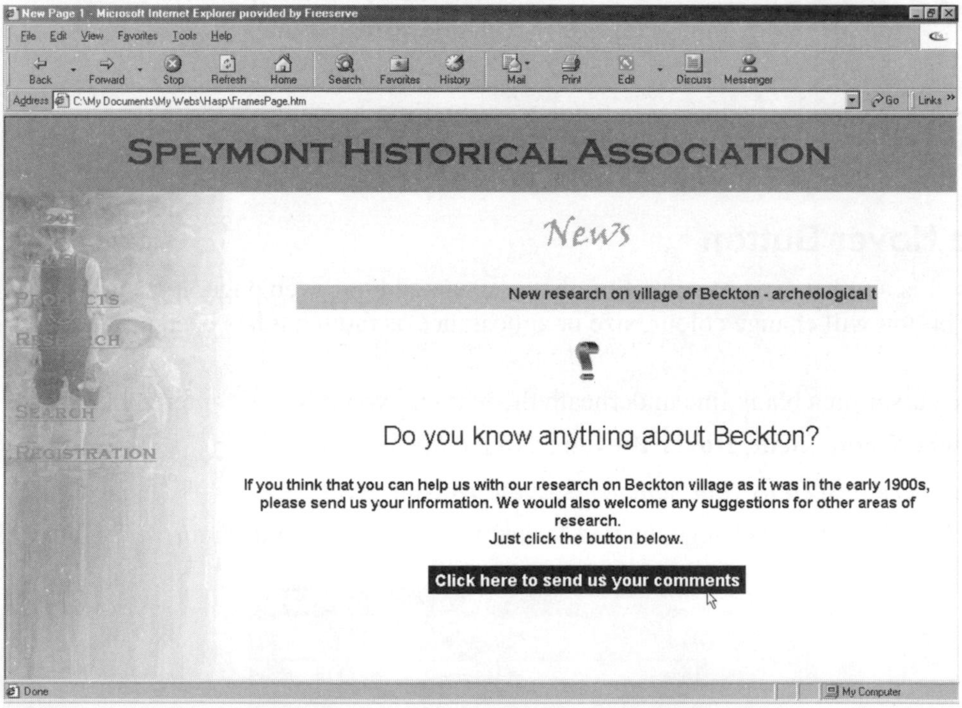

Figure 9.9: The News page in a browser

You may need to move the DHTML field in Design view. (Drag it when the mouse pointer changes to crossed arrows.)

- With the News page open in the browser, try testing out the Hover button. What happens?

The button should work and take the user to the Feedback page. However, when the Feedback page appears, the Frame page disappears. This is because the hyperlink has not been set to change the page in a specific frame – in this case, the main frame.

Setting the target frame

- Go back to Normal view in FrontPage. (Make sure that the frames are visible as in Figure 9.6.)

- Right-click on the **Hover** button.

- Select **Hover Button Properties** from the pop-up menu.

- Click the **Browse** button in the **Hover Button Properties** window as if you were once again setting the page to be displayed when the button is clicked.

- Now click the **Change Target Frame** button in the bottom right corner of the **Select Hover Button Hyperlink** window.

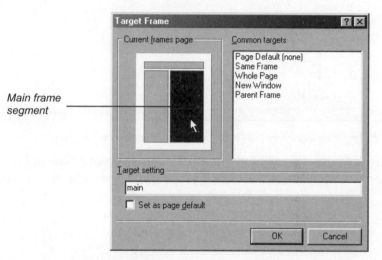

Figure 9.10: Setting the target frame for a hyperlink to change

- In the **Target Frame** window, click the main frame segment of the frames page diagram. The target setting will change to say **main**.

- Click **OK** on each of the option windows to confirm the setting.

- **Save** the page and return to the browser to view your page.

- Click the **News** page button and then click the Hover button again to test it. Only the main section of the page should change now.

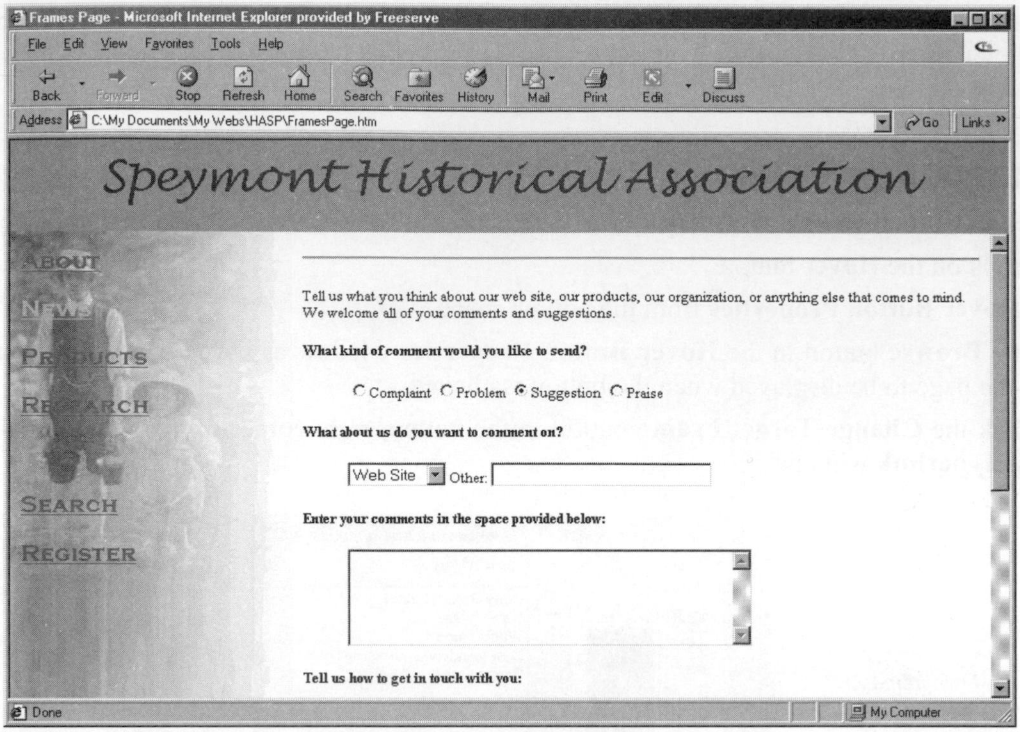

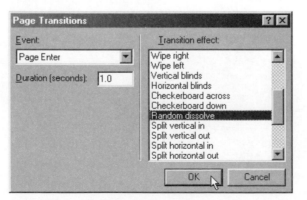

Figure 9.11: The Feedback form appears in the main section of the page

The layout of this page has already been designed for you since it was selected as one of FrontPage's own template designs. You can modify the design of the form if you wish, in the same way as you would edit any other page.

Page Transitions

Page transitions can be added to animate an entire page as it opens. For example, you can make a page appear as if it were descending from above or appear from the sides like theatre curtains.

Like the Dynamic HTML text mentioned earlier in the chapter, Page Transitions are used in both PowerPoint and FrontPage.

* Click the **Navigation** button on the left of the FrontPage window.
* Double click the **Home** page to open it.
* Click **Format**, **Page Transition** on the main menu.

Figure 9.12: Adding a page transition

- Select **Page Enter** as the **Event**.
- Scroll down to find the **Random Dissolve Transition Effect** and enter a **Duration** of **1** second.
- Click **OK**.
- Repeat the steps and apply the same effect to the **Page Exit Event**.

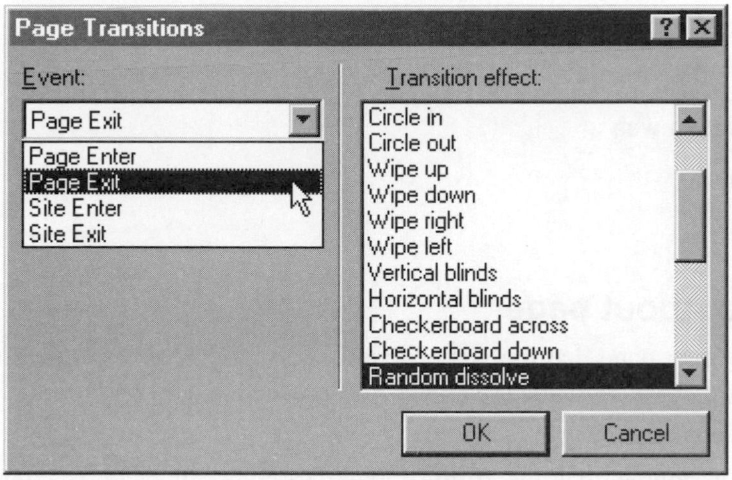

Figure 9.13

- Click **OK** on the **Page Transitions** window to close it and confirm your selection.
- **Save** the web page and view it in a browser. The new effects will not be instantly apparent but when you click on a link, exiting the page, it will fade out and the Frames page will fade in as if it were already underneath. If you click the **Back** button, the Home page will fade back in because the dissolve effect was also applied to the **Page Enter Event**.
- **Close** the browser window and **FrontPage**.

Chapter 10 – Java Applets

Objectives

By the end of this chapter you will have learned how to:

➤ modify the web's file structure

➤ insert an applet into a web

➤ add a hit counter

Working on the About page

The About page is the first page that the visitor to your site will see when they click the graphic on the Home page. In this chapter you will add content, a Java applet and a hit counter to the page.

- **Open** the **HASP** web to start work.

- In **Navigation** view, double-click the **Home Page**. Ctrl-click this page to enter the site. This will automatically display the **About** page in the main section. It will appear as blank because nothing has been added to it yet.

- Position the cursor on the top line of the page and type About the Association.

- Select the title and make it size **36pt** in **Viner Hand ITC** font. **Center** it and make it orange. (It will probably wrap to two lines.)

- Press **Enter** to go to the next line.

Java applets

Java applets are programs that work with graphics to create different special effects – for example, a flag flying in the wind, water rippling across a pond etc. You may have seen some very clever examples of applets if you have looked at other sites on the web.

A Java applet usually has the extension **.class**. If it includes different graphics, it will find these via its parameters.

The applet that is going to be used in this site produces a smooth slideshow of different images. We will customize it to display photographs provided by the Historical Association.

There are thousands of Java applets available for you to download, and this one was downloaded from www.javafile.com. The best way to find any sites with applets is to type 'Java applets' in to the search box of a search engine.

Modifying the web's file structure

Organisation is all-important in Web site maintenance, so we are going to create two new folders in which to keep the images and files that we need

- Click the **Folder List** button to view the files currently in your web.

- Click on the main (root) web folder to select it (e.g. **C:\My Documents\My Webs\Hasp**).

- Select **File, New, Folder** from the menu. Rename it *Java*.

- Click the **Images** folder to select it and click **File**, **New**, **Folder** again to create another folder.
- Call this one *Fader*.

The top portion of the new file structure should look Figure 10.1 below:

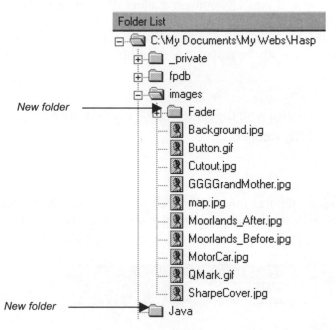

Figure 10.1: Modifying the web's file structure

Importing files into a web

The applet file and the graphics files it uses need to be imported into the web before the slideshow will work. Unfortunately FrontPage will not do this automatically like it does when you insert a graphic in the usual way, so it needs to be done manually.

- Click the **Java** folder in the **Folder List** to select it.
- Select **File**, **Import** from the main menu.
- You will see the Import window appear. Click **Add File**.

Select the **imagefader.class** file from the location you downloaded it to on your hard disk. You will need to have downloaded this file from www.payne-gallway.co.uk/frontpage.

- Click **Open**.

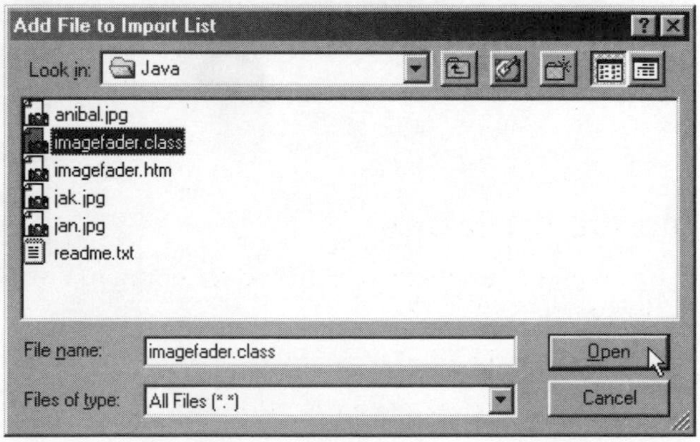

Figure 10.2: Adding the applet file to the Java folder in the web

- You will see the file appear in the **Import** window. Click **OK**.

Note: The files shown in figure 10.2 are all the files that were downloaded with the applet. Applets are normally downloaded in Zip files and will typically contain a **.class** file, which is the applet file itself, a **readme.txt** file with instructions on how to run the applet, a **.htm** file which is usually a working example of the applet (when run in a browser) and any necessary graphics files that it uses. In this case there are 3 **.jpg** files with it. These can usually be replaced with graphics of your own choice – check with the **readme.txt** file.

We are going to replace the images supplied with the applet with four of our own.

- Select the **Fader** folder and click **File**, **Import**.
- Click **Add File**.
- Select the **koblenz.jpg** file.
- Hold down the **Ctrl** key and select the other files that will be used with this applet: **scarboro1.jpg**, **scarboro2.jpg** and **stagecoach.jpg**. In the screenshot below, the files are being imported from the folder where they were stored by the scanning program.

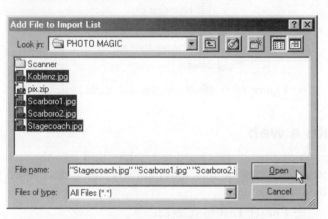

Figure 10.3: Selecting multiple files

- Click **Open** to put them into the Import window.

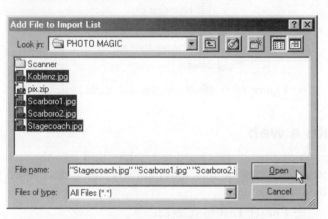

Figure 10.4: Importing multiple files

- Click **OK**. The files will be added to the **Fader** folder in **Folder List**.

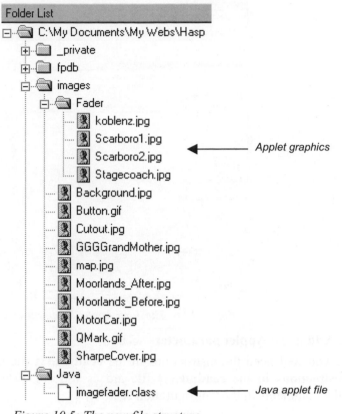

Figure 10.5: The new file structure

Inserting an applet into a web

Now you can insert the applet into the About page.

- With the mouse cursor on the line below the title, select **Insert**, **Advanced**, **Java Applet** on the main menu.

You will see the Java Applet Properties box appear.

- In the **Applet source** box, enter the name of the applet file as *imagefader.class*.

- In the **Applet base URL** box, enter the pathname **./java/**

This means "starting at the current folder (the single dot) go down to the Java folder". The **./** is not required by most browsers but is included to make the code universal.

Some browsers may not be able to support Java so you can enter a message for people using these in the next box. See figure 10.6.

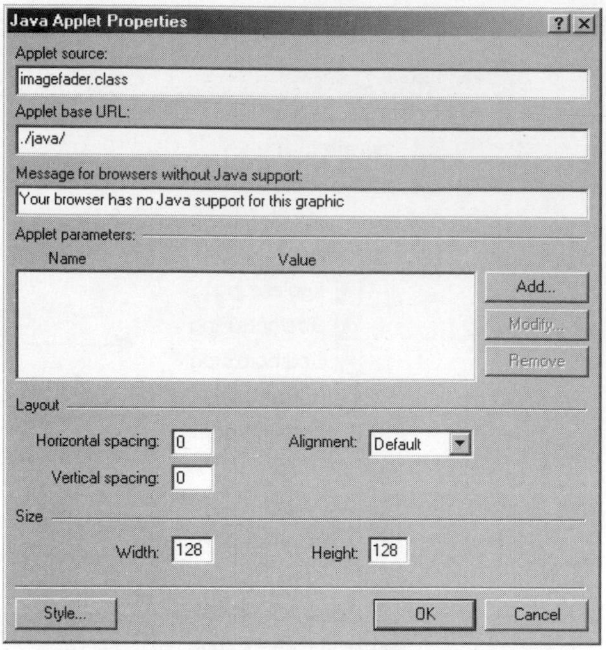

Figure 10.6: The Java Applet Properties window

- Now click **Add** in the **Applet parameters** section.

This is where you will need the instructions in the **readme.txt** file that came with the applet. For this applet, the instructions in the **readme.txt** file are as follows. (The meanings of the parameters are explained in the comments in the Configuration section)

```
*** Documentation about Demicron's "Imagefader" java-applet ***
********* Version 1.0, programmed by Anibal Wainstein *********

Licence agreement:

The registration number for this applet is A00012.
Note that Demicron doesn't take any responsibility against damage this
applet may do to your system or another. The applet is freeware and
may be used commercially by anyone. It may not be altered in any way.

Description:

If you want a nice slideshow then you should use this applet. The
applet collects a number of equal-sized pictures and shows them by
fading one to another in a cycle. You can also specify an URL
connected to the picture that is applied when the user clicks on the
picture. Note that the applet space MUST be of the same size as the
pictures and ALL the pictures MUST have equal dimensions.

Configuration:

* "demicron" (must be "www.demicron.se") Required parameter.
* "reg" (must be "A00012") Required parameter.
* "width" (integer number) Applet and picture width.
* "height" (integer number) Applet and picture height.
```

```
*  "sleeptime" (integer number) The time a picture will be shown before
   it fades to another.
*  "step" (floating point number) The detail of the fade in percent. A
   lower number gives best detail. Should be around 0.05.
*  "delay" (integer  number) Fade delay. Should be around 20.
*  "maxitems" (integer number) Number of images and URLs.
*  "bitmapxx" (text) The name of the picture xx.
*  "urlxx" (text) The URL of picture xx. If you dont want any, just
write a " " (space character).
```

Here is an example of a HTML-configuration:

```
<APPLET CODE="imagefader.class" WIDTH=80 HEIGHT=107>
<PARAM name="demicron" value="www.demicron.se">
<PARAM name="reg" value="A00012">
<PARAM name="maxitems" value="3">
<PARAM name="width" value="80">
<PARAM name="height" value="107">
<PARAM name="bitmap0" value="anibal.jpg">
<PARAM name="bitmap1" value="jak.jpg">
<PARAM name="bitmap2" value="jan.jpg">
<PARAM name="url0" value="http://www.nada.kth.se/~nv92-awa/">
<PARAM name="url1" value="http://www.nada.kth.se/~nv92-jak/">
<PARAM name="url2" value="http://www.nada.kth.se/~nv92-jfu/">
<PARAM name="step" value="0.05">
<PARAM name="delay" value="20">
<PARAM name="sleeptime" value="2000">
</APPLET>
```

Having pressed the **Add** button on the Java Applet Properties window, you will see the Set Attribute Value window appear. This is where you will state which pictures you want the applet to display in the slide show, how big the pictures are, how many pictures there are and so on. You can enter the parameters in any order – they will automatically be rearranged alphabetically.

- Enter **bitmap0** (zero, not the letter 'O') in the **Name** box.

- Enter **./images/fader/koblenz.jpg** in the **Value** box. This is where the applet can expect to find the first picture – The **Koblenz.jpg** picture, in the **Fader** folder, in the **Images** folder in the web.

Figure 10.7: Setting the first attribute for the applet

- Click **OK**. The parameter will be added to the list.

- Click **Add** to repeat these steps to add the rest of the parameters below. These parameters are all adapted from the bottom section of the **readme.txt** file above. The meanings of each of the parameters are also explained in the text above.

Name:	Value:
bitmap1	./images/fader/scarboro1.jpg
bitmap2	./images/fader/scarboro2.jpg
bitmap3	./images/fader/stagecoach.jpg
delay	20
demicron	www.demicron.se
height	181
maxitems	4
reg	A00012
sleeptime	2000
step	0.05
url0	*Just enter a single space here*
url1	*Just enter a single space here*
url2	*Just enter a single space here*
url3	*Just enter a single space here*
width	280

Note that once again the single dot in the pathnames for **bitmap1**, **bitmap2** etc means "starting at the current directory, (the single dot) go down to **images**, then to **fader**, then down to the image in question".

- Once you have added all of the Applet parameters, set the **Width** to **280** and the **Height** to **181**.

Note: It is important to make sure that the slideshow applet and all of the graphics used in the slideshow are of identical size. The **Width** and **Height** boxes on the **Java Applet Properties** window are measured in pixels. Your window should look like that in Figure 10.8:

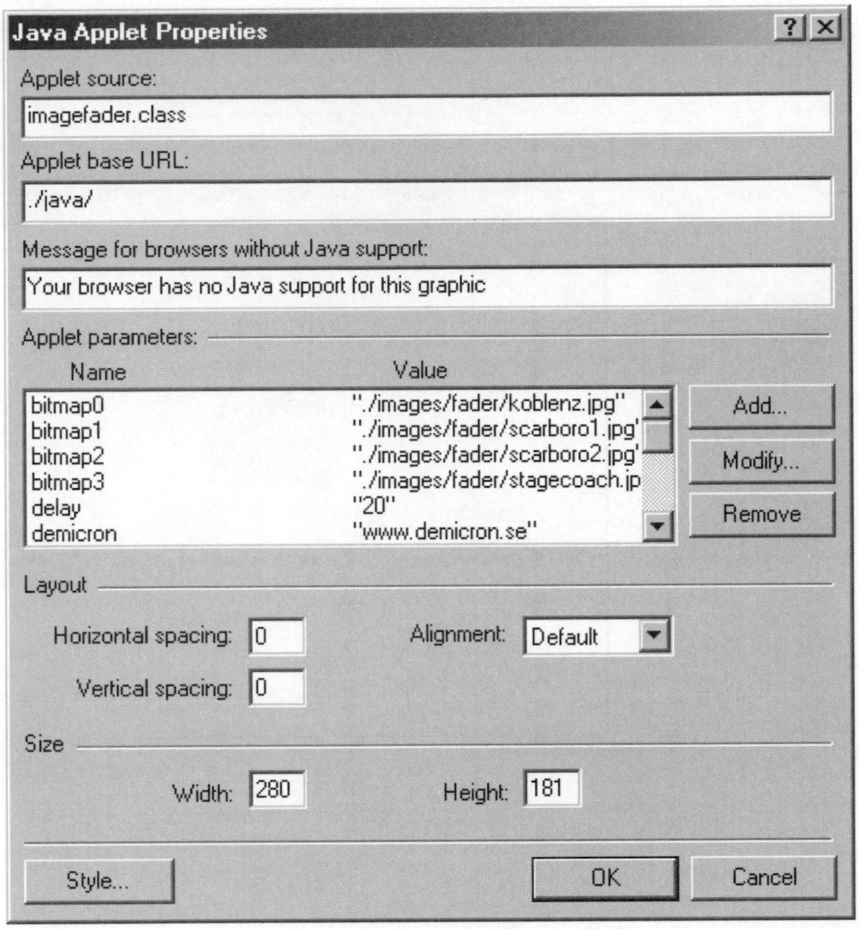

Java Applet Properties

Applet source:

imagefader.class

Applet base URL:

./java/

Message for browsers without Java support:

Your browser has no Java support for this graphic

Applet parameters:

Name	Value	
bitmap0	"./images/fader/koblenz.jpg"	Add...
bitmap1	"./images/fader/scarboro1.jpg'	
bitmap2	"./images/fader/scarboro2.jpg'	Modify...
bitmap3	"./images/fader/stagecoach.jp	
delay	"20"	Remove
demicron	"www.demicron.se"	

Layout

Horizontal spacing: 0   Alignment: Default

Vertical spacing: 0

Size

Width: 280   Height: 181

Style...   OK   Cancel

Figure 10.8: The completed properties window

- Click **OK**. The applet filename will appear underneath the 'J' icon on the page. The applet won't actually work until the web is published so this is as far as you can go here for now.

- Press **Enter** to go to the next line.

- Enter the following text:

The Speymont Historical Association aims to provide everyone with the opportunity to learn from, contribute to and purchase various publications on historical topics relating to the local area. It also organises tours of local areas of historical interest and talks by members on all sorts of fascinating historical topics!

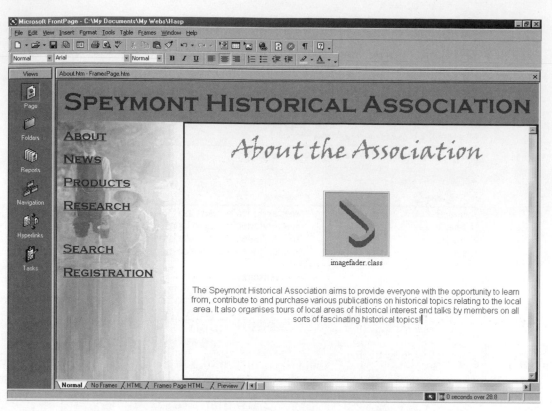

Figure 10.9: The page so far (without the Folder List)

Adding a Hit Counter

A hit counter can be useful for telling you how many visits there have been to the site. This is another feature which will only work when the web is published so you will have to wait to see the effect!

- Set the cursor on a new line beneath the text about the association.

- Click the **Center** button to put the cursor in the middle of the line.

- Select **Insert**, **Component**, **Hit Counter** from the menu.

- Select the second number style.

- Check the **Fixed number of digits** option and set it to **5**. It is unlikely that this Web site is going to have more than 99,999 hits in its lifetime!

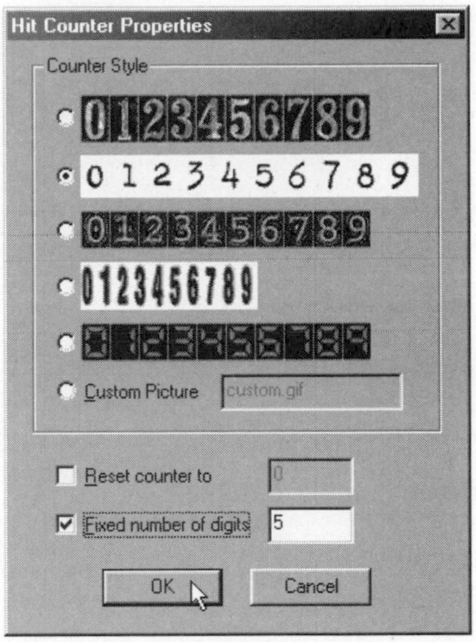

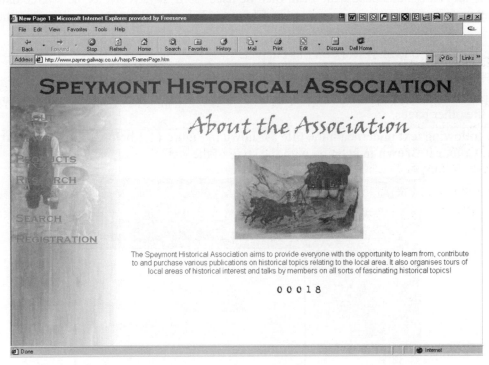

Figure 10.10: The Hit Counter Properties window

- Click **OK**. **[Hit Counter]** should appear at the bottom of the page.

You cannot see the Java applet or the hit counter working until you publish the web, but when you do, you will see a slideshow of the pictures you imported, each one remaining on the screen for a few seconds and then fading into the next. The hit counter is displayed at the bottom of the screen. Eighteen and rising!

Figure 10.11: The published web page

- **Save** the page and **Exit** FrontPage.

Chapter 11 – Database Forms

Objectives

By the end of this chapter you will have learned how to:

➤ insert a form in a web page for a user to fill in

➤ validate the data entered by the user

➤ send the information to a Microsoft Access database

➤ send user feedback to an e-mail address

Collecting mailing list data

A Web site can be a very useful means of collecting data to add to a mailing list. If people voluntarily fill in a form on your site, giving their names and addresses, it probably means they will be quite receptive to any information you send them advertising activities, new products etc. A well-targeted mailing list is worth its weight in gold to any organization!

FrontPage has a facility to create a form which the user can fill in, and when they press **Submit**, the data will be sent to an Access database which can then be used from, say, Word as the source data for a mail shot. This latter part of the project is covered in Chapter 13. In this chapter we will create the data input form.

- **Open** the **HASP** web to start work on this chapter.

- In **Navigation** view, double-click the **Home Page** and open the **Registration** page.

- At the top of the page type *Registration* in **Viner Hand ITC** Font, size **36pt**. Colour it **Orange** to match the other pages.

- Enter the following text underneath the title as shown in Figure 11.1 below. Format it to **Arial**, size **12pt**. Colour it **Brown** in keeping with the style of the web.

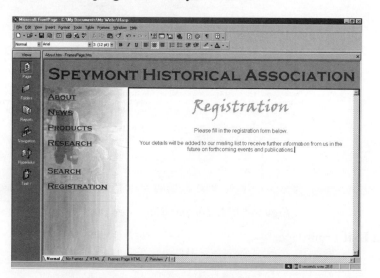

Figure 11.1: The Registration page

Inserting a blank form

- Position the cursor on a new line under the text and click **Insert**, **Form**, **Form** on the main menu. An empty form will appear.
- Position the cursor in front of the two buttons and press **Enter** to add a blank line above them.

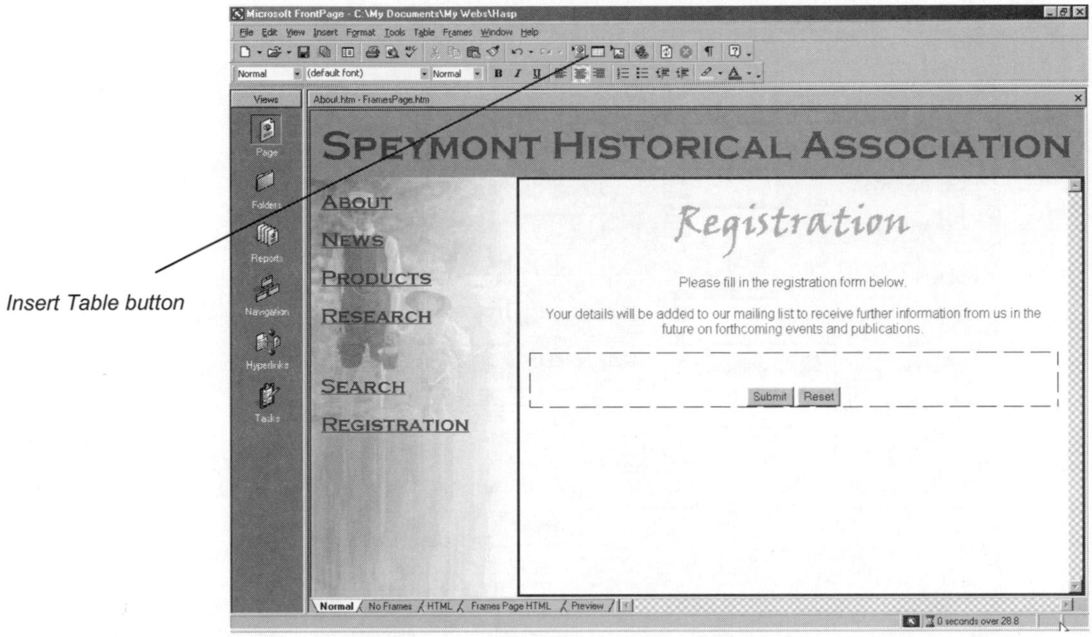

Figure 11.2: Creating a form

- Click the **Insert Table** button and select a **6 by 9 Table** (by dragging out the grid). Using a table is good way to ensure that all the fields and field titles line up neatly.
- Rearrange the table by merging and resizing cells to look like the one shown below. Add the field titles.

Please fill in the registration form below.
Your details will be added to our mailing list to receive further information from us in the future on up coming events and publications.

Title:		Forename:		Surname:	
Address:	Street:				
	Town:				
	County:				
	Post Code:				
	Country:				
E-Mail:			Telephone:		
Area of special interest:					

Submit Reset

Figure 11.3: Creating a table for the form fields

Modifying a table's appearance

- Right-click the table and select **Table Properties** from the pop-up menu.

- Change the **Borders** size to **0** to remove them altogether and select **Cream** as the shade for the table's **Background Color**.

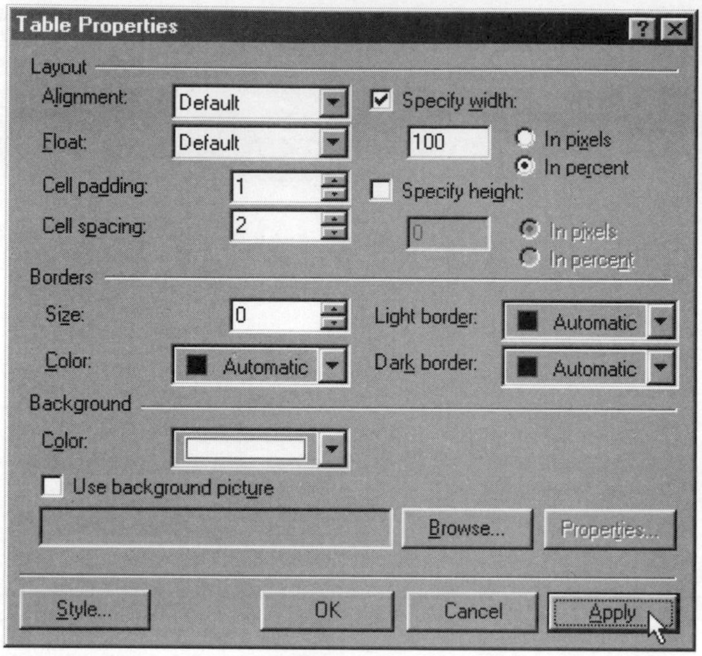

Figure 11.4

- Click **OK** to confirm the settings and close the window. (Clicking **Apply** confirms the settings without closing the window.)

Adding Drop-Down Menu fields

The form fields can be added next. The visitor will enter their details into the fields, and these will automatically be collected in an Access database created by FrontPage.

- Position the mouse cursor in the cell to the right of **Title** and select **Insert**, **Form**, **Drop-Down Menu** from the main menu. A field will appear in the cell.

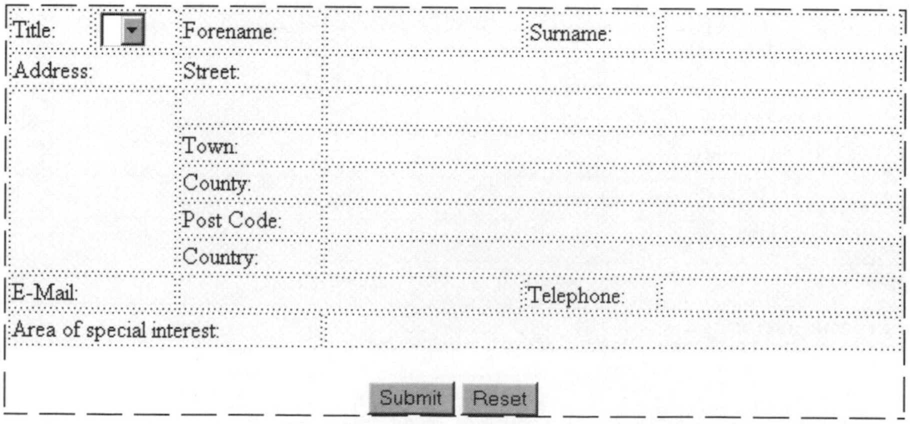

Figure 11.5: Adding a Drop-Down Menu field

Naming a field

It is important to name the fields so that the headings in the database table that will be created have meaning.

- Right-click the field and select **Form Field Properties** from the menu.
- Enter *Title* as the **Name**.
- The **Tab Order** sets the order in which the cursor jumps to each field when the **Tab** key is pressed by the user. Set this to **1** since this will be the first field to be filled in.

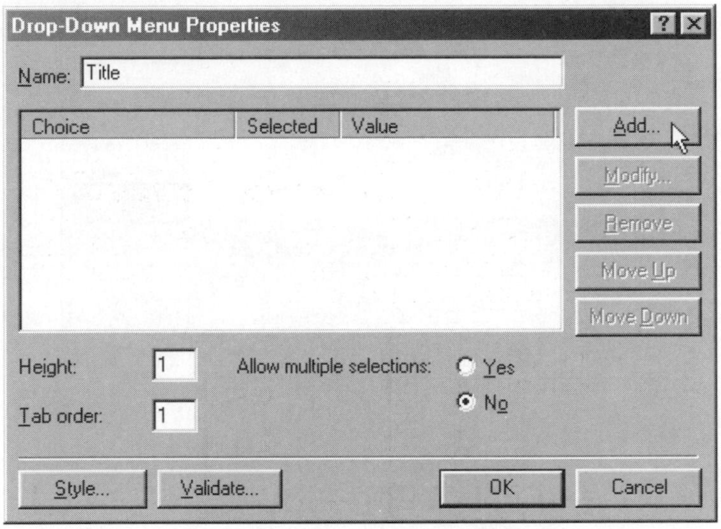

Figure 11.6: Naming a field

The **Allow Multiple Selections** field should stay as **No** because a person can only have one title, e.g. Mr, Mrs, Miss etc.

Adding values to a Drop-Down Menu field

- Click **Add** to add a field value to the drop-down list for the user to choose from. This field will contain choices of Mr, Mrs, Miss, Ms and Dr.

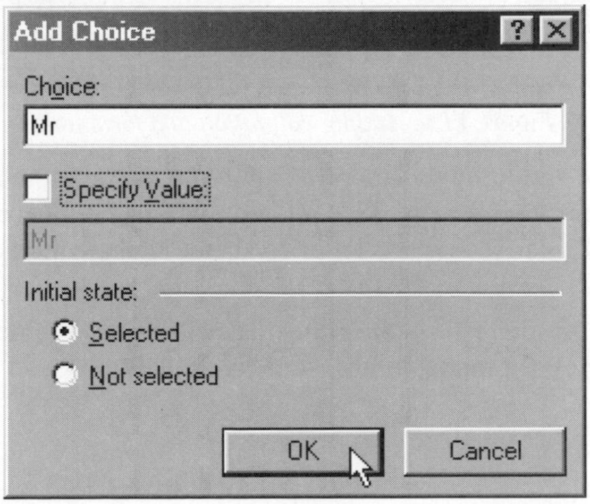

Figure 11.7: Adding a value to the Drop-Down Menu

- Enter *Mr* as the **Choice** and click the Selected option. This will automatically select **Mr** as the default option. (Statistics show that the majority of Internet users are male!)

- Click **OK**.

Repeat the operation to add *Mrs*, *Miss*, *Ms* and *Dr* to the list of choices. The **Initial State** on these choices will be **Not Selected**.

- Click the **Validate** button on the **Drop-Down Menu Properties** window.

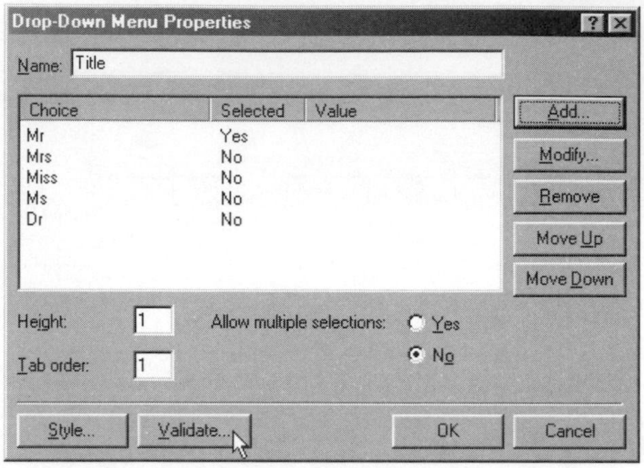

Figure 11.8: A full set of choices has been added

Adding Drop-Down Menu validation

Validation will help to ensure that the correct information has been entered in each of the fields. You can also specify that certain fields may not be left blank.

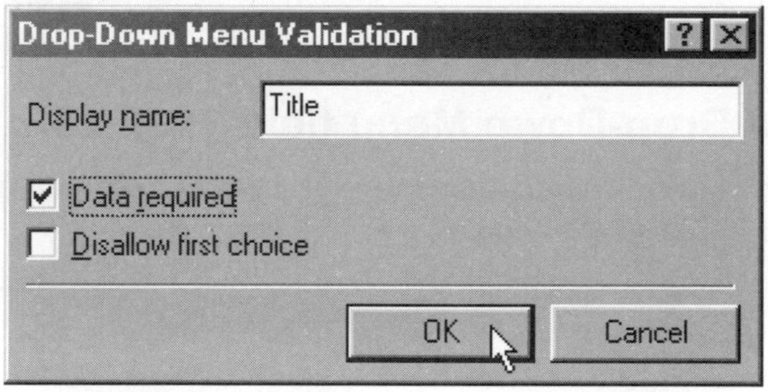

Figure 11.9: Adding validation to a form field

- Check the **Data Required** option box. This means that the user will be required to fill in this field before they can submit their details. This is an important field because without knowing someone's title you cannot easily write a letter to them. A mail merge letter, for example, generally starts with "Dear <<Title>> <<Surname>>".

- Enter *Title* as the **Display Name**. This is the name that will be used to refer to this field in any error messages that pop up if, for example, the field is left blank.

- Click **OK**.

Adding a One-Line Text Box field

A One-Line Text Box field acts in much the same way as the Drop-Down Menu field. You can name it and add validation in much the same way but the user does not get a predetermined list of possible entries.

- Position the cursor in the cell to the right of **Forename** and select **Insert, Form, One-Line Text Box** from the menu.

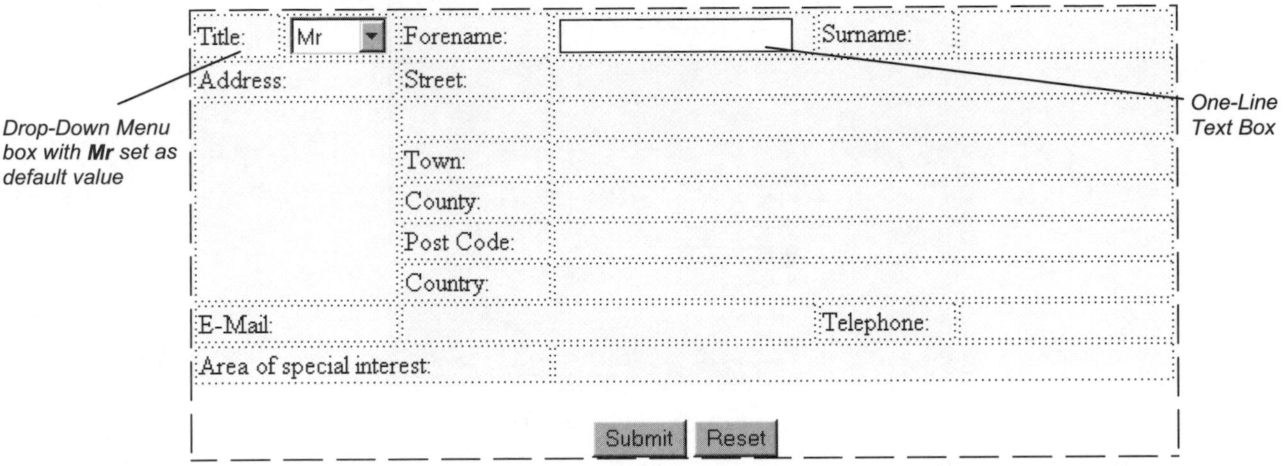

Figure 11.10: A One-Line Text Box

- Right-click the new field to bring up the shortcut menu. Select **Form Field Properties**.
- Change the **Name** to **Forename** and set the **Width in Characters** to **15**. It is unlikely that you are going to get any names longer than say 11 characters, like 'Christopher' for example, but 15 should take care of any others.

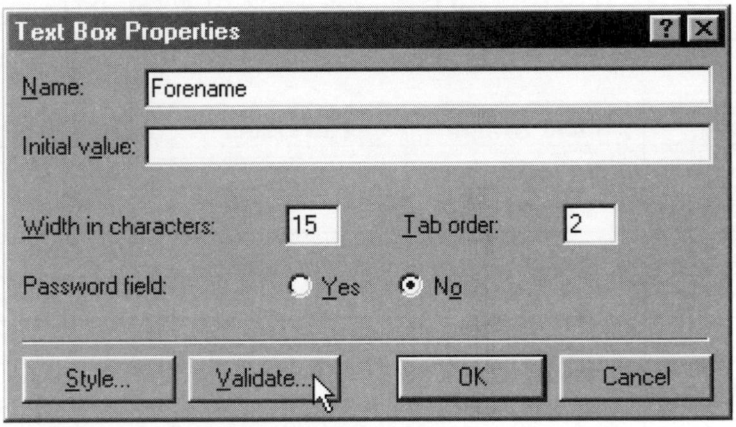

Figure 11.11

- Set the **Tab Order** to **2**. This will be second field that the user will fill in.
- Click the **Validate** button.

Adding validation to a One-Line Text Box

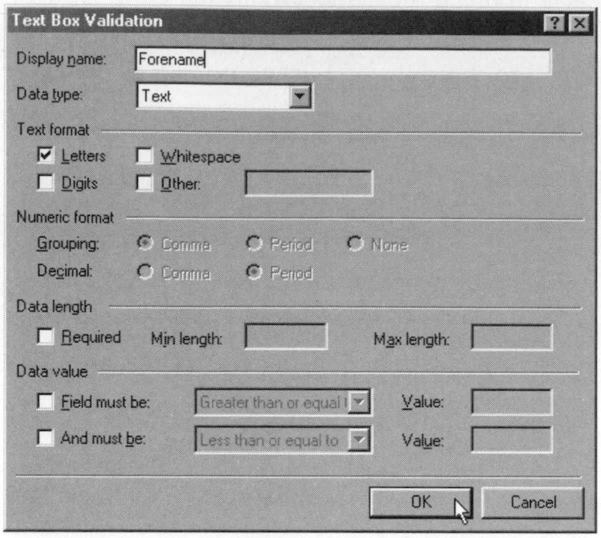

Figure 11.12: Adding validation to a One-Line Text Box

- Change the **Data Type** to **Text**.
- Select **Letters** as the **Text Format**.
- Enter **Forename** as the **Display Name**. Click **OK**.
- Click **OK** again on the **Text Box Properties** window.
- Use **Insert, Form** to add the rest of the fields shown in the table below as **One-Line Text Boxes**. No validation is necessary for these other than being 'required' in some cases. It is difficult to validate name and address fields since they can take virtually any combination of letters and numbers.

Field Name	Field Length	Tab Order	Required
Surname	20	3	Yes
Street	40	4	Yes
StreetLine2	40	5	
Town	30	6	Yes
County	20	7	
PostCode	8	8	
Country	30	9	
EMail	30	10	
Telephone	25	11	

Figure 11.13

Once you have added all the fields listed in Figure 11.13, you can add the final field for the **Area of Special Interest**. This will be a Drop-Down Menu box like the **Title** field, saving the user the chore of typing in their choice.

- Insert a **Drop-Down Menu** field into the **Area of Special Interest** cell.
- Right-click the field and select **Form Field Properties**.

- Enter *Interest* as the field name.
- Press the **Add** button to fill in the choices shown in figure 11.14.

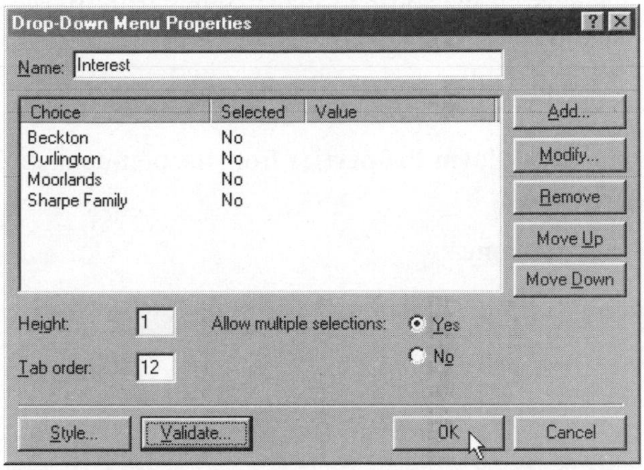

Figure 11.14

- Set the **Tab Order** to **12**.
- Select **Yes** to **Allow Multiple Selections**. This will let the site user choose more than one area of interest by holding down the Ctrl key when they are making their selections.
- Click **OK**.
- Next to the field, type in a short instruction on how to select more than one choice from the Menu box.

In the screenshot below, the Views bar has been hidden. Depending on the size and resolution of the screen you are using, you may have to scroll to see all the fields. You should take into account, when designing your Web site, that many viewers will not have large, high-resolution screens!

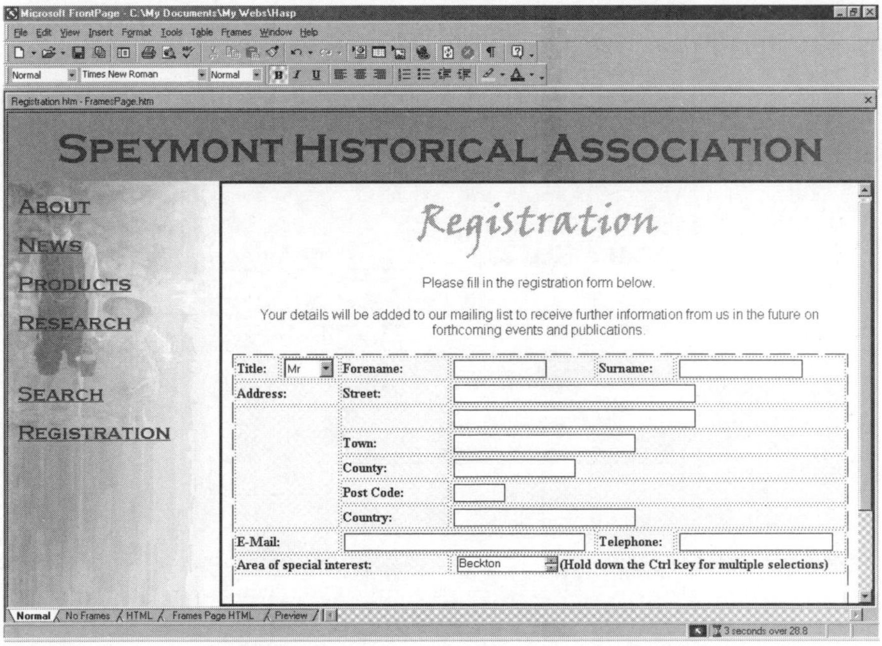

Figure 11.15: The finished registration form

- **Save** the page so far.

Submitting the information to an Access database table

Once you have set up a form on a web page, you need to know how to retrieve the data that visitors submit. By default, FrontPage sets up the form so that it sends data to a text file or Web page on the server. To retrieve the form data, you open the Web page in FrontPage.

However, you can change these defaults, and in this exercise, you will route the data to a database residing on the Web server.

- Right-click on the form and select **Form Properties** from the pop-up menu.
- Select the **Send to Database** option.
- Enter *Registration* as the **Form Name**.

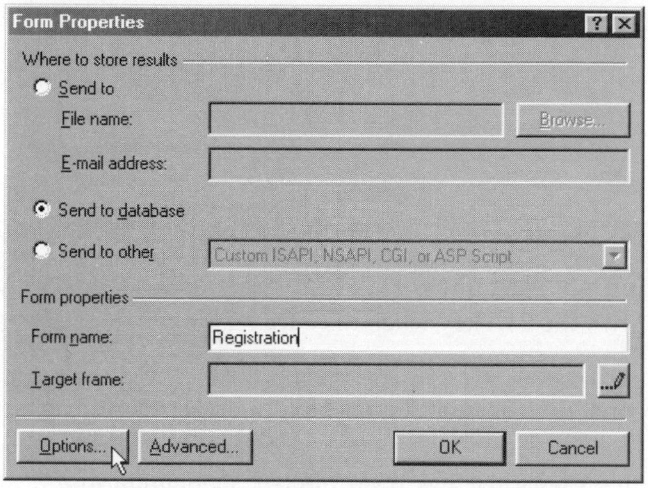

Figure 11.16: Sending the form data to a database

Now the database table that will receive the form data needs to be created. FrontPage will do this automatically.

- Click **Options**. The Options for Saving Results to Database window will appear.

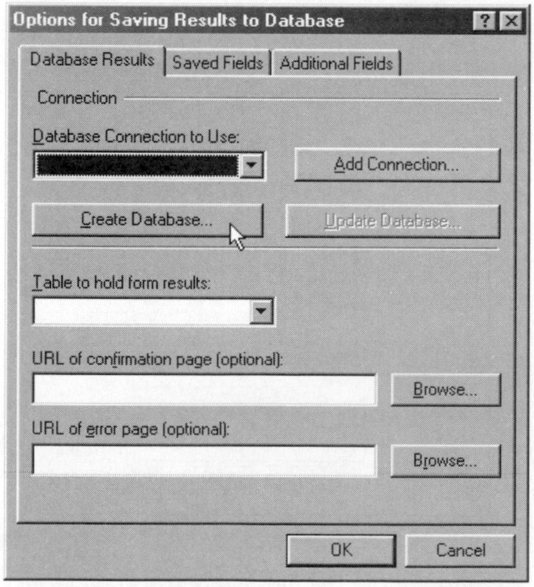

Figure 11.17: Creating a database table for form data

- Click **Create Database**. FrontPage will create a table called **Registration** in which to store the form data.

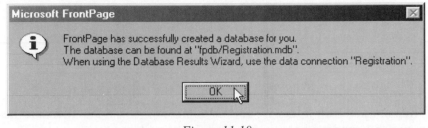

Figure 11.18

- When the database has been created, FrontPage will display a confirmation dialogue box. Click **OK**.
- Click **OK** again twice to close the database creation windows and confirm your actions.

Active Server Pages

FrontPage will recommend that you save or rename the Registration page with a different file extension for it to function properly. It is what is known as an Active Server Page and requires a **.asp** extension.

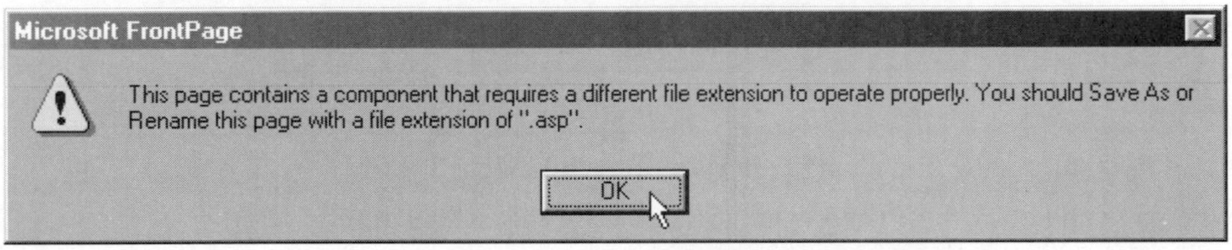

Microsoft FrontPage

⚠ This page contains a component that requires a different file extension to operate properly. You should Save As or Rename this page with a file extension of ".asp".

OK

Figure 11.19

- Click the **Folder List** button on the toolbar to view the files in your web if they are not already in view. 
- Right-click the **Registration.htm** file and select **Rename** from the shortcut menu.
- Rename it **Registration.asp**.

Products.htm
QMark.gif
Registration.asp
Research.htm
Search.htm
Sharpe.htm
SharpeCover.jpg

Figure 11.20

FrontPage and all Microsoft programs will warn you that changing a file's extension may make it unusable. This is to stop users from accidentally changing it.

- In this case you need to make the change so click **Yes** to confirm.

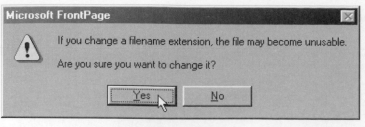

Figure 11.21

The links to the Registration.**htm** file will not function now since the filename has been changed. FrontPage can automatically update these links to find the **.asp** file instead.

- Click **Yes** to update the hyperlinks.

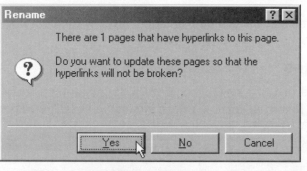

Figure 11.22

- Highlight the entire table and change the **Font** to **Arial**. Make it **Bold**.
- **Save** the page and click the **Preview** tab to see the form as it will appear.

Note: This page will not send data to the database until it is published on a FrontPage-compliant Web server. If you try to look at it in a Browser, you will see the following message:

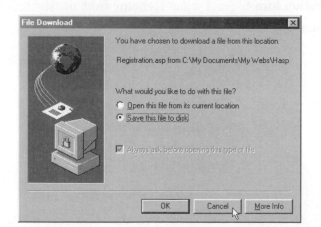

Figure 11.23: Attempting to look at the Registration page in a browser

- Click **Cancel**, and close the browser.

We will continue looking at how to collect the data submitted by visitors to the site in Chapter 13.

The Feedback form

Although this form has already been created automatically by FrontPage's Template Wizard, it still needs to be told where to send the information it collects. By default, all the feedback will be stored in a text file on the web server. As we have already seen, you can route it to a database, and as a third alternative, you can have it sent directly to an e-mail address. This is a suitable option for visitor feedback, provided the user does not get snowed under with hundreds of e-mails every day.

Ideally, it would be good to have it sent directly to an e-mail address you specified. First you need to add a new title to the page.

- Open the **Feedback** form by double-clicking on the **Feedback.htm** file in the **Folder List**.
- Replace the purple coloured text at the top of the page with the text *Feedback*.
- **Center** it, colour it orange, make it **36pt** and **Viner Hand ITC** style font.

Sending form data to an e-mail address

- Right-click the form (the area within the dashed border) and select **Form Properties** from the menu.

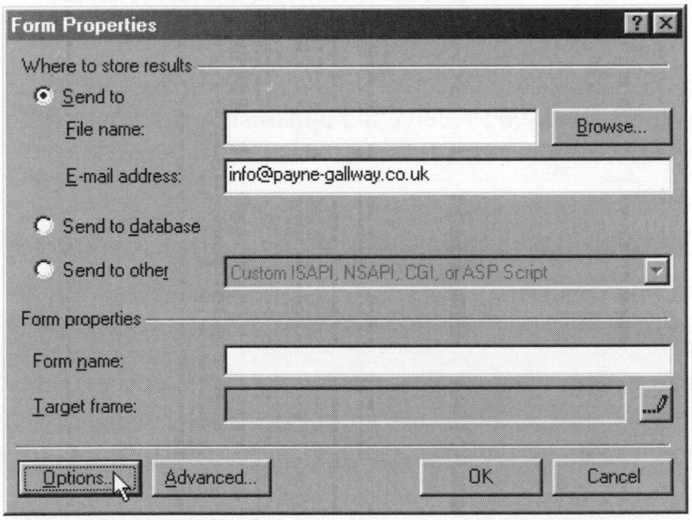

Figure 11.24: Sending data to an e-mail address

- Delete the file name in the **File name** box and enter an **e-mail** address you would like to have the feedback sent to instead. (Use your own e-mail address for testing purposes.)
- Click the **Options** button and select the **E-mail Results** tab.

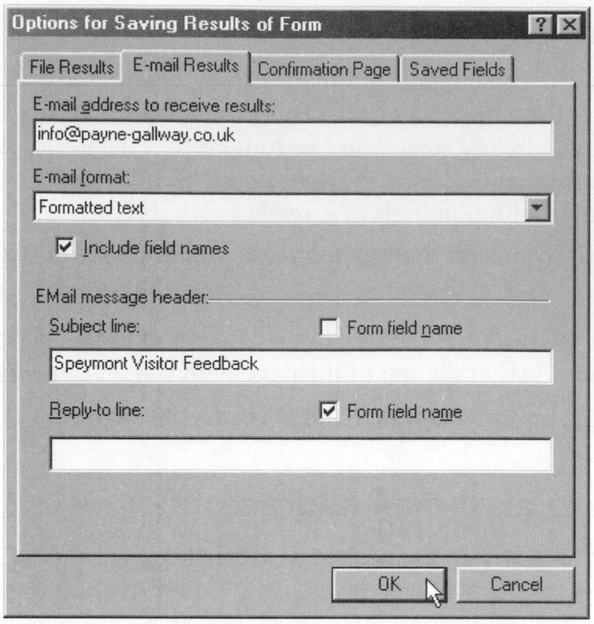

Figure 11.25: Sending data to an e-mail address

- Enter *Speymont Visitor Feedback* as the **Subject line** of the **Email message header**. This will put this line as the subject when you receive the e-mail so you know it is from a visitor and what it is likely to contain before you read it.

- Click **OK**, and **OK** again.

- You will see the following warning message. Click **No**. This will be fine once the web has been published.

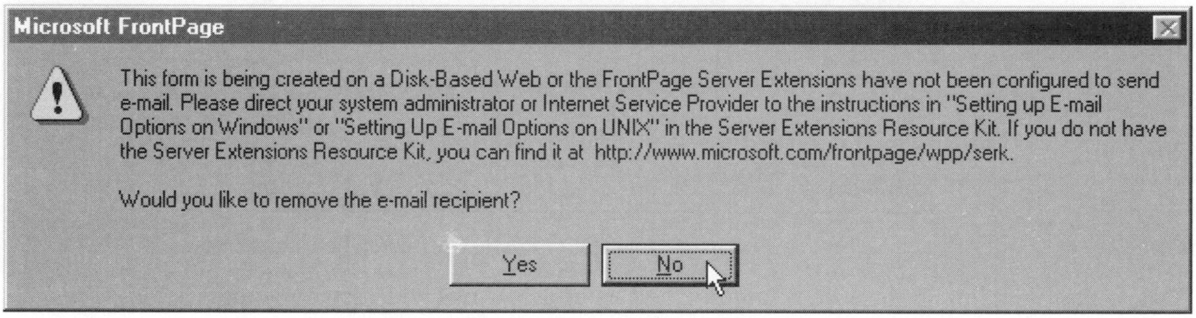

Figure 11.26: Warning!

- **Save** and **Close** your web.

Chapter 12 – Publishing the Web

Objectives

By the end of this chapter you will have learned how to:

➤ select a Web Presence Provider

➤ publish your web

➤ open the web online

➤ delete files from a published Web site

A glossary of terms

Publishing your Web site is a relatively easy process. However, it is common to encounter problems which may be the fault of the designer or may be due to the setup provided by the Web host.

Here is a glossary of basic terms in web publishing to help your understanding of the acronyms etc.:

Name or Acronym	Full Name	Description
ISP	Internet Service Provider	An ISP is a company such as Freeserve, AOL or CompuServe which gives or sells access to the Internet, providing your computer with a connection.
Browser		A Browser is piece of software like Microsoft Internet Explorer or Netscape Navigator that allows you to download and display a Web site on your computer.
Web Server		A Web Server is a computer connected to the Internet. Browsers can access the Server to find and display different pages of a web.
Web Host		A Web Host is a company that can provide space on a Web Server for you to publish a web.
Search Engine		A Search Engine is a program like Yahoo or AltaVista that is used to search the Internet for specified sites.
FTP	File Transfer Protocol	A File Transfer Protocol is a set of instructions common to all computers on how to send files from one machine to the other.
IE5	Microsoft Internet Explorer version 5	An example of a Browser.
WPP	Web Presence Provider	A Web Presence Provider is a Web Host that provides the FrontPage Server Extensions.

Several of the advanced features used in this site require FrontPage Server Extensions to operate properly. Without these, some of these features (e.g. the Search form) will be displayed but will not work, and other features such as the hit counter will not be displayed at all.

FrontPage Server Extensions

FrontPage Server Extensions are extra files that operate advanced web components such as those listed below. They also provide the ability to maintain and edit a web online. There are several features of FrontPage which require the extension files to work. Some of these have not been used in this site, but they are:

> **Page Banners**
>
> **Hit Counters**
>
> **Confirmation Pages**
>
> **Scheduled Pictures**
>
> **Scheduled Include Pages**
>
> **Search Forms**

Where to publish your web?

A good place to start looking to publish a web is your ISP. These often act as host as well. Companies such as Freeserve, AOL or CompuServe offer limited space for you to publish your own site as part of the service included in your contract. If you plan to use one of these companies to host your web, you will need to contact their technical support department to find out how much space you are allowed and if they support the FrontPage Server Extensions. Freeserve does not, for security reasons, and others take a similar stance.

Another place to look is on the Web. There are companies that offer to publish Web sites free of charge on condition that they can put some of their advertising banners at the top of each page. If you do not mind having someone else's advertisements on your pages, this might be a good choice.

The alternative is to go to a dedicated host. A dedicated host can provide as much space as required and will often use faster equipment. There is a wide selection of dedicated hosts that you could go to but they will charge. A host that supports the FrontPage Server Extensions is often referred to as a Web Presence Provider or WPP. FrontPage has a facility for finding a selection of these automatically on the Web for you to choose from.

This chapter is based on the methods that have been used in publishing this Web site. I used a dedicated web host that charges for its services. The host supports FrontPage Server Extensions – an essential requirement to get all the included features to work. The browser used was IE5.

Important: If your circumstances do not match these, you may still find parts of the chapter useful in publishing your own web. Bear in mind that every instance of web publishing is likely to have slightly different circumstances, involving slightly different processes.

Selecting a Web Presence Provider

Make sure that you are using a computer with a connection to the Internet.

- Open **FrontPage** and the **Hasp** web.
- Make sure that the **Folder List** is visible.
- Click the **Folders** button on the **Views** bar.

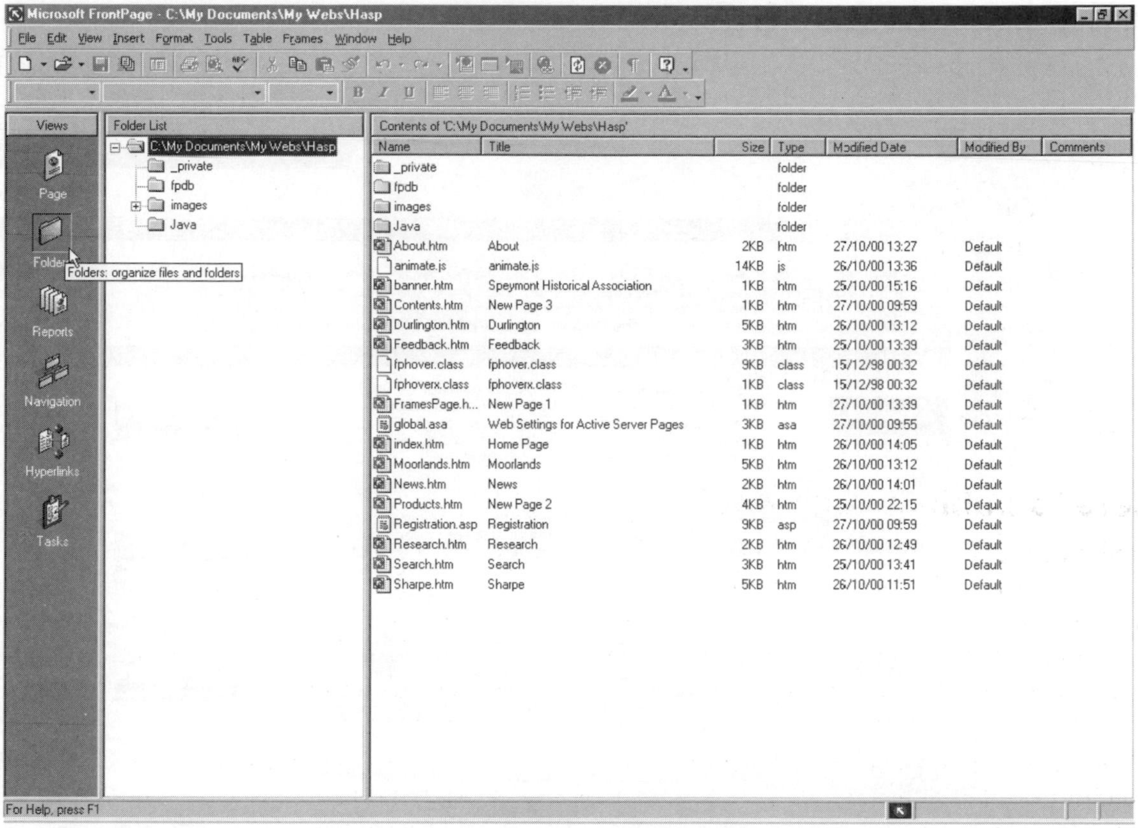

Figure 12.1: The files and folders in the web

Now you need to load your browser. I am using **IE5**. Previous versions of Internet Explorer will behave differently. If you need to get the latest version, it is available to download free of charge from the **Microsoft** Web site under the **Upgrades** link.

- Double-click on the **Internet Explorer** icon. **IE5** will open.
- Return to FrontPage.
- Click **File**, **Publish Web** on the menu.

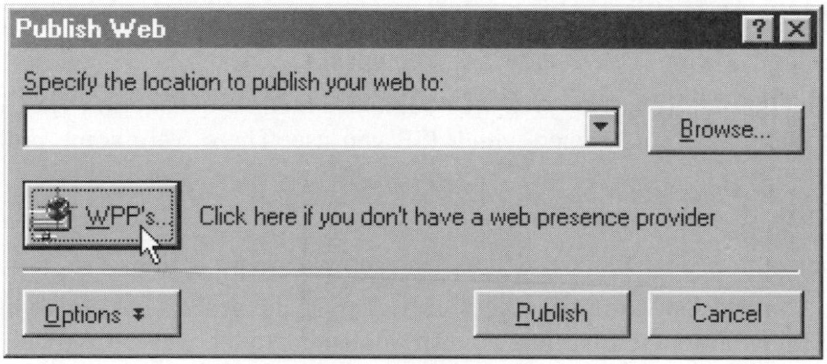

Figure 12.2: Finding a WPP

- Click the **WPP's** button. This will open a page on the Microsoft Web that will allow you to search for a suitable WPP. Select United Kingdom providers if you are using this book in the UK and look at the list it gives you. EasyNet is one of the better known WPP's.

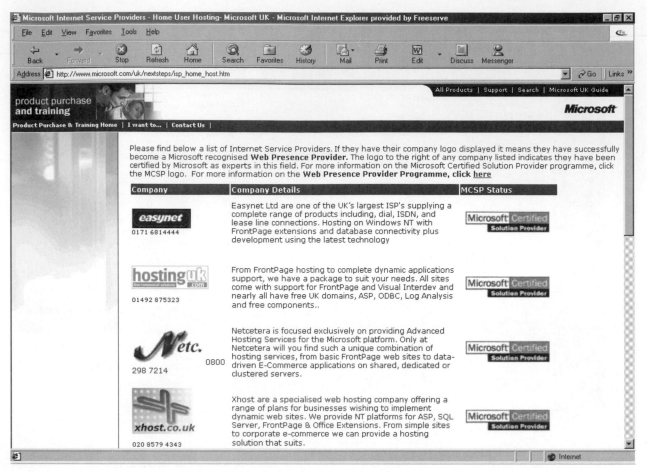

Figure 12.3: Selecting a WPP

- Listed on this site are some of the major WPPs. This Web site is published on a smaller independent server, **www.lightspeed.co.uk**. Smaller companies often provide you with a better and more personal service if you encounter problems.

Publishing the HASP web

Now you can publish the Hasp Web site that has been created.

- Make sure FrontPage is running with the Hasp web open.
- Connect to the Internet via IE5. This web was published using a connection via CompuServe but it shouldn't make much difference which ISP you use. There were some problems with Freeserve.
- Select **File**, **Publish Web** from the menu.
- Click the **Options** button. The window will expand showing more options.

The default option is to **Publish changed pages only**. This is the best one to stick with since it can save time in transferring files. If it is the first time you are publishing to the web, FrontPage will publish all the pages. The Server Extensions make a comparison between the files at the specified location you are publishing the files to and the web in FrontPage on your computer. FrontPage then publishes only those pages that differ.

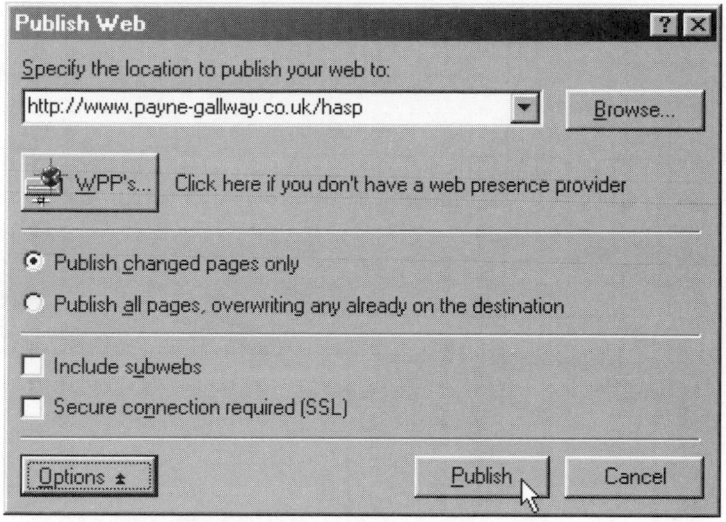

Figure 12.4: Publishing the web

You will need to have found out from your host the location you can publish your files to, and the username and password to access the location. The password may not always be applicable.

- Enter the web location of the site by typing http://www.(the name of the site) in the top box of the Publish Web window. (See Figure 12.4.) This Web site is being published to http://www.payne-gallway.co.uk/hasp. You will be able to see it there if you log on.

- Once you have specified the location you wish to publish your web to, click **Publish**.

- If you are asked for a password, type it in and continue.

- The files will begin to fly across to the new location on the Web.

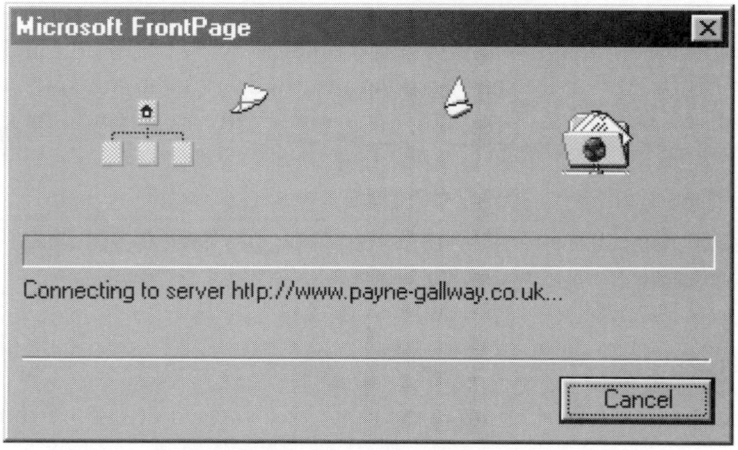

Figure 12.5: Transferring the web files

You should now be able to log on to the location you specified and see your web fully functional. Try looking at some of the features that previously didn't work before it was published.

If you encounter any problems, try checking properties and parameters. With Java applets, for example, incorrect pathnames are the most common fault. If you still can't fix it yourself, try asking your host if they could have a look. It might be something they need to do at their end.

Opening the web online

To open your web whilst it is on the World Wide Web, open FrontPage. This will *only* work with the Server Extensions enabled.

- Select **File**, **Open Web** from the menu.
- Click the **Web Folders** button on the left of the window and select the Web location you published your web to.

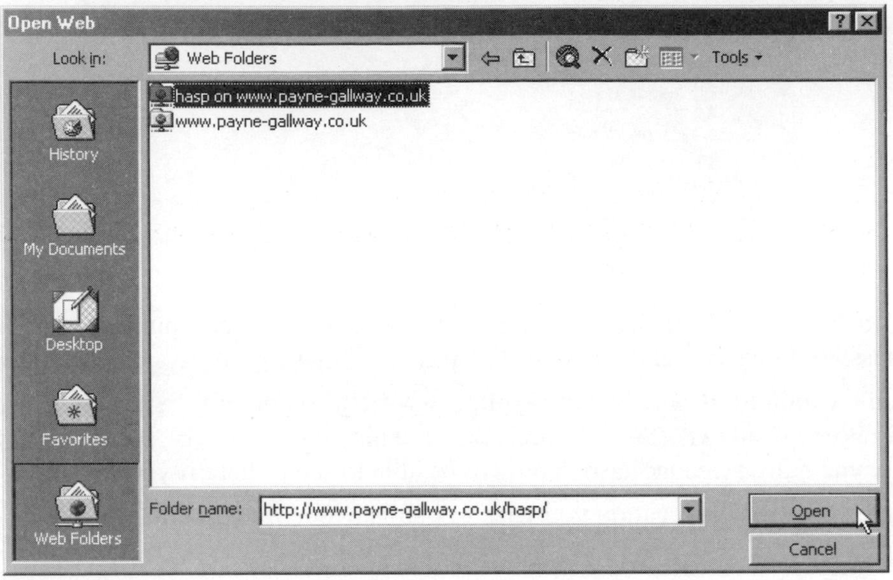

Figure 12.6: Opening a Web site on-line

- Click **Open**.

Your Web site will open in FrontPage whilst it still on the Web. You can edit and make changes to this version as you would offline. It is not usually a good idea to do this though since the version of the web on your computer will not remain in sync, but it's a quick way to try out changes without having to republish every time. When you've finished, update the master version on your computer.

> **Note:** You cannot easily copy updated files from your Web site back to your hard disk. For this you will need an FTP program, something which this book does not cover.

Deleting web files

You can delete files you have put on the web in the same way you would do in FrontPage *off* the web.

- Follow the instructions for opening the web online.
- Select a file you wish to delete and press the **Delete** key. You will be given a warning. Click **OK** and your file will be deleted.

Some providers prefer you to let them delete files so you had better check with them first.

- Log off the Internet and close the current web in FrontPage.

Search forms

Search forms rely on an index of all words in the web built automatically when it is published to find what you are looking for. Many hosts do not enable indexing without you asking specifically because of the potential, albeit minor, extra overhead.

Promoting your site

The final step in getting your site on-line is to make sure that people will find it in a search engine when they type in relevant keywords. You will also want a short description of your site to appear telling people what it is all about before they enter the site.

Metatags

Metatags are the things that provide the search engines with an idea of what your site is about. It is these tags that they use to draw up a list of matches when someone types in a keyword to search on in the search engine.

- Open the Hasp web on your hard disk in FrontPage
- Double-click the **index.htm** file to open it in Page view.
- Click the **HTML** tab at the bottom of the page. You will see the following text or something very similar:

```
<html>
<head>
<meta http-equiv="Content-Type" content="text/html; charset=windows-1252">
<meta http-equiv="Content-Language" content="en-us">
<title>Home Page</title>
<meta name="GENERATOR" content="Microsoft FrontPage 4.0">
<meta name="ProgId" content="FrontPage.Editor.Document">
<meta http-equiv="Page-Enter" content="revealTrans(Duration=1.0,Transition=12)">
<meta http-equiv="Page-Exit" content="revealTrans(Duration=1.0,Transition=12)">
</head>

<body>
<p align="center"><a href="FramesPage.htm"><img border="0" src="images/Cutout.jpg"
width="671" height="522"></a></p>
<p align="center"><font face="Arial" size="5">    <font
color="#663300">Welcome
to the Speymont Historical Association Web site</font></font></p>
</body>
</html>
```

Description metatag

This will provide the search engines with a short description of the site.

- After the head tag `<head>`, create a new line and type the following:

```
<meta name="description" content="
```

- Now enter a short description of the Web site and end it with `">`. (Don't type the full stop.)
- The metatag for this Web site is:

```
<meta name="description" content="The Speymont Historical Association, based in
Durlington, UK, is concerned with researching the families and history of the
area.">
```

Keyword metatag

Keyword metatags will provide the search engines with keywords to match against search topics entered.

*   After the description metatag create a blank line and type:

    ```
    <meta name="keywords" content="
    ```

*   Now enter keywords that people might use in a search engine to find your site or relevant sites. Separate each keyword by a comma and a space. At the end of the list type `">`. (Don't type the full stop.)

*   The keyword metatag for this Web site is:

    ```
    <meta name="keywords" content="speymont, sharpe, moorlands, durlington, speymont
    historical association, beckton">
    ```

*   Now **Save** the page.

You will need to publish this page again to submit these changes to the web.

Note: The tags may not work for two or three weeks after they have been published because it will take a while for the web crawler to find your new site and update its index with the new keywords.

---

*   Close the web and FrontPage.

Chapter 13 – Creating a Mail Merge

Objectives

By the end of this chapter you will have learned how to:

➤ look at the database table created by FrontPage to receive the form data from the Registration page

➤ collect the Registration data

➤ export the data to an Access database on your hard drive

➤ delete the data from the original table once it has been exported

➤ create a mail merge letter

➤ use the Registration data in the mail merge letter

Processing data in Access and Word

If you are doing an 'AS' Level course, it may be beyond the scope of the project to go into the processing of data that you have collected from your Web site. However if you are doing a major project for an 'A' Level course, you might consider creating a Web site and also developing an Access application which processes the data collected on the site. This chapter assumes that you have a basic knowledge of Access, and takes you through the steps of exporting data from the database on the Web server to your own hard drive. It does not, however, go into any detail about developing a fully-fledged system using Access. For that, you need to look at 'Successful ICT Projects in Access' by P.M.Heathcote.

Consult your teacher and the mark scheme for the relevant Examining Board to make sure you are fulfilling the requirements for a Grade A project.

What is a Mail Merge?

Mail Merge is the term used for merging a list of names and addresses with a standard letter to create personalized letters. It's a very useful technique whenever you want to send the same letter to several different people – for example all the people who have registered with the Speymont Historical Association via the Web site. Their information will have been automatically inserted in a table in Microsoft Access which can be used as the data source for the mail merge performed in this chapter.

The Access database table created by FrontPage

FrontPage will have put the Access database in a subfolder of your web folder called **fpdb**. You can open this database in Access to see the structure of the table created by FrontPage.

• **Open** the **HASP** web in FrontPage to start work.

• To see this table, click the **Folder List** button if the file structure is not already visible.

• Now double-click the **fpdb** folder.

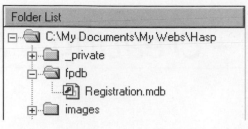

Figure 13.1: The Access database table

- Double-click the **Registration.mdb** file. This will automatically open Access (if it is installed on your computer) and display the table name (**Results**) in the Database window.

Note:	You may not be able to open Access using this method. If not, open Access in the normal way from the **Start** menu or the icon on the desktop, and open the database.

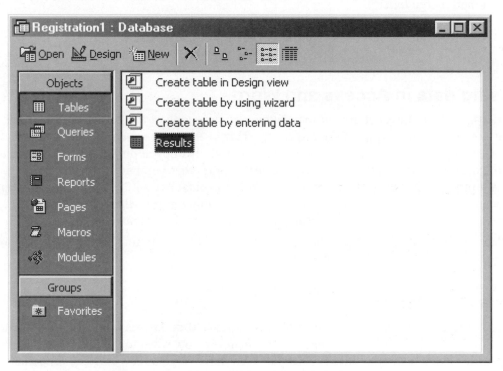

Figure 13.2: The table shown in Microsoft Access

- Double-click the **Results** table to see it as a datasheet.

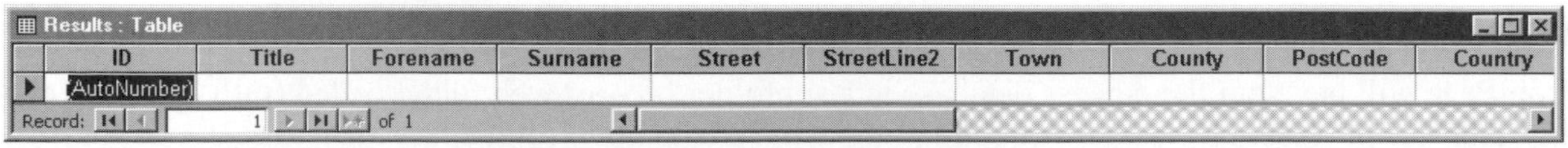

Figure 13.3: The table in Datasheet view

To see the table's structure you can view it in Design view.

- Click the **Design View** button.

Field Name	Data Type	Description
ID	AutoNumber	
Title	Text	
Forename	Text	
Surname	Text	
Street	Text	
StreetLine2	Text	
Town	Text	
County	Text	
PostCode	Text	
Country	Text	
EMail	Text	
Telephone	Text	
Interest	Text	
Remote_computer_name	Text	
User_name	Text	
Browser_type	Text	
Timestamp	Date/Time	

Field Properties

General | Lookup

Field Size	Long Integer
New Values	Increment
Format	
Caption	
Indexed	No

A field name can be up to 64 characters long, including spaces. Press F1 for help on field names.

Figure 13.4: The table in Design view

You will notice that there are several extra fields that have been added. These are automatically added by FrontPage to provide more information about where the data came from and when. They will not affect the data collection in any way.

- Close the database, but leave Access running.

When visitors register...

The data that people submit will be kept in the **Registration** database on the Web server. You will need to export this data (held in the table called **Results**) to another blank database on your computer.

- Log on to the Internet and go to the address <u>www.payne-gallway.co.uk/hasp</u> or the address of your own site.

- So that you have some test data on which to perform your mail merge, go to the **Registration** page and submit 3 or 4 records of test data.

Creating a blank database to hold the data exported from the web

- Return to Microsoft Access.

- Select **File**, **New** from the menu to create a new database. Create or select a suitable folder to save the database in – this is not part of your web so save it in a completely separate folder. For example, it could be saved in a subfolder of My Documents called **HaspData**.

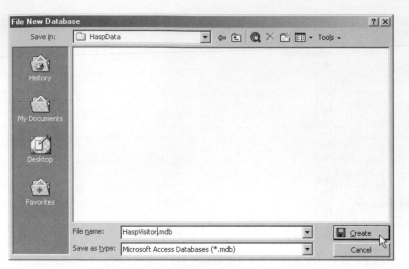

Figure 13.5: Creating a blank database

- Name the new database **HaspVisitor.mdb**.
- Click **Create**.
- **Close** the database but leave Access running.
- Return to FrontPage and close the **Hasp** web.

You have now set up a blank database on your computer in which to store the data collected on the Web site. It is easy to become confused about what is held where, so here is a short recap.

When you publish the web, a copy of the web is made on the web server, which could be anywhere in the world. Changes to either copy of the web have no effect on the other. So for example when you make changes to the web stored in the My Webs folder on your hard disk, it will not affect the published web until the updated version is republished.

Similarly, if data is entered by visitors to your published Web site, the data will be stored on the Web server, and will not appear on your hard drive until you download it. In order to retrieve this data, you have to be logged on to the Internet. In the next step, we will be going online to open (in FrontPage) the web stored on the Web server.

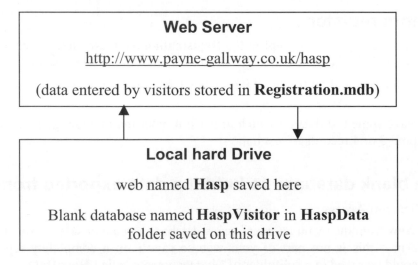

Figure 13.6

Exporting the registration data from the Hasp web

- Log on to the **Internet**.
- When you are connected, go back to **FrontPage** and select **File**, **Open Web** from the menu.
- Select the **Web Folders** button and click the web address where your web is stored or enter the address in the Folder Name box (in this case, **http://www.payne-gallway.co.uk/hasp**).

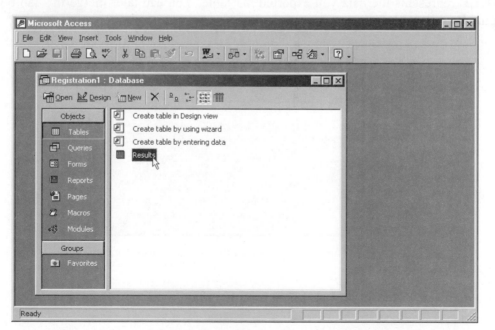

Figure 13.7: Opening the Hasp web on-line

- Click **Open**.
- Click the **fpdb** folder to expand it.
- Double-click the **Registration.mdb** database. It will open in Access.
- Double-click the **Results** table in the **Database** window to open it and check that the records you entered are there.

Figure 13.8: The on-line database table

- If all is well, close the table. If the records are not there, try again!
- Click **File**, **Export** from the menu.
- Select the **HaspVisitor.mdb** database that you created on the hard drive of your computer in the **HaspData** folder.

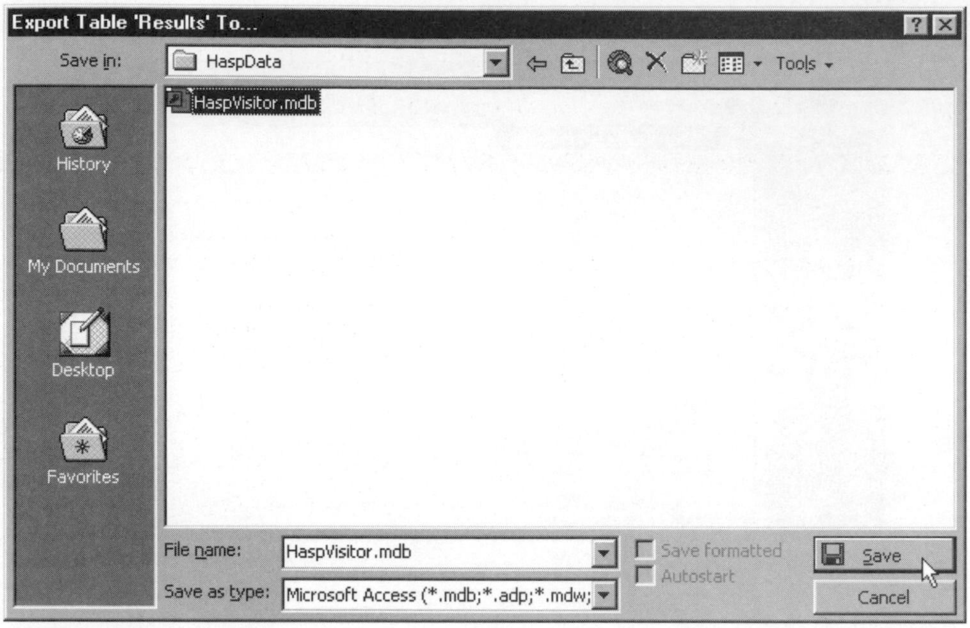

![Export Table 'Results' To... dialog box showing Save in: HaspData, with HaspVisitor.mdb file, File name: HaspVisitor.mdb, Save as type: Microsoft Access (*.mdb;*.adp;*.mdw;](data)

Figure 13.9: Exporting the on-line database table to the local hard drive

- Click **Save**.
- The Export window will appear. You can leave the default table name as **Results**. However, the next time you export data, you will have to change the table name if you do not want to overwrite existing data. You could call it, for example, **Results(DD,MM,YY)** where **DD,MM,YY** represents the data you exported the table. You can later merge this table with the original **Results** table.

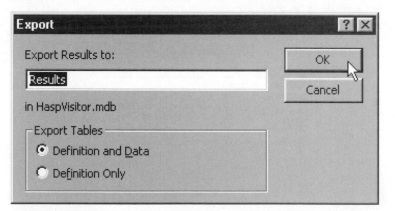

Figure 13.10: Selecting the new table name for the exported data

- Click **OK**.

This creates a duplicate of the on-line table on your hard drive.

Deleting information in the database table

You now need to delete the data that is held on the Web server so that you only copy new data to your database next time you export data. You could of course export all the data, but as people logging on to a Web site often try out registration forms by entering x's or silly names, you will probably have to 'clean up' the data each time you export it. People often register twice 'just to make sure' that their data has been saved.

- Double-click the on-line **Results** table in the **fpdb** folder of the **Hasp** web.

- When it appears in the **Database** window in **Access**, double-click it again to open it.

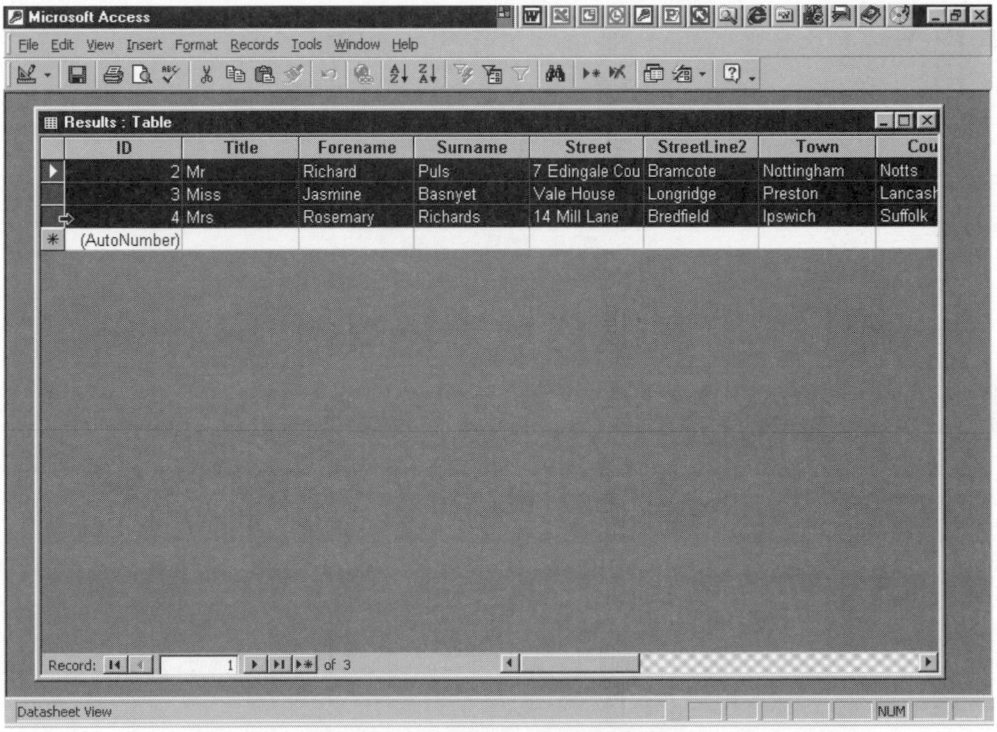

Figure 13.11: Deleting records on-line

- There are data from 3 people's submissions shown here. Select all the records and press the **Delete** key.

- A warning message will appear telling you that the changes will be permanent and you cannot get the information back again. Click **Yes**.

Figure 13.12: Warning message

- Log off the **Internet**.
- **Close Access**.

If you do not delete the old online data after exporting it, the next time you export data, it would overwrite any changes you had made to the original set of data. For example, if you had been through the previous table deleting any rubbish records that people had submitted, they would once again be replaced with the rubbish that you had removed.

This is an important step in maintaining the integrity of your data.

Creating the Mail Merge letter

- Open **Microsoft Word**. Version **2000** is used in this chapter but it will work with previous versions.

- Select **Tools**, **Mail Merge** from the menu. The **Mail Merge Helper** will appear.

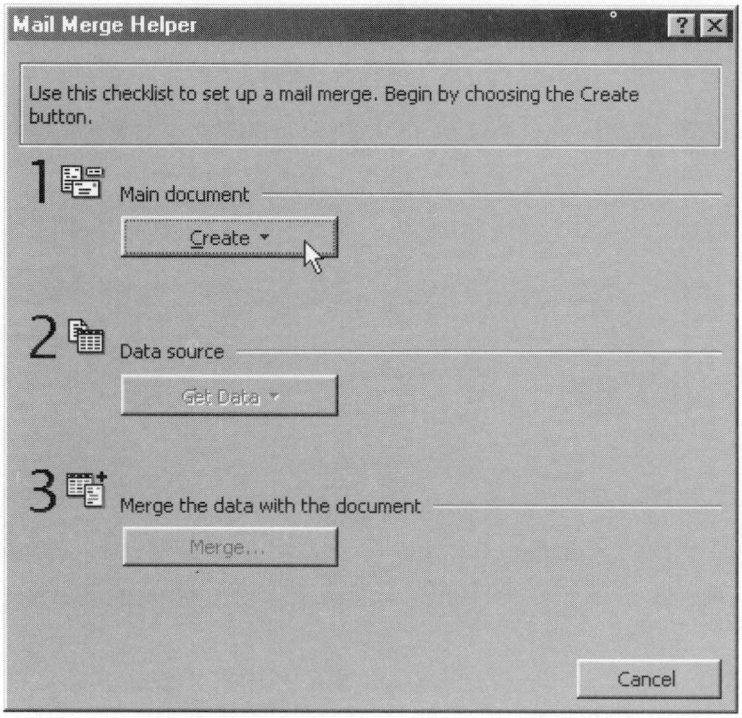

Figure 13.13: Setting up a Mail Merge

- Click **Create** under the **Main Document** heading.

- The following window will appear. Click **Form Letters**, then **Active Window**.

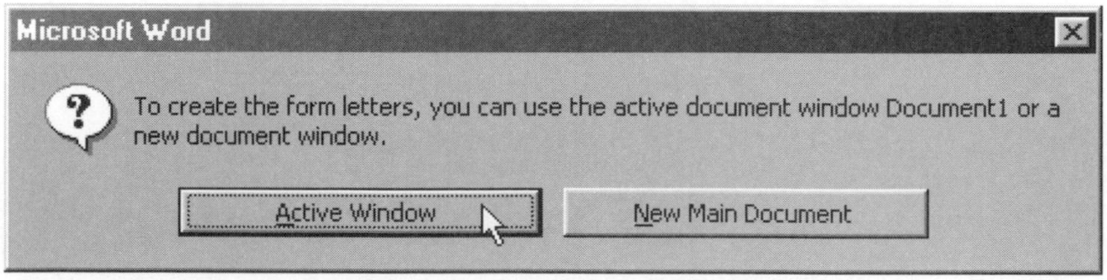

Figure 13.14: Setting up a Mail Merge

You will be returned to the **Mail Merge Helper**.

- Click the **Get Data** button under the **Data Source** heading.

- Select **Open Data Source** from the menu.

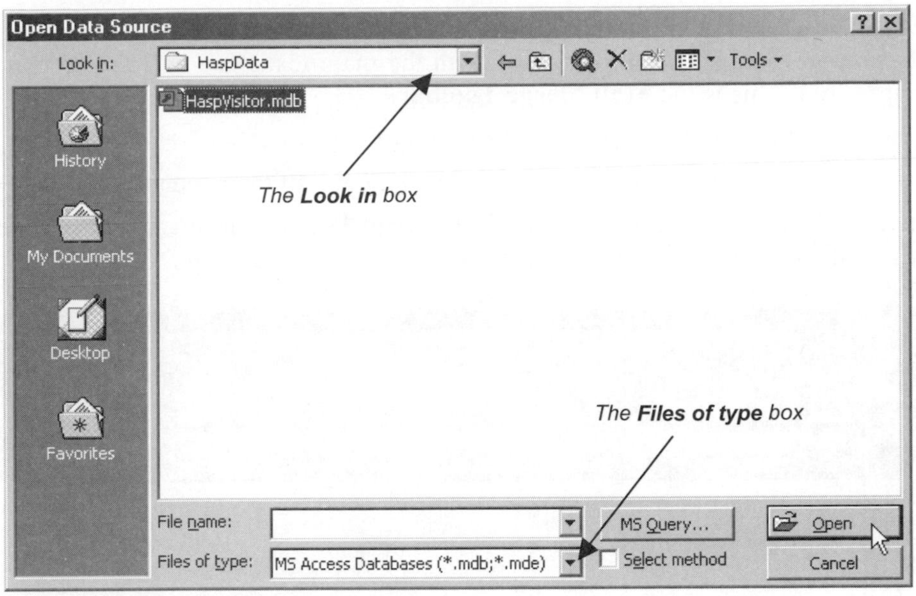

Figure 13.15: Selecting the data source for the mail merge

- In the **Look in** box, find the folder where you created your Registration database earlier in the chapter.
- You will need to change the **Files of type** option at the bottom of the **Open Data Source** window to **MS Access Databases (*.mdb;*.mde)**. This will display the database file.
- Click **Open**.

Figure 13.16: Selecting the database table to use for the mail merge

- Select the **Results** table containing the registration data (or whatever you have named it) and click **OK**.

You will see the following message:

Figure 13.17

- Click the **Edit Main Document** button. This will take you back into Word to insert the fields in the database table into the document along with the main text. You will notice that a new toolbar has appeared. This is the **Mail Merge Toolbar**.

- Type in a heading at the top of the page like the one shown below:

- Press Enter a couple of times to move the cursor down the left of the page a little.

- Click the **Insert Merge Field** button on the **Mail Merge Toolbar**. Insert the **Title** field. This will display the title of the person in the first record of the database table.

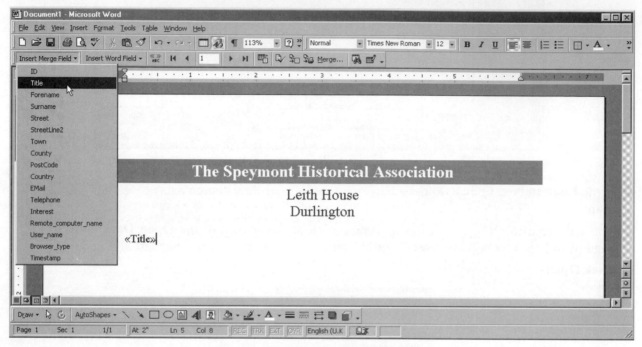

Figure 13.18: Setting up a Mail Merge

- Insert the rest of the fields to make up a full name and address. Copy the letter below to complete it.

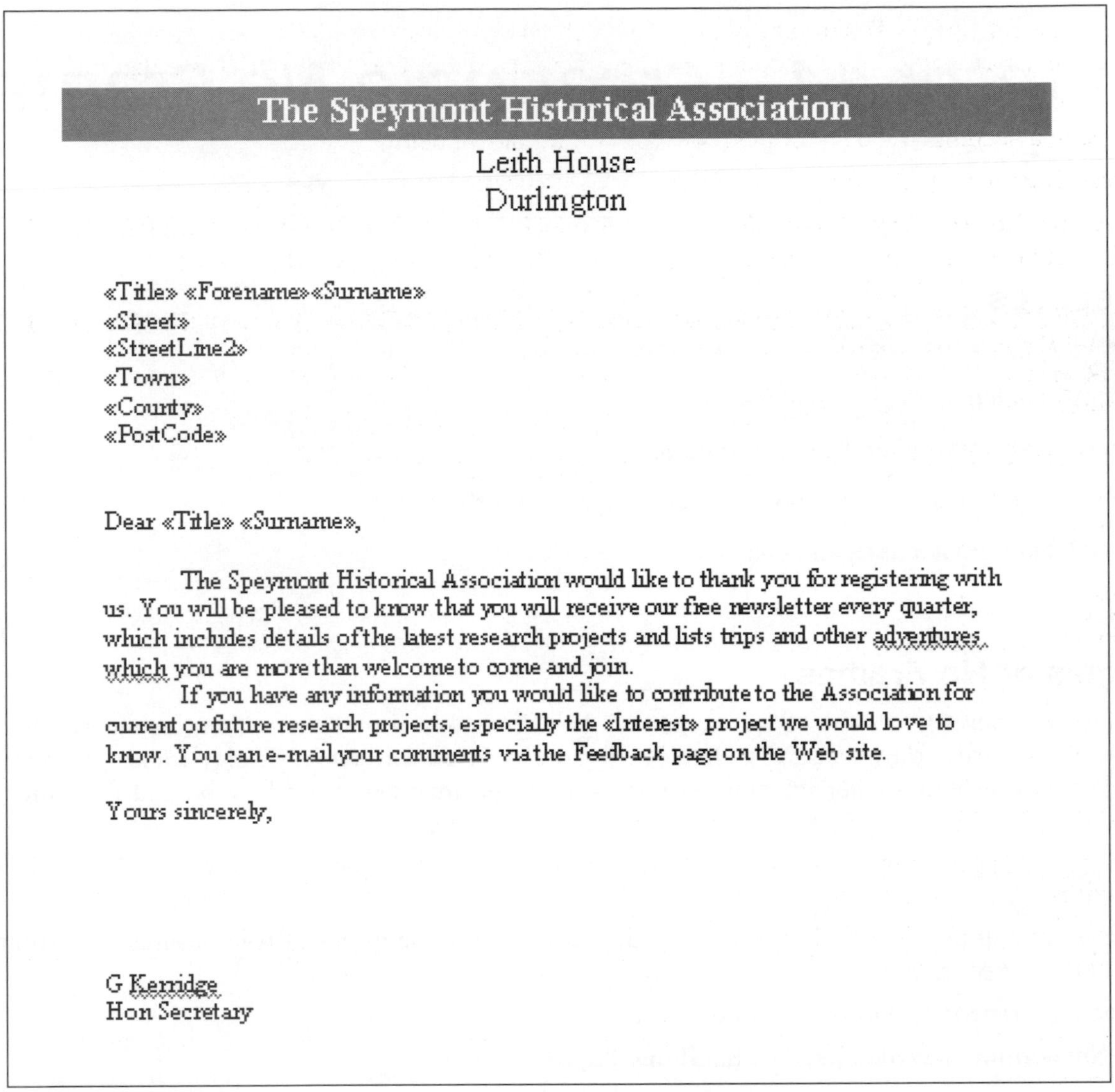

The Speymont Historical Association

Leith House
Durlington

«Title» «Forename» «Surname»
«Street»
«StreetLine2»
«Town»
«County»
«PostCode»

Dear «Title» «Surname»,

     The Speymont Historical Association would like to thank you for registering with us. You will be pleased to know that you will receive our free newsletter every quarter, which includes details of the latest research projects and lists trips and other adventures, which you are more than welcome to come and join.
     If you have any information you would like to contribute to the Association for current or future research projects, especially the «Interest» project we would love to know. You can e-mail your comments via the Feedback page on the Web site.

Yours sincerely,

G Kerridge
Hon Secretary

Figure 13.19: The mail merge letter

- Click the **View Merged Data** button to see how the letter will look with the actual data.

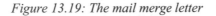

- Scroll through the records using the **Next Record** button.

If it is all OK, you are ready to start the merge.

- Make sure that your computer is connected to a printer and that the printer is switched on.
- Click the **Start Mail Merge** button on the **Mail Merge** toolbar.

You have successfully completed a mail merge!

- **Save** and **Close** all open documents and applications.

Chapter 14 – Creating a No Frames Web

Objectives

By the end of this chapter you will have learned how to:

➢ copy content from one web to another

➢ create a web without the use of frames

➢ create and remove shared borders on the pages of a web

➢ add and format a navigation bar

Frames or No Frames?

This chapter shows what sort of web pages can be achieved in FrontPage without using frames in the design. Some earlier browser such as Internet Explorer 4 or earlier cannot display frames, therefore No Frames pages generally cater for more visitors. This is an important consideration and one which you should discuss with your user before starting on a new Web site.

A No Frames page is simpler and easier to create than a Frames page but offers fewer design choices and capabilities.

This chapter will build a small 3-page web that will show you the basics of web designing in FrontPage without the use of frames.

• **Open** the **HASP** web to start work on this chapter.

• In **Navigation** view, double-click the **Home Page** to open it.

Copying content from one web into another

We are going to create the beginnings of a new Web site for the Speymont Historical Association, with exactly the same content as the original version but without frames. The quickest way of doing this is to copy the content of each page from the old web to the new one.

• On the Home page, highlight the picture and the text beneath it. Right-click the highlighted area and click **Copy**.

• Select **File**, **New**, **Web** from the menu. This will be the new 3-page web.

• Select **Empty Web** from the choices and specify the location of the new web. If you type in the name of a folder that doesn't exist, it will be created for you. This web has been called **HASPNF** – Hasp No Frames, but you may think of a different name to use.

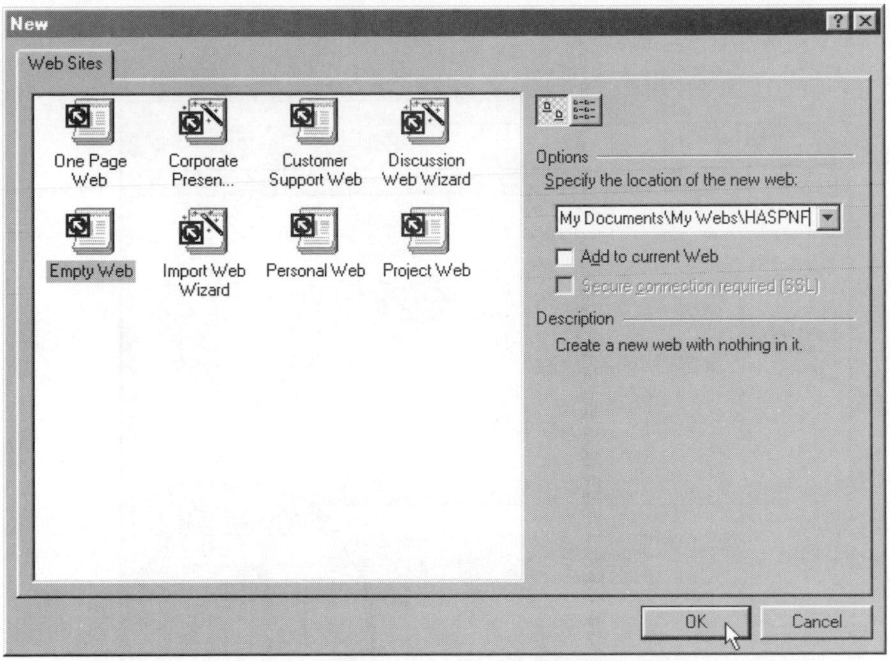

Figure 14.1: Creating an empty web

- Click **File**, **New**, **Page** on the new web to create the **Home Page**.

- Open the new Home Page by double-clicking it.

- Right-click the blank page and select **Paste** from the menu. The original Home Page will appear as the new Home Page.

- Go back to **Navigation View**.

- Click **File**, **New**, **Page** to add another new page.

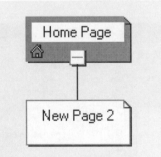

Figure 14.2: Adding a new page to the web

- Right-click the new page and **Rename** it **About**.

- FrontPage will automatically rename the **new_page_2.htm** file **About.htm** as well. Check in the Folder List that it has done so. If it has not, rename it yourself. (If you can't see it, click the **Refresh** button.)

- Select **Window**, **index.htm** to go back to the Home Page in Page View.

- Right-click the image and select **Hyperlink Properties** from the menu.

The hyperlink will currently link to the original Hasp Web site where you copied the page from. This needs to be changed to the new **About.htm** page that has been created in this Web site.

- Click the **About.htm** file and click **OK**.

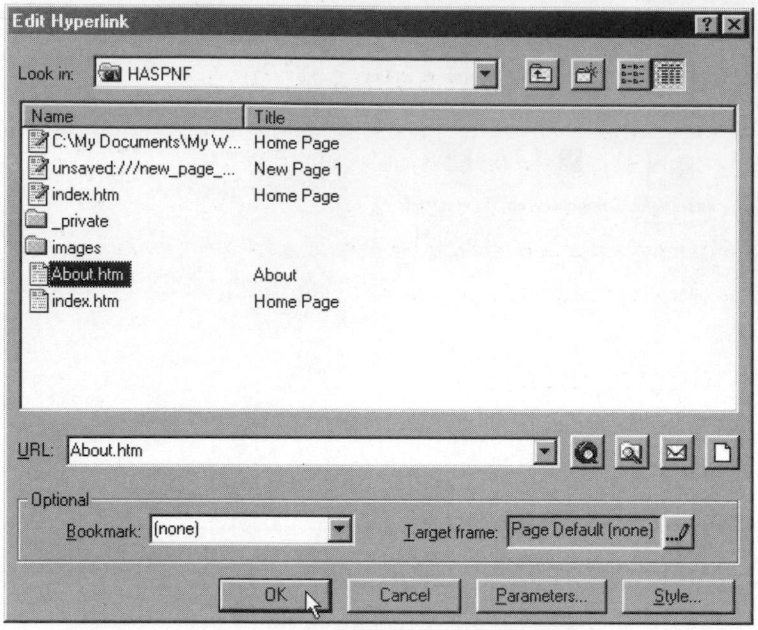

Figure 14.3: Editing a hyperlink

- Ctrl-click the image to test the new link. You should see a blank page. This is the About page with no content.

Adding shared borders

- Select **Format**, **Shared Borders** from the main menu.
- Make sure that the **All Pages** option is selected.

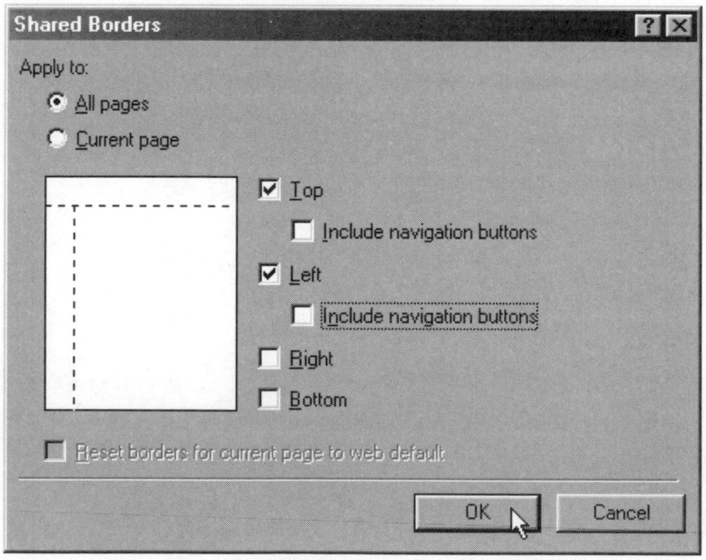

Figure 14.4: Inserting shared borders

- Select **Top** and **Left** from the choices below that and click **OK**.

A thin box will appear across the top and down the left of the screen. This is the shared border. Anything you put within these borders will appear on every other page in the site.

Removing shared borders from selected pages

- Select **Window, index.htm** to go back to the Home page. You will notice that the borders appear here too. This is the only place that they are not wanted.
- Select **Format, Shared Borders** from the menu.
- Select the **Current Page** option and deselect the **Top** and **Left** option boxes.
- Click **OK**. The borders on this page will now have disappeared.

Creating the Products page

- Click the **Navigation View** button.
- Select the **About** page and select **File, New, Page** from the menu.
- Rename the page **Products**.
- Click the **Refresh** button on the standard toolbar. Your new page should automatically have been renamed **Products.htm**. If it has not, rename it yourself.

The web structure will now look like the one below:

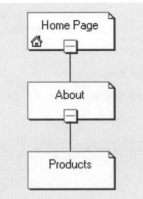

Figure 14.5: The web structure

Copying more content from another web

- Double-click the new **Products** page.
- Open the original **Hasp** web and open its **Products** page.
- Highlight all the content in the page (**Edit, Select All**) and click **Edit, Copy** on the menu.
- Open the **HaspNF** web again and click the mouse cursor back on the centre of the blank **Products** page.
- Select **Edit, Paste**. The contents of the original products page will appear in the new Products page.

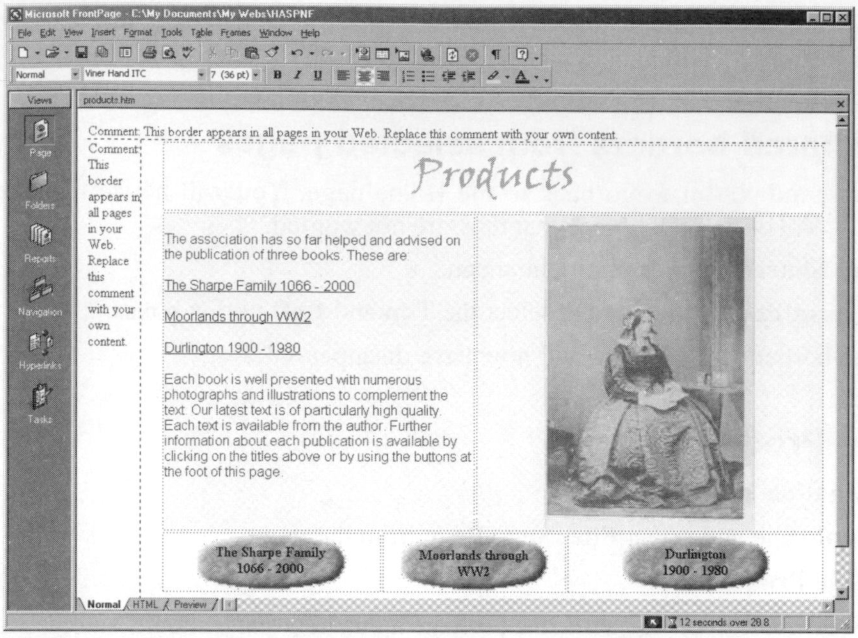

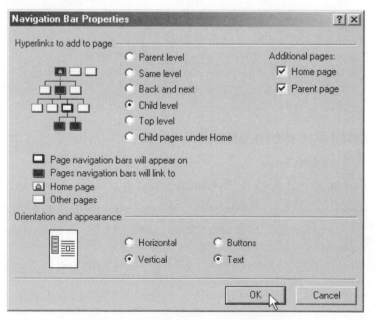

Figure 14.6: Copying from another web

Adding navigation bars

- With the **Products** page open, click the purple text in the left hand border to select it.
- Press the **Enter** key to delete it and insert a blank line.
- Select **Insert**, **Navigation Bar** from the menu.
- Click the **Child level** option and the **Home page** and **Parent Page** options to the right of the window.

Figure 14.7: Inserting a navigation bar

- Select the **Vertical** orientation option and the **Text** appearance option.

- Click **OK**.
- Two new hyperlinks will appear in the border. **Home** and **Up**. These will take to the visitor to the Home page or the About page when clicked. They have automatically been given hyperlinks to these pages.

Formatting the navigation bar

- Click the purple text in the top border and replace it with *Speymont Historical Association*.
- Centre the text and make it **36pt**.

Now you can format the **Navigation Bar**. Navigation bars don't offer very much flexibility compared to when you add links manually but they can be formatted.

- Select the navigation bar links by clicking on them. Make them **Copperplate Gothic Bold**, size **18pt**.

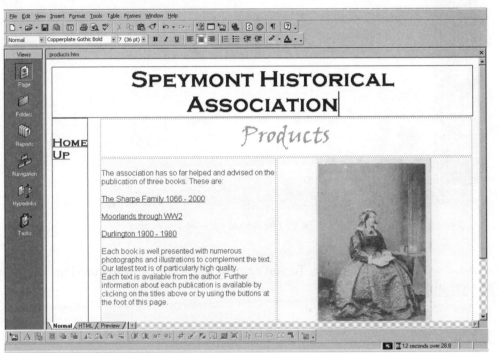

Figure 14.8: Adding a title

- **Save** the page. You will need to save the graphics embedded in the main content of the page as well.
- Click the **Preview in Browser** button.

Note: You can change the navigation bar properties by double-clicking the navigation bar. Try the effects of setting different options in the Navigation Bar Properties window.

The buttons and links in the main content of this page will still link to the appropriate pages on the original Hasp Web site. These would need to be changed as more pages are added to this web.

Try scrolling up and down the page. One of the main advantages of Frames pages over No Frames pages is that they scroll independently of one another. With the shared borders, the title will disappear off the top of the page as you scroll down.

Working on the About page

- Try Ctrl-clicking the **Up** link in the navigation bar. You will see the About page appear although it will be blank.

- Enter some text as shown below.

- Click the **Preview** tab.

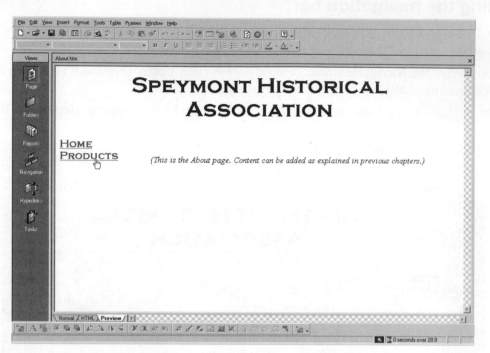

Figure 14.9: The About page in Preview

This is as far as we will go in this chapter. To add content and features, you would use the same techniques as have already been covered.

Part 3
Tackling the Project

In this section:

Chapter 15 – Project Stages

Objectives

By the end of this chapter you will have considered the following stages in completing your project:

➢ the definition of a problem in information technology terms

➢ the specification of the tasks to be completed

➢ the completion of appropriate design work from which to implement the solution

➢ the determination of a schedule of activities

➢ the determination of a test plan

➢ the implementation and testing of the solution

➢ the evaluation of the solution against the requirements of the user

Introduction

The advice in this chapter is aimed primarily at students working on a project for the AQA AS Level ICT specification. However, it can be adapted for any coursework project so long as you bear in mind that you must follow the advice and mark scheme of the particular Examination Board and course that you are studying for.

Anyone completing an ICT or Computing project will go through similar stages:

❑ finding a suitable user with an appropriate project idea

❑ interviewing the user to ascertain exactly what the requirements are

❑ deciding on how the project will best be implemented

❑ designing the detailed solution

❑ implementing and testing the project

❑ evaluating it against the original specification

❑ completing all the documentation.

As this is likely to be the first time you have tackled a project in FrontPage, you may well be learning more about the software as you go along and this will affect the way in which the project is implemented. You can gain extra credit by identifying improvements as the project progresses and documenting these in a Project Log, which should be included with your project report.

Definition of the problem

The first thing you will have to do is to identify a user who would like you to build a Web site for them. Since almost every business or organization, large or small, now deems it essential to have its own Web site this really should not be too difficult – much easier at any rate than finding a user with a desperate need for a database or spreadsheet application. Your school, local sports club, scout or guide group, hairdresser, corner shop, restaurant, plumber or doctor's surgery may all be queueing up for your services.

Once you have made your selection, you need to get down to ascertaining the objectives. Remember the two questions which were mentioned right at the beginning of this book:

❑ Who is the target audience?

❑ What is the Web site designed to accomplish?

Specification of requirements

Once you have selected a project, you must ascertain in detail exactly what the requirements are. To do this you need to interview the user and write down the answers you receive, as well as keeping any documents you are given for reference – for example a company letterhead from which you can scan a logo, or graphics/photographs which are to be included in the Web site.

You will presumably have some idea of the requirements (what the Web site is for) before you set up a more formal interview, and you should prepare a list of questions in advance. You may be able to suggest ideas for the site which the user had not thought of or did not know was possible, like collecting names and addresses of people 'registering' on the site and automatically adding them to a database. Questions that you could consider asking could include the following:

❑ What information do you want to put on your Web site?

❑ What information do you want to gather from people visiting your site?

❑ What use do you want to make of that information?

❑ Do you have a logo that you want to appear on the Home page, or even every page?

❑ Will the information on the Web site change very frequently?

❑ Who will update the Web site?

❑ Have you got an ISP or should I organise that for you?

❑ Do you have enough proficiency in FrontPage to maintain and update the site yourself or would you like me to do this for you?

❑ Is it important that everyone can view your Web site, no matter what browser they are using? (This has implications for the design, i.e. whether or not to use frames, which cannot be viewed in older browsers)

You can probably think of lots of other questions. In addition, you may have to find out whether the user's ISP supports FrontPage Server Extensions, and any other technical details.

Design

Before you start work on the computer, you need to sit down and do some planning. There are several points to consider and each of these needs to be documented.

❑ What information will go on each page and how will the pages link together?

❑ User interface considerations – how will the pages be given a consistent look and feel?

❑ Method used to construct the Web site – if you are using FrontPage, will you use frames, shared borders, or neither?

A good way to plan the layout of a Web site is to take a large sheet of paper and a pad of Post-it notes. Use a separate Post-it for each page of the Web site, jotting down its title and an outline of its contents. Then stick these onto the sheet of paper. You will be able to rearrange them as the planning process continues, and once you are satisfied you can type up the final plan. Figure 4.1 in Chapter 4 shows an example.

You should justify your use of frames, shared borders etc. If you are posting the site to a school Intranet, you will be familiar with the capabilities of the browser used.

You also need to consider what type of hardware the majority of visitors to your site will be using. If you develop your pages on a very high resolution screen, you may find that what fits perfectly on your screen is only half-visible on a lower resolution screen, and the viewer will have to scroll both sideways and downwards to view the whole contents of the page.

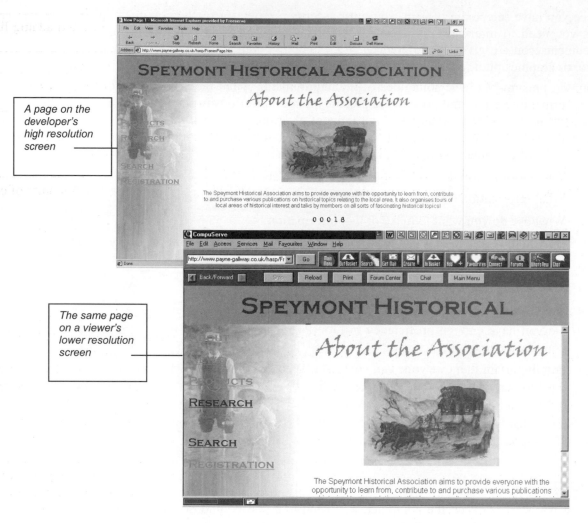

Figure 15.1: The same page viewed on two different screens

You do not need to decide on the details of each page at this stage. Once you have the basic plan it will be easier to develop your ideas as you go along. You may decide that a particular page will benefit from a scrolling marquee or other special effects, for example.

Schedule of activities

You have a relatively short time in which to complete the project, and it is absolutely essential to write down a plan of how and when you intend to complete each stage. Everything will take longer than you think, and you cannot allow yourself to get behind because, for example, your user is out of town and you can't interview her to ask a vital question. You can always be getting on with another task, such as finding out how to set up navigation bars, how to include a Java applet, how to send data to a database, how to publish to the Web, etc.

Time management is of the utmost importance in successfully completing a project! Here is a sample schedule of activities, but of course each person's schedule will be unique to their own project.

Week Beginning	Activity
8th January	Plan Web site, interview the user and finalise initial design ideas.
15th January	Begin to design site. Start with building the structure of the site and adding links between the pages. Design pages for each different frame.
22nd January	Design the three products pages. Sharpe, Moorlands and Durlington.
29th January	Design the main Products page and Research page. Scan in graphics for these pages.
5th February	Design News page and add animation.
12th February	Design database registration form on Registration page. Test.
19th February	Design About page and add Java applet. Test.
26th February	Test entire site thoroughly. Record test data, expected results and outcomes of each test.
5th March	Evaluate site with user and comment on possible improvements. These can be added if needed.
12th March	Write up the user manual.

Test strategy and test plan

There are marks in the Specification section for devising an appropriate test strategy and a test plan. Your strategy may well be to test each page and the links therein as you go along. You will also have to test out any HTML code or Java applets that you include, and you will have to test the whole site once it is published to a server. It is as well not to leave this too late – you need to try accessing the site from different hardware and using different browsers. You may find that using some browsers the site appears differently. You will then have to decide whether to tolerate this or whether you will have to change your implementation.

Having decided on your test strategy, you need to write down a list of individual tests that you intend to carry out together with the expected results. In the Testing section you can then show evidence, usually in the form of screenshots, that each test gave the expected results. You can develop and add to the test plan as you implement the project, since you will almost certainly identify areas which you can improve and which need further testing.

Look at the sample project for an example of a test strategy and test plan. You can use a different format, but where data is involved, your test plan must include, for each element to be tested:

  ❑ The test data to be used

  ❑ The reasons why this data has been selected

  ❑ The expected outcome.

'Data' in the case of a Web site may be a mouse click on a particular hypertext link, or it may be actual data to be collected and saved in a database, for example.

Implementation and testing

You are expected to document the implementation of the project. The project log that you keep will be included in this section. Use this to document your progress, the trials and tribulations you faced, how you overcame certain problems, any major change in design that you made and why, etc. Try to discipline yourself to write up the log every week or every time you do some work on the project or hit a problem that needs to be solved. You can explain here, for example, that you used a wizard in Week 3 to set up your basic design. By Week 4 you may have found that this was not a good idea and you can write in the log the reasons why you have decided to abandon this approach and use a particular template instead.

You can include in this section a summary of how the solution was implemented, any major hurdles overcome and a description of the advanced features of the software that you used. Remember that not every moderator will be familiar with the capabilities of the software you have chosen, and it will help them to appreciate what you have achieved if you spell it out.

Evaluation

In this section you should give a realistic evaluation of how well your Web site meets the user's expectations and how effective it is likely to be in achieving its purpose, whatever that may be. Try to be objective, and be honest about its shortcomings. If a particular graphic takes 3 minutes to download, say so and explain why you have left it in or taken it out. If the site is difficult to navigate, suggest how you think it could be improved. If certain pages cannot be viewed in some browsers, explain why you have left them in the format you have chosen. Discuss any limitations that your site has, and suggest solutions or improvements. You will get credit for showing an awareness of how effective your solution is and how well it meets the original requirements specification.

It is a good idea to show evidence that you have been interacting with the user of the Web site. For example, you may include a brief summary of the initial interview with them. You should show them the web while it is under construction and get some feedback which you can report in the Implementation section. Once you have finished designing the Web site and shown it to the user, you should try and obtain a letter from the user telling you their thoughts and ideas of your final solution. This should be included in your report.

User guide

The user guide is aimed at the owner of the Web site. You will not be expected to explain to the user how to use FrontPage to update the site, but you need to tell them how to log on, how to view any 'hidden' pages, how to get in touch with their ISP if problems arise, etc. Illustrate the user guide with plenty of screen shots, as this will add to the evidence of having successfully completed the project.

Chapter 16 – Writing the Project Report

Introduction

This chapter will give you some advice on how to set about writing the project report. Remember that the moderator will not actually see your system running – the report has to provide all the evidence of what you have achieved.

It will help you to look at the sample project as you will see how the report could be laid out and get some idea of what should be included in each section.

The mark scheme

Turn to the Appendix at the end of this book, which contains the AQA instructions and guidance for project work. You will see that the mark scheme in Section 20 is divided into five sections: **Specification**, **Implementation**, **User Testing**, **Evaluation** and **User Documentation**. You could organise your project report into these five major sections, but you may choose to vary this. Analysis and Design, for example, may be included in the mark schemes for other specifications. Spend some time familiarising yourself with the mark scheme so you know exactly what you are aiming for. Ultimately the decision on how best to structure the report is yours.

Creating an outline for your project

Word has a useful feature called **Outlining**. This feature enables you to create an outline for your entire project, breaking it down into sections and subsections, which you can then fill in as you build up your project. You can easily add, delete or rearrange headings at any stage, and at the end of it all you will be able to create an automatic Table of Contents.

In this chapter you will use Word's Outline feature to create an outline for your project. You can do this even before you have selected your project. It will help you to get a clear idea of the kind of task you should be setting yourself.

- Open a new document using the **Normal** template and save it as *Project.doc*.

- Click the **Outline View** button at the lower left corner of the Word window.

Outline View

Figure 16.1: The Outline View button

- The Outline toolbar pops up, the Style box displays Heading 1 style, and a fat minus sign appears in the left margin.

Figure 16.2: The Outline toolbar

- Type your first heading *Specification* and press **Enter**.

- Now type the first subtopic heading, *Description of the Problem*. It also gets Heading 1 style, just like the first heading. Since you want it to be a subtopic, click it and then click the **Demote** tool on the Outline toolbar. That makes it a Heading 2 style.

- Type the other headings for the Specification section. These could include:

    User Requirements
    Web Site Design
    Data Collection and Storage
    Test Strategy
    Test Plan and Expected Outcomes

- Press **Enter** after *Test Plan and Expected Outcomes*, click the **Promote** tool and type the next major heading: *Implementation*.

- Most of the marks in this section will be given for the actual implementation which you will demonstrate to your teacher. The project log should be included in this section. Useful evidence of the implementation should also be present in the user documentation. In this section, you can include, for example:

    Overview of the Web Site

    Description of the User Interface

    Justification of Hardware Used

    Justification of Software Used

    Project Log

    Advanced Software Features Used

    Problems encountered

    Do not follow these suggestions slavishly – they may not be appropriate for your particular project. Take note of Section 19.1.2 in the AQA Mark Scheme if you are following this specification:

    "Documentation is expected on the implementation work completed, which will contribute to the assessment of whether the candidate fully employed their package skills in an effective and appropriate manner. Also, that the selections of the chosen hardware and software facilities have been fully justified in relation to the solution developed. The project log recommended in the specification for Module 3 is expected to contribute towards the evidence for this aspect."

- Add these headings and subheadings to your outline. At this stage your screen should look something like Figure 16.3.

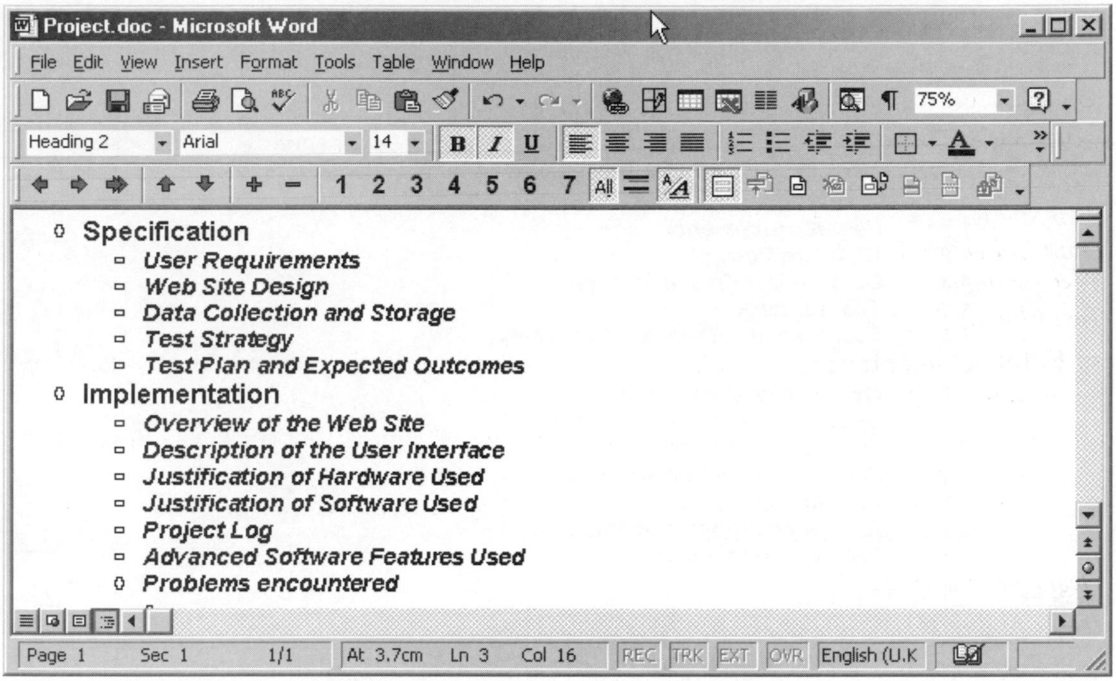

Figure 16.3: Outline for Analysis and Design

- Now enter the headings for the next four major headings: *Testing*, *Evaluation* and *User Documentation*. These are all at Heading 1 level.

This completes the project outline. Naturally, you will probably want to amend it as you develop your own ideas.

Reordering topics

If you decide that you want to change the order of topics in your project, do the following:

- Select for example *Project Log*. To move it up to the top of the Design section, click the **Move Up** button several times until it reaches the top of the section.

Adding numbers to the headings

- Select **Format, Bullets and Numbering**.

- Click the **Outline Numbered** tab and select a numbering format or customise one to your own liking. Your outline will appear something like Figure 16.4.

Note: If you decide to move your outline headings up or down it's a good idea to remove the numbers first and then re-apply them.

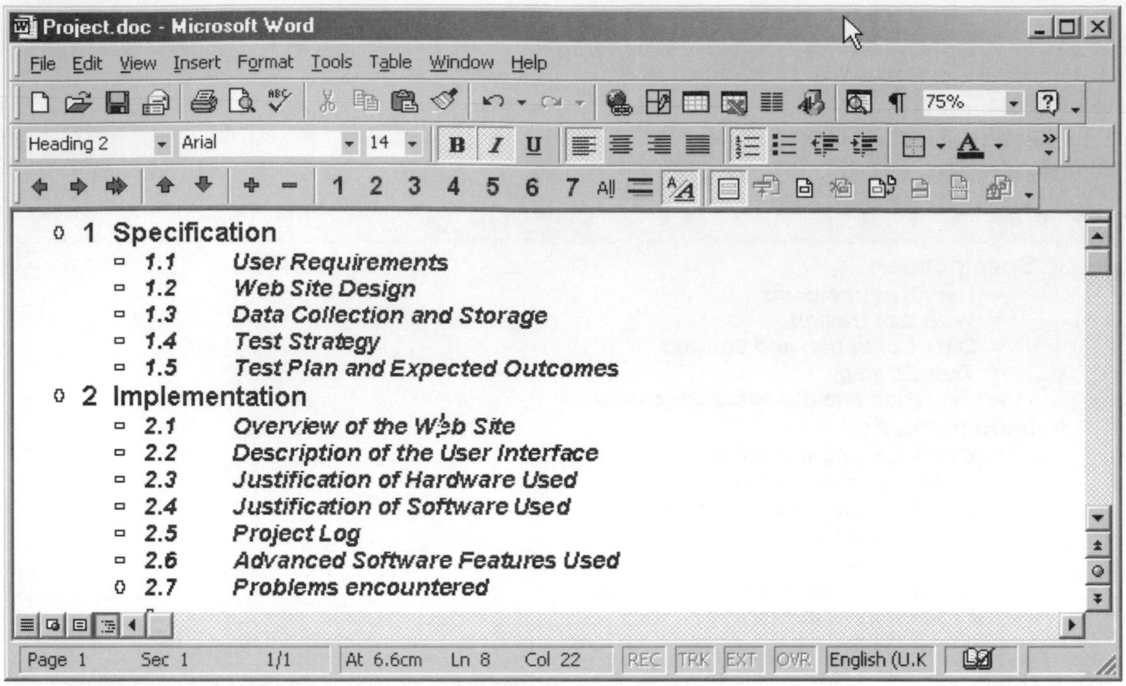

Figure 16.4: Adding numbers to an outline

Turning the outline into a document

The outline IS the document. Just click the **Print Layout View** button at the bottom of the window, and start entering text. You may want to change the indent and make a new style for the document text.

Adding a header and footer

You should add a header and footer to your project documentation. For example, the header could contain the Project title and the Section title, and the footer could contain your name and the page number.

- Insert page breaks between each of your major sections by pressing **Ctrl-Enter** wherever you want a page break.

- With the cursor at the beginning of the project outline, select **View, Header and Footer**.

- On the left hand side of the header, type your project title.

- Tab twice to get to the right hand side of the header. We need to insert a field here so that the name of the section is inserted.

- Select **Insert, Field**. In the **Categories** box select **Links and References**. In the Field Names box, select **StyleRef**.

- After the word STYLEREF, enter the style name *"Heading 1"* in quotes as shown in Figure 16.5.

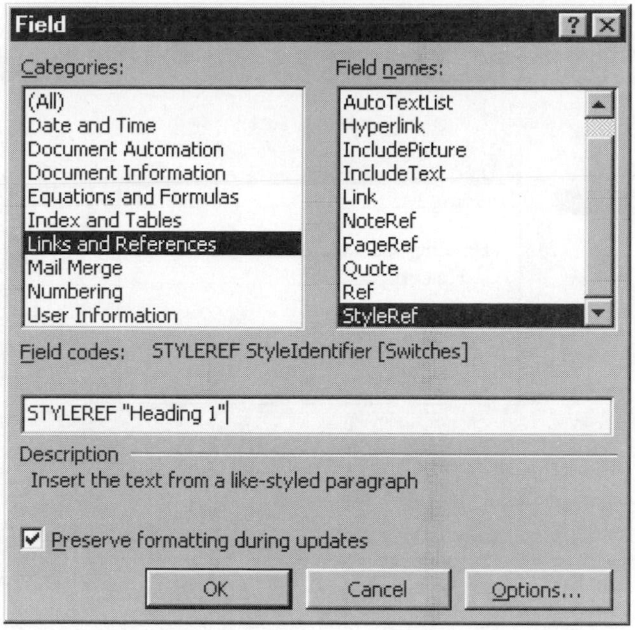

Figure 16.5: Inserting a field into the header

- Click **OK**. The header should appear as in Figure 16.6.

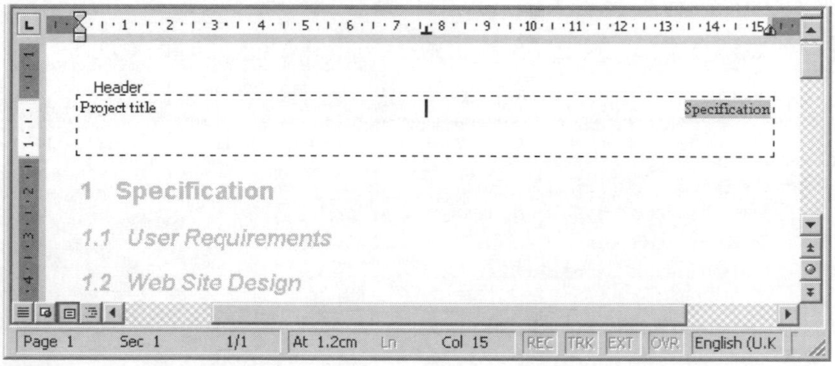

Figure 16.6: Header containing Section name

- Click the **Switch between Header and Footer** button and insert your name.

- Tab once or twice and insert the page number using the **Insert Page Number** button on the Header and Footer toolbar.

Inserting a Table of Contents

You can now insert a Table of Contents at the beginning of your project. This can be automatically updated at any time by clicking in it and pressing F9.

- Insert a page break in front of the heading *Specification*. (You can do this by pressing **Ctrl-Enter**)

- Click the **Normal View** button in the bottom left of the Word window (or select **View, Normal**).

- With the cursor at the beginning of the document, click **Insert, Index and Tables**.

- Click the **Table of Contents** tab. Leave the other defaults as shown in Figure 16.7.

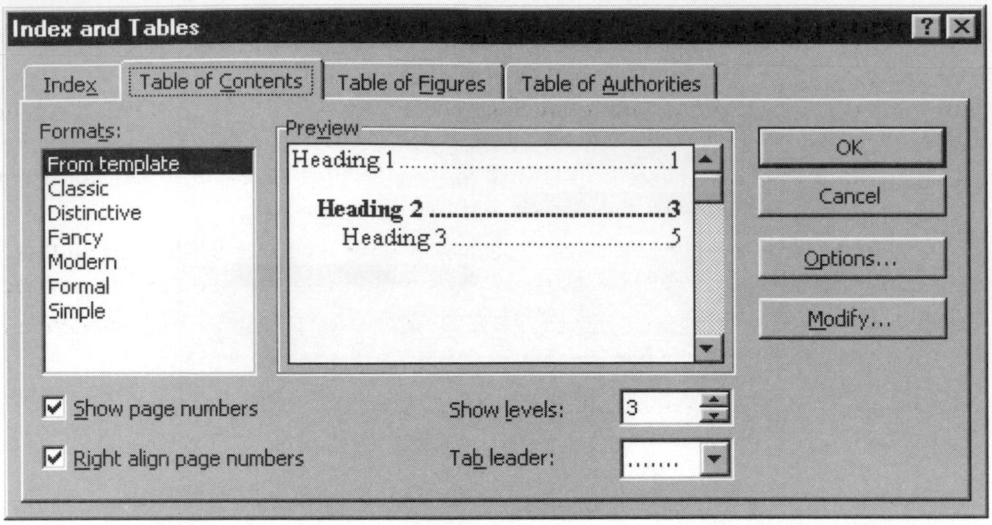

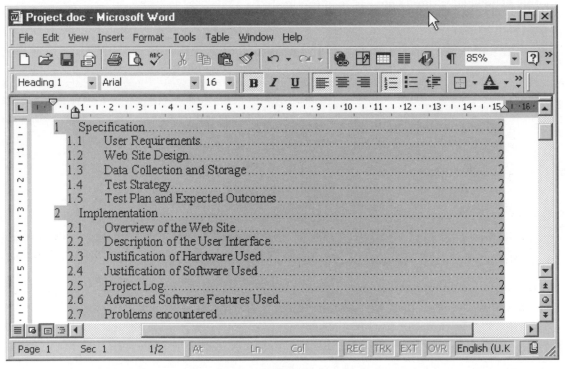

Figure 16.7: Inserting a Table of Contents

- The table of contents will appear as shown below.

Figure 16.8: The Table of Contents

- You can change the styles of TOC1, TOC2 etc. which are used in the Table of Contents using **Format**, **Style**.

- You can also change the styles of Heading 1, Heading 2 etc.

That's about it for your project outline. In the next few paragraphs we'll flesh out each section.

Specification

FrontPage is a suitable software package to use for an AS Level or Advanced VCE project. If you combine it with data collection and create a database system as part of your project, it could fulfill the requirements for an 'A' Level project. It will be written up according to whatever mark scheme you are following, and you should be very careful to follow the mark scheme closely. Do not assume that the sample project has exactly the headings that you should use.

Try to write a good clear list of objectives, as the success of your project may depend on this. After all, if you don't really know what you are trying to achieve, how will you know whether you have achieved it?

"The objective of my system is to create a user-friendly Web Site which will be attractive and easy to use."

Does this tell you what I am setting out to build?

For an example of a list of objectives, have a look at the sample project.

Design

This forms part of the 'Specification' section in the AQA mark scheme for an AS project. The design should be specified in sufficient detail that a competent third party (even a second party) could implement it. Planning is essential, even though you may have to alter your design if it doesn't work.

Your test strategy (see Chapter 15) will be documented in this section, as well as your test plan and test data. If applicable your test data should include valid and invalid data, data on the boundaries of acceptable values. Write down any test data that you intend to use and include it in your project report. You will probably need to add to it as you discover further aspects that need to be tested.

Many tests for a Web site project will not involve sample test data, but will involve thorough testing of all the hyperlinks and special features or add-ins such as applets or hit counters. Note that many special features cannot be tested until the web is published; some features will require the server to have FrontPage extensions and others may require the co-operation of your service provider to enable them.

Implementation

Keep a diary of how the implementation goes, and include this in a 'Commentary on Implementation'. This provided valuable evidence that you have actually done the work. Explain why you have performed a task in a certain way or why you have not implemented something as you originally designed it. It is perfectly acceptable to include evidence of difficulties encountered in implementation, and to discuss reasons for the difficulties if possible.

To gain high marks in this section you must show that you have actually solved the user's problem effectively, and that you have used advanced features of the software.

Testing

You must show evidence of testing in the form of screenshots or printed output. This output must be cross-referenced to the original test plan – it is a complete waste of time and paper including page after page of output with no meaningful comment as to what it is supposed to show. Handwrite on the output, use a highlighter pen, or any other means to help the reader understand what your test is designed to show, and how it actually shows it.

Evaluation

Refer back to the objectives and state to what extent these have been achieved. Also give some suggestions as to how the system could be enhanced, or what its weaknesses are – it's no good pretending that a rather feeble project is exactly what the user always wanted for Christmas, the moderator is unlikely to be fooled. Much better to show that you realise there are weaknesses and write about how you feel it could be improved. Honesty pays!

User documentation

This is for a non-technical user and should explain clearly all the functions of your system. Use plenty of screenshots to illustrate the text. These can also provide valuable evidence of the fact that your system actually works. Many moderators look at the User Guide early in the moderation process to help them understand the project better.

Handing it in

You must include a title page and a Table of Contents, and number every page – by hand if necessary.

Don't spoil it all by handing your project in as a collection of loose pages paper-clipped together, or stuffed into a single plastic pocket intended for a single sheet. Take pride in what you have achieved – spend 50p on a plastic folder in which the pages can be securely held.

Heed this advice from the 1998 Examiner's report:

"All projects must be securely bound; a thin folder or punched holes and treasury tags work well. Slide binders are often inhibiting to reading all the text, or they come off in the post. Ring binders, lever arch files and individual plastic pockets must not be used at all. They add unnecessary bulk and weight. The practice of using multiple sheets in poly pockets should cease."

Don't forget to include a signed cover sheet giving your name, candidate number and centre number.

Best of luck!

Appendix A

Sample Project

Speymont Historical Association

Web Site

Project by:
A. Student
Any College
2001

Table of Contents

Specification

Description of the Problem

Create and use styles for section and paragraph headings. Then you will be able to automatically generate a Table of Contents. 11 or 12 point Times Roman is a good choice for body text. (The text here is 11 point.)

The Speymont Historical Association is an organisation which helps individuals publish and market their books on local history. It also holds meetings and organises trips to site of local historical interest.

The organisation needs some sort of advertising medium which can be used to get their message across to individuals interested in the local history of the area. It should also provide the opportunity to collect the names and addresses of people who might like to be added to the mailing list and receive information about forthcoming events and current research. Since personal data is being collected, the Association will have to register as a data user to conform with the Data Protection Act.

Include an introduction to give some background information about the organisation.

Then give an overview of what the project is about.

The President of the Association believes that a web site would be an effective way of promoting their activities and reaching a wider audience. Web sites for similar organisations in other parts of the country have been visited by people from all over the world who have a connection with the area – for example a grandfather was born there, or they live in a village of the same name in Australia.

User Requirements

Two types of user can be identified in this project – the owner of the web site and anyone who visits the site. We will consider the requirements of these two users separately.

1. **The owner of the web site (The Speymont Historical Association)**

   a. There must be some means for visitors to enter their name, address and areas of interest if they wish to receive further information.

   b. The data entered by the users must be validated and automatically entered into a database. From here it can be used to create mail-merge letters. (This will not form part of this project.)

   c. There needs to be a facility to log the number of visitors they have had on the web site.

   d. They want it to be a good source of information of the society's activities.

   e. They are hoping that people from all over the world will be able to contribute to research projects.

   f. The Association hopes that the Web site will increase sales of the books it advertises.

   g. The user wants to be able to update the site himself.

   h. People must be able to easily find the site when using a search engine.

2. **The general public**

   a. People need a site that loads quickly.

   b. They need a site that is easy to use, navigate around and understand.

c.   People need to know who to contact if they need further information.

d.   They must be able to easily get ordering information if they wish to buy a book.

e.   Visiting the site should be an interesting, pleasurable and rewarding experience.

f.   It should be possible to view the site using many different browsers and versions of browsers.

Web Site Design

There should be sufficient information in this section so that if you gave it to an experienced Web developer, they could create a site which matches the requirements specification.

The basic structure of the web site will be as follows:

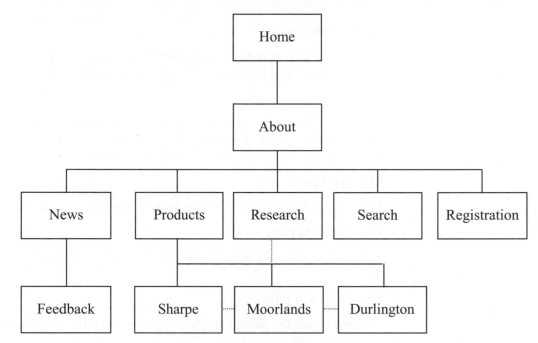

The web will use frames pages so that links to the pages on the second and third tiers of the structure will always be visible in a Contents frame down the left hand side of the page. This means that the user can go to any of these pages from any of the others if they want to. The Association name will also be permanently visible in a banner at the top of each page.

The problem here is that for an 'A' or 'AS' Level project you want to demonstrate knowledge of the advanced features of web design software, but some features will not be viewable in an older browser. Whatever you decide, you must justify your decision.

I discussed with the user the implications of using frames – i.e. that the use of frames would help to create a smart web site but that people with older browsers would not be able to view it. The user thought that most people would have fairly new browsers and that as this is not a commercial site it would not be too serious if a few people could not view it as intended.

There will be links from the About and Research pages to the Feedback page, indicated by the dotted lines. The Research page will also link to each of the three product pages, Sharpe, Moorlands and Durlington. There will also be links between each of these product pages.

E-mail links from the Product pages will provide the visitor with the ability to correspond directly with the authors of the books advertised. Clicking on an e-mail link automatically opens an e-mail program such as Microsoft Outlook Express.

The Home page

This page will display, without frames, a picture relating to the Association. The picture will act as a hyperlink to the rest of the site.

The About page

This page will display text about the Association and a hit counter telling users how many previous visits to the site there has been. It will have a scrolling marquee, dynamic text effects and a JavaScript Slide Show displaying photographs provided by the Association.

The Search page

This will be a built-in page from FrontPage's library of page templates. Its purpose is to search the site for a specified keyword and locate pages containing it.

The Registration page

This page will contain a form that users can fill in and submit to an on-line database created by FrontPage. The data entered by the user will automatically be saved in an Access database. See *Data Collection and Storage* below.

The News page

This page will contain any text on current activities and items of interest.

The Products page

This will act as a catalogue of the various products available, with links to each of them.

The Feedback page

This will allow the user to contribute any information about the current projects.

The Research page

This will have details of any research projects currently being undertaken by the association with links to books already published and the feedback form.

The Sharpe, Moorlands and Durlington pages

These pages will describe the different publications currently available.

Data Collection and Storage

The following data will be collected:

Title (This will be a combo box which will automatically validate it.)
Forename
Surname
Address
Post Code
Telephone
E-Mail Address
Areas of Specific Interest

FrontPage automatically saves the data on the Web server from where it can be downloaded to the user's computer. It can then be used in a mail merge operation.

Test Strategy

It is important to include user involvement in your test strategy. Clearly you could not hand over a completed Web site without the user having had an opportunity to see it, comment on it and ask for any changes they want made.

Each page and every link will be tested as the web site is developed. Some of the advanced features of the website will not work until it is published so this will be done relatively early on in development. Special features such as Java applets and HTML code can then be tested.

Further tests will be carried out using different computers with lower specification hardware and different browsers e.g. Netscape (most recent version), Internet Explorer 5, and earlier versions of each.

The user will be asked to log on to the published Web site and comment on any difficulties experienced, features that did not work as expected or additions that they would like made.

Test Plan and Expected Outcomes

The following tests will be carried out:

Be sure to include tests which relate to every point in the user requirements list. There are some missing here – for example using a search engine to find the site. You would lose a mark for this.

Test Number	Test	Method of Testing	Expected Outcome
1	Log on to the site	Log on using a browser and type in the web address.	Association's Home page is displayed
2	Page transitions	Click on the Home page or log on to the site	Page should fade in or out
3	Enter site	Click on the image on the Home page	User enters main site and should see the About page as the initial page displayed in the main section
4	Java applet	Open About page	Applet slideshow will be displayed
5	Site hyperlinks	Click on hyperlinks in Contents page	User should see chosen pages appear in Main section of page
6	Hit counter	Log on and open About page, note the number of hits. Exit site and re-enter	Number of hits increases by at least 1. (Someone else may have logged on while this is being tested!)
7	Rollover effects	Move mouse pointer over links in Contents page	Links should change colour

8	Hotspots on Research page	Click on different areas of the image map to check links	Each separate area will take the user to another page
9	Scrolling marquee and animated GIF	Open the News page	Scrolling marquee should display scrolling text. Question mark graphic should rotate
10	Dynamic HTML	Open the News page	Text should scroll in from the left
11	Feedback page	Send some test feedback	Test feedback will be received as an e-mail
12*	Registration and data collection (See test data below)	Fill in Registration form and submit test data	Test data will appear in Access table on server
13	Export data from server to offline Access database	Log on, open Registration database online and export Results table	Data will appear in Results table in HaspVisitor database offline
14	Buttons	Click on buttons on Products pages	Buttons will link to alternate product pages
15	Compatibility with different browsers	Open Web site using different browser software	Site opens satisfactorily
16	Compatibility with different hardware / resolution settings / screen sizes	Open Web on different machines	Site opens satisfactorily, and looks and feels the same.
17	Internal site search	Click on Search page and enter *Durlington* in search box	Site finds pages with Durlington mentioned
18	Download time	Open Web and surf through various pages	Time to download each page will be within reason
19	Bookmarks	Open a product page and click on the Ordering Information link	Page will jump to the bottom to show ordering information
20	E-Mail hyperlinks	Open a product page and click on the author's e-mail link	E-mail program will open with author's address in Send To box

You should
document the
appropriate invalid
data for testing all
of the validations
incorporated in the
form. Also test
special features like
multiple selection
combo boxes.
The test data
shown here does
not really explain in
sufficient detail
exactly what is
being tested and
why, and what the
expected outcomes
are.
Up to you to do
better!

* Test data for Registration form:

a. Mr, Richard, Puls, 7 Edingale Court, Bramcote, [omit required **Town** field].

b. Miss, Jasmine, [**Surname** blank], Vale House, Longridge, Preston.

c. Mrs, Rosemary, Richards, [**Street** blank], Bredfield, Ipswich.

d. Repeat test b, with **Surname** - Basnyet, area of special interest – Beckton.

e. Repeat test c, with **Street** – 14 Mill Lane, areas of special interest – Moorlands and Durlington.

Implementation

Selection of Hardware and Software

In this section, you must fully justify the chosen hardware and software facilities.

There are several packages that can be used to implement a web site including Dreamweaver, FrontPage and Word 2000. Dreamweaver is a very expensive, sophisticated package but is not available to me. Word 2000 does not have enough of the features required for me to implement the solution. FrontPage is available and has all the capabilities I need to fulfil the design specification.

I implemented the solution using the hardware that was available to me at home, namely a Pentium PC with a 17" monitor. This is a large high resolution screen and may result in the pages I design not being fully visible without scrolling on some smaller, lower resolution screens. The alternative is to design it on a smaller, lower resolution screen meaning that people with better screens will see a large blank area on the pages. It is impossible to cater for everyone in the best way and the user is satisfied with my proposed implementation hardware.

Summary of Implementation

The Web site was implemented using frames which permit common sections, such as the navigation bar or contents bar, to appear on every page. Although older versions of some browsers cannot display pages with frames, these versions are virtually obsolete these days.
The reason that frames were preferred is that they provided cohesion between the pages and always remain visible while the main content of the page is scrolled up or down independently.
The same cohesion can also be obtained with the use of shared borders rather than frames but these do not scroll independently of the main section, being part of the same page.

Project Log

(For the purposes of this book, the Project Log is included here. In practice you would probably include your handwritten log in an Appendix and refer the reader to the appropriate page at this point.)

Date	Work Done	Problems Encountered or resolved
8th Jan	Interview with President of Speymont Historical Association. Designed the basic web site. Scanned in photographs for the site provided by the President.	
15th Jan	Started the project using the Corporate Presence	I didn't like the look of it so decided to start

	Web Wizard.	*the web from scratch using my own designs.*
22nd Jan	*Inserted all of the links between the pages and added the rollover effects so they change colour when hovered over or clicked on.*	
29th Jan	*Designed the Products pages and inserted the scanned photos.*	*Scanned photos as .tif type graphics - file size was too big. Had to re-scan as .jpg which were far more compressed. This meant that web pages loaded more quickly.*
5th Feb	*Added button to the products pages and linked them to each other.*	*Buttons caused entire page to change rather than just the main frame. This was corrected by changing the target frame in the hyperlink properties.*
12th Feb	*Added hit counter, Java applet and other special features to enhance the site*	*Applet did not work.*
19th Feb	*Published the site, tested the search page.*	*Had trouble finding ISP with FrontPage Server Extensions. Search page did not work - will need to sort this out.*
23rd Feb	*E-mailed Paul at Lightspeed to consult him about Search Page, Java applet and database problems.*	*Paul explained what the problems were and I have now sorted them - see copy of e-mail below.*
26th Feb	*Created the registration forms to submit visitor data to an Access database.*	*Need to upload to Web for testing.*

28ᵗʰ Feb	Showed user the site. He tested all links and the Registration page. He did not think that the Search page added much to the site and it may be removed.	The Search page does not work. This is something that needs to be tweaked at the server end. All things considered, we may decide to remove it.
5ᵗʰ March	Finished final testing of the Web site.	
12ᵗʰ March	Wrote up user manual.	

E-mails to and from Web Host manager

Include any evidence in this section of problems with implementation and how you solved them, interactions with the user, web host etc

Paul,

The web site was working very well.

I tried to recreate the applet myself having seen what you had done but it doesn't work again.

I think that i am almost there but there is probably something very
small that i must have missed? I have changed the graphics it finds and the
height and width. The height and width of all the graphics are the same at 181 and 280 pixels. - same as applet.

Please could you find time to look at this.
Your help is very much appreciated,

Rob Heathcote

(Reply from Paul)
Paths again.

I'd put the html files in a sub directory and set the paths accordingly.
In particular the paths to the images were set as
../images/fader/koblenz.jpg, etc.

In plain English this means "go up one level (the .. bit) then down to
images, then down to fader, then down to koblenz.jpg"

Similarly, the path to the code base was set as
../java/

which means "go up one level then down to java"

You moved the files back into the root of the sub web. This means that

the paths specified in the html were no longer correct.
../images/fader/..... and ../java/ addressed folders in the
root of the main PG site. Folders that weren't there, hence
the blank applet of death.

Interestingly, if your site hadn't been a sub-web it wouldn't
have
mattered because going up one level from a root web is not
possible. The
code goes up as far as it can (to the root) and then works
down from
there (in effect it defaults to the root) and it would have
found the files.

I have set the paths to ./images/fader/..... and ./java/.
This means
"starting at the current directory (the single dot) go down
to images,
then down to fader, then down to the image in question".
With some
browsers it would work without the "./" prefix. However not
with all so it's recommended

Re the database.

It's better to create it on-line as it creates the global.asa
file
automatically with the correct links and so on for the server
the
frontpage web is hosted on. ODBC Data sources are a whole
tangled
subject in themselves. Frontpage takes care of most of it
without
bothering the user, building the global.asa file which
controls the
connection and so on. DO NOT Attempt to edit this file.
Data sources
are usually not portable between computers so your locally
produced data connection probably won't work on the server.

Regards
Paul

You can press Alt + Print Screen to put a picture of the screen on to the clipboard. This can then be pasted into your document where it can be cropped or sized.

Testing

Test 1: Log on to the site

As the user does not yet have an ISP (Internet Service Provider) the site has been published on the Payne-Gallway website at www.Payne-Gallway.co.uk/hasp.

Test 1: Logging on to the Web site

Page appears as expected.

Test 2: Page transitions

When the image on the Home page is clicked on, it will fade away to display the main site.

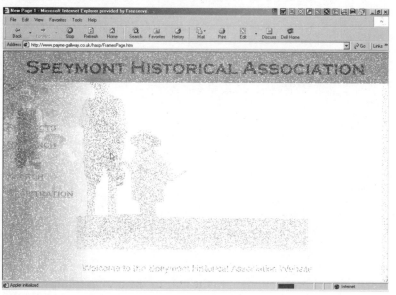

Test 2: Page Transition

Test 3: Enter site

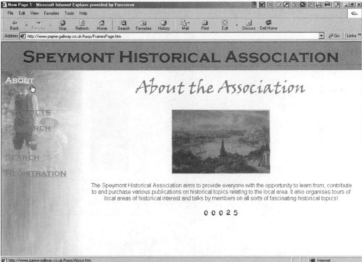

Test 3: Entering site to display About page

The site appears as expected and the About page is displayed first.

Test 4: Java applet

Test 4: Java applet displays a slideshow of 4 images

Document any corrective action you took when a test did not give the expected result. You can if you wish show a screenshot of the unexpected result and then the corrected version.

The screenshot shows a transition between two images in the slideshow.

I had a problem getting the Java applet running. To solve this I asked Paul, my ISP manager, to tell me what I had done wrong and he told me that I had the pathnames of the pictures wrong. (See e-mail in Implementation Section.)

Test 5: Site hyperlinks

All the links on the left side of the page work successfully. Links to some of the pages are slightly slow. This is owing to the speed of the modem and the graphics on the page. This problem will not be evident using more modern modems. The graphic files were also reduced by re-sampling them in FrontPage using the Resample button on the Pictures toolbar. This works by keeping the file size proportionate to the size of the picture on the screen – if the picture size is reduced, it can be re-sampled, thus reducing the file size and causing it to download more quickly.

One of the hyperlinks to the Feedback page caused the page to appear without its frame. This was fixed by changing the Target Frame setting in the Hyperlink Properties window to Main.

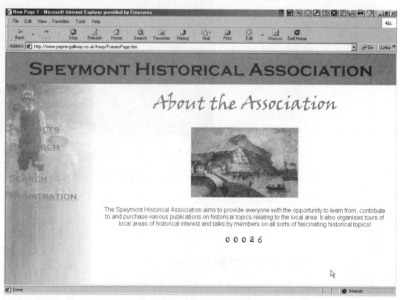

Test 5: Setting the Target Frame

Test 6: Hit counter

The site was logged on to and the number of hits was recorded as being 25 (See test 3). The site was re-visited and the hit counter had increased to 26.

Test 6: The Hit Counter

This only worked once the Web site had been published on a server supporting the FrontPage Server Extensions. The counter did not increase when I opened another page and returned to the About page. In fact, I had to log off altogether and log back on again to increase the hit counter.

Test 7: Rollover effects

Rollover effects are seen when the mouse cursor hovers over a link, clicks a link or visits a page via a link. The link in each case should change colour depending on what action has been taken. The unvisited link colour is not displayed because they have all been visited on this computer.

Link colour of visited page

'Mouse-over' link colour

Link colour of active page

Unvisited link colour not shown

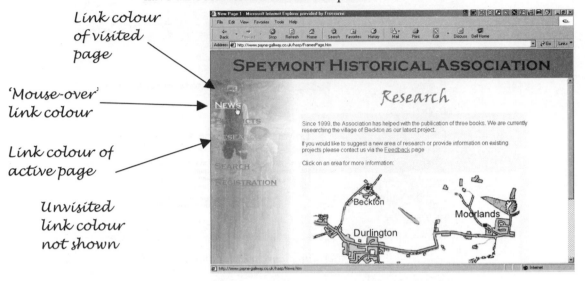

Test 7: Text Rollover Effects

Annotate your tests by hand to explain in more detail what is being tested in each screenshot.

In this site, the links begin as dark brown and change to light brown if they have been visited in the past. If the page associated with a link is currently visible, the link will turn gold. If the mouse is hovering over a link, it will turn a cream colour. This works successfully with all links.

Test 8: Hotspots on Research page

The hotspots on the map graphic worked well. They all linked to the appropriate pages and were in the right places. This could be seen in editing as well in a browser.

Mouse cursor over Moorlands area – Link to Moorlands page displayed in browser

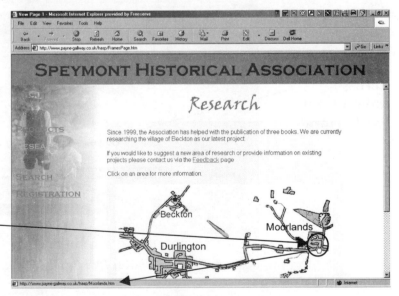

Test 8: Hotspots

Test 9: Scrolling marquee and animated GIF

The text in the marquee successfully scrolled across the screen repeatedly. The question mark graphic underneath the marquee rotates.

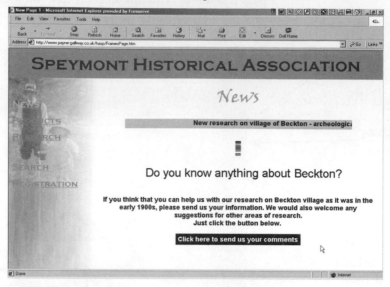

Test 9: Scrolling marquee and animated GIF

Test 10: Dynamic HTML

The sentence "Do you know anything about Beckton" wipes across the screen from left to right. This part is successful but unfortunately there seems to be no way to ensure that it is always in the centre of the screen, independent of the screen size or resolution.

Text wipes across screen from left to right

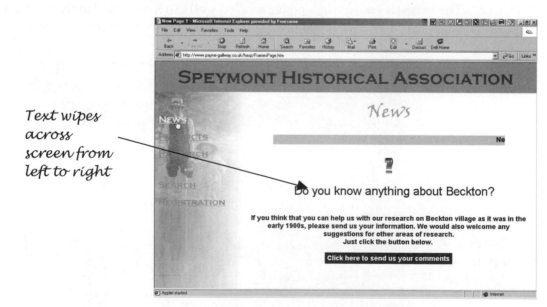

Test 10: Dynamic HTML

Test 11: Feedback page

A test message was entered into the Feedback page and submitted.

Test message entered into Feedback form →

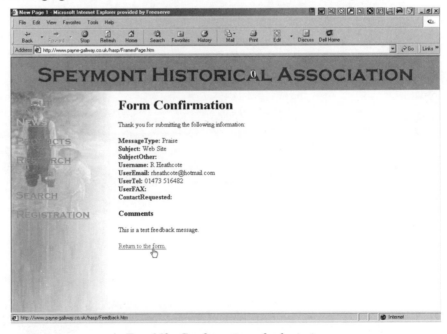

Test 11a: The Feedback page and test message

The message gave confirmation that it had been sent to the recipient.

Test 11b: Confirmation of submission

The recipient then received the message shortly afterwards.

Test 11c: Message received by recipient

Test 12a – 12e: Registration and data collection

Tests 12a to 12e should all be documented. 12b to 12d have been omitted here for resons of space in this book!

Test data has been chosen to test all of the validations and the effect of selecting one or multiple areas of interest. The first test highlights the effects of omitting the Town details and gives an error message when the user tries to submit the form.

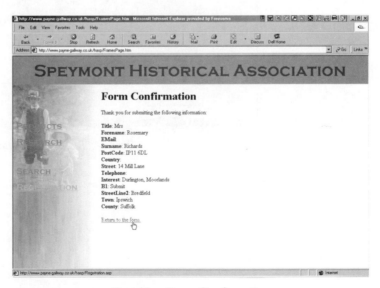

Test 12a: Validation message to show Town must be entered

Test 12e: Multiple areas of special interest

This test involved entering two different areas of interest. Both were submitted to the database.

Test 12e: Form Confirmation

Test 13: Export data from server to offline Access database

The test data was successfully exported to the HaspVisitor database.

	ID	Title	Forename	Surname	Street	StreetLine2	Town	County	PostCode	Country	E
	2	Mr	Richard	Puls	7 Edingale Cour	Bramcote	Nottingham	Notts	NG12 7BR		
	3	Miss	Jasmine	Basnyet	Vale House	Longridge	Preston	Lancs	PR14 7MS	United Kingdom	jbasny
▶	4	Mrs	Rosemary	Richards	14 Mill Lane	Bredfield	Ipswich	Suffolk	IP11 6DL		
*	(AutoNumber)										

Test 13: Export to offline database

Test 14: Buttons

The buttons at the bottom of each of the product pages successfully displayed the appropriate publication when clicked on, except one. This was subsequently fixed in the Hyperlink Properties box.

Test 14: Testing the buttons

Test 15: Compatibility with different browsers

The Web site was opened in Compuserve and NetScape. Both applications successfully displayed the website.

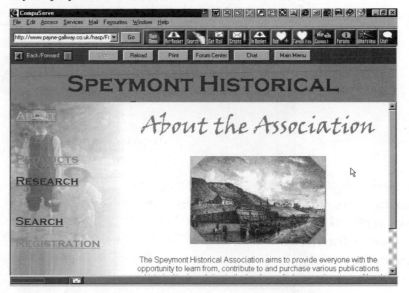

Test 15:The Web site displayed in CompuServe

Test 16: Compatibility with different hardware / resolution settings / screen sizes

The user will have to scroll sideways on some pages to see the full content. This is because a lower resolution screen was used and a smaller screen size. See screenshot above.

Test 17: Internal site search

This does not work because it requires the ISP to set up an indexing facility for your web site. The ISP has been contacted and it has been enabled but is not yet up and running. This is an extract of the e-mail from the ISP about indexing:

`Indexing.`

```
This is normally an option on setting up a FP / internet
information server (IIS site) Many ISPs don't select it
(it is unticked by default) because of the potential
(albeit minor) extra overhead. I have now enabled it for
you subweb but haven't quite got it working yet.
```

Test 18: Download time

All of the pages downloaded fairly quickly and did not cause me any frustration in waiting for them. The About page took the longest since it contains the Java applet which needs to be loaded.

Test 19: Bookmarks

The bookmarks on each of the products pages work successfully. Each of them take the visitor to the bottom of the page and the ordering information.

The Ordering Information bookmark takes the user to the information they need.

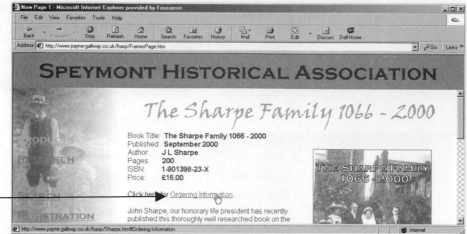

Test 19: Testing the bookmarks

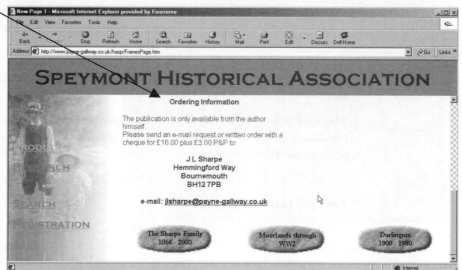

Test 19: The ordering information found by the bookmarks

Test 20: E-Mail hyperlinks

The e-mail address shown in test 19 was clicking on and the following screen appeared:

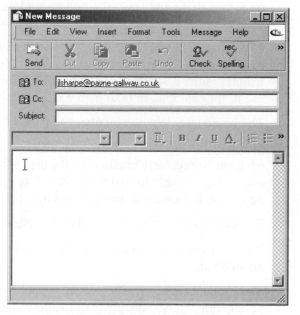

Test 20: E-mail hyperlinks

The e-mail address in the Web site was automatically entered as the 'mail to' address in the New Message window of the e-mail client on the computer.

User Testing

The user logged onto the Web site and thoroughly tested all the links. He also tested the Registration and Feedback pages. The Search page did not work and if the ISP cannot set the necessary parameters to make it work, I will remove this page as it does not really add anything to the site.

Evaluation

The Evaluation
Section should
include direct
reference to the
requirements
specification.
Identify any
limitations in your
solution.

The Web site has now been fully tested and is up and running. Visitors can register on the database and leave their name, address and area of specific interest. The data entered is validated as fully as possible.

The data can be retrieved from the server and stored on a database on the user's hard disk. However, this part of the project has not been further developed and would require a separate self-contained system to analyse the data, maintain it and use it, for example, in mail merge letters.

The hit counter logs the number of visitors to the site.

The web site has a news page which shows the society's current activities. This needs to be regularly updated by the user who is currently learning FrontPage. The site is fairly simple to maintain but will require modification when, for example, a new book is published. Buttons and new pages will need to be added.

The site loads within 10 seconds on a computer using a 28Kbs modem.

Various people have tried it out and found it fairly easy to use, navigate around and understand.

The Products state clearly who to contact for further information on various publications. It was decided not to allow visitors to buy books online because this is not a secure site and they would had to have provided their credit card details to make a purchase. This would pose a security risk.

The site has many features which make it interesting and maintain the visitor's interest, e.g. a slideshow, photographs, an animated gif and page transition effects.

It is possible to view the site with different browsers. However, using an older browser, the frames pages cannot be viewed and a text message is displayed to this effect. As this was discussed with the user before the design was finalised, this cannot be considered a major flaw. When viewed on a lower specification screen than the one on which the site was developed, the viewer must scroll horizontally and vertically to see the content of some of the pages. This is a drawback but the alternative would be to build a site whose pages only filled half the screen on higher resolution screens. In the end, I used the equipment that was readily available to me.

User Manual

You need to consider who the user is for a Web site project. As the site visitor is exceptionally unlikely to see your user documentation, it is safe to assume that the user is the person who has commissioned you to build the site!

The user manual is not a technical guide to using FrontPage, even if the user is going to be updating and maintaining the site.

Introduction

This Web site has been designed especially for the Speymont Historical Association. Its purpose is to provide information about its activities and collect names and addresses of people who would like further information.

Publications sponsored by the association are advertised on the site and visitors are invited to purchase one of these or contribute to current research.

The site was developed using Microsoft FrontPage 2000 on a Pentium PC. It has been published on the Payne-Gallway website as a sub web with the address www.payne-gallway.co.uk/hasp.

This manual explains the layout of the site, how to gather information entered by visitors to the site and how to update and republish the web.

The Home page

When a visitor first logs on to the site, they will see the Home page as shown below.

Figure 1: The Home page

The visitor can then click anywhere on the graphic to be taken to the About page in the main site.

The About page

The site is built using frames and the About page shows as one of four different frames on the page - the Banner, the Contents, the Main section (the About page), and the Frames page containing all three of these. Only the main section of the site changes when a link is clicked on – the Banner and Contents remain visible on every page visited.

Frames Page – This page will never actually be seen. It is the container in which the Banner, Contents and main page are held.

Contents Page – This page will always be visible and will contain many of the links to display other other pages in the main page.

Banner Page – This is currently active, indicated by the thicker border. This page is always visible.

Main page – This page will change according to which links are pressed on the Contents page.

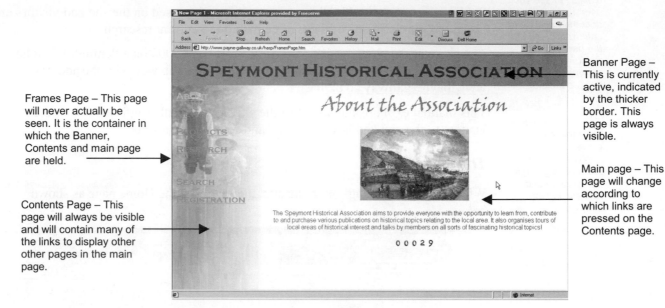

Figure 2: The main site

The page features a slide show of photographs collected by members of the Historical Association which automatically fade from one to the other.

The hit counter displays the number of visits that have been made to this site.

The News page

This page features a scrolling marquee in which you can add or change the text to advertise the latest activity or trip planned for the Association members. (See Technical Manual.)

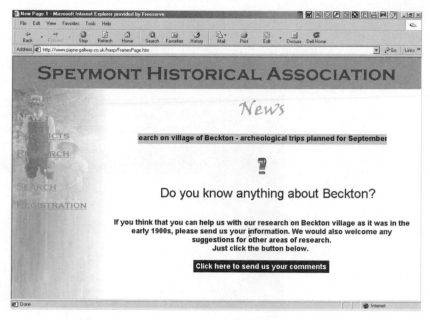

Figure 3: The News page

When the visitor clicks on the Hover button at the bottom of the page to send their comments, they will be taken to the page shown below: (The only other page that this page can be accessed from is the Research page.)

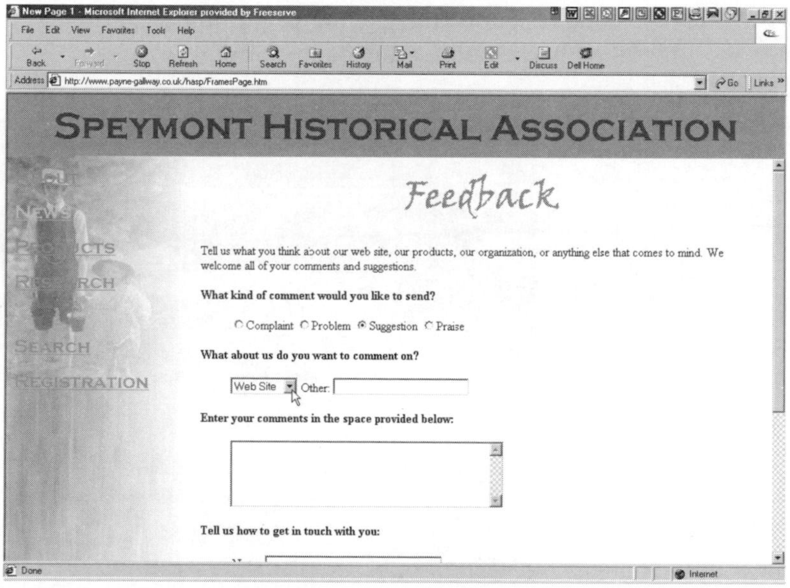

Figure 4: The Feedback page

Obtaining the visitor feedback

The feedback submitted by the visitors will automatically be e-mailed to you at info@payne-gallway.co.uk.

The Products pages

Clicking the Products link in the Contents list will take the visitor to the Products page. This describes and has links to all the current publications sponsored by the association.

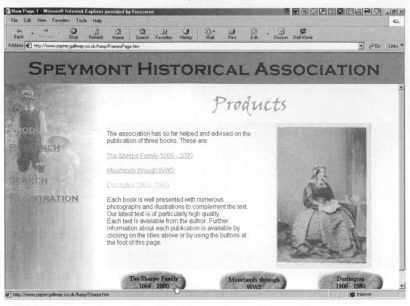

Figure 5: The Products page

The links in the main text of the page and the buttons at the foot will perform the same function and take the visitor to that particular publication. For example, see the Sharpe publication page below.

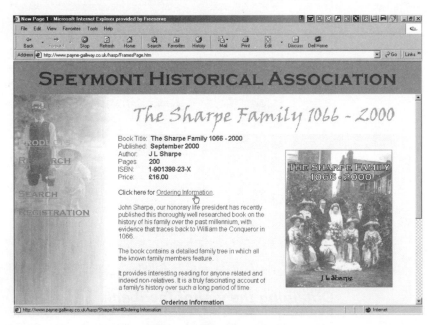

Figure 6: The Sharpe page

If the visitor clicks on the Ordering Information link, they will be taken lower down the page to an address and e-mail link to the author for further information.

Ordering Information

The publication is only available from the author himself.
Please send an e-mail request or written order with a cheque for £16.00 plus £3.00 P&P to:

**J L Sharpe
Hemmingford Way
Bournemouth
BH12 7PB**

e-mail: jlsharpe@payne-gallway.co.uk

Figure 7: Ordering Information

Clicking on the e-mail address will open an e-mail program installed on the visitor's computer such as Microsoft Outlook Express.

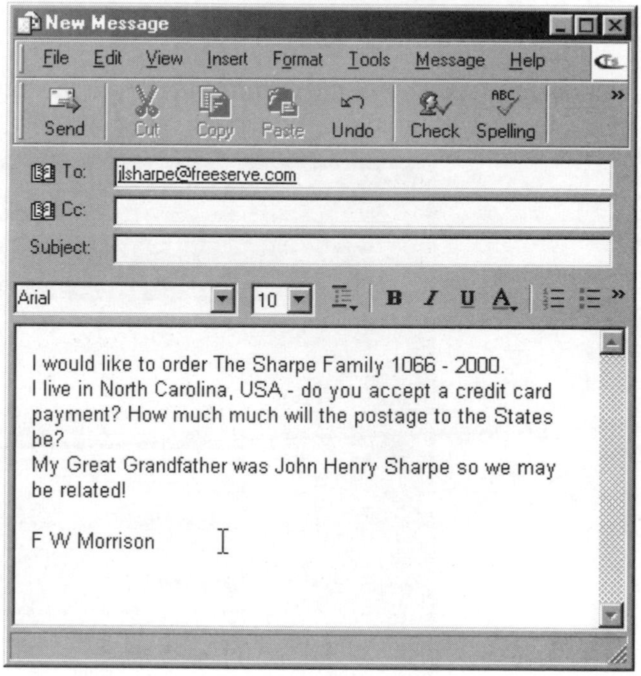

Figure 8: E-mailing the author

The Research page

The Research page displays a map of the local area. Hotspots on the map link the visitor to the various publications associated with the area they have clicked on.

If they click on an area for which there is no associated publication they will be taken to the Feedback page where they will have the opportunity to contribute their own ideas or comments.

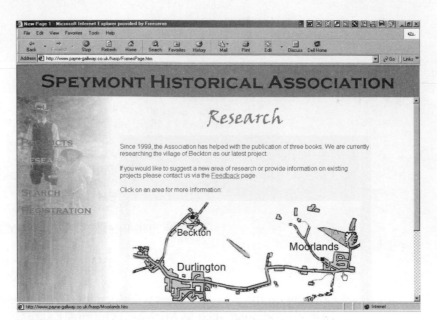

Figure 9: The Research page

The Search page

This page allows the user to enter a search string and search the site for the keywords entered.

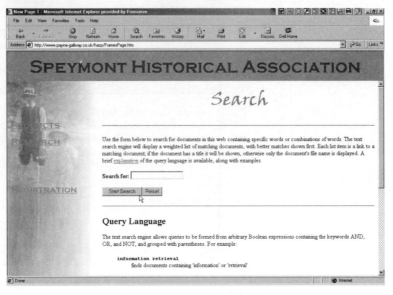

Figure 10: The Search page

The page should return links to pages containing text matching that entered in the search for box.

The Registration page

This page allows the user to enter their name, address and are of interest if they wish to receive further information from the Association. The data will be stored in an Access table on the Web and be downloadable to form the basis of a mailing list.

Using this table, a mail merge can then be created and sent out to all registered members.

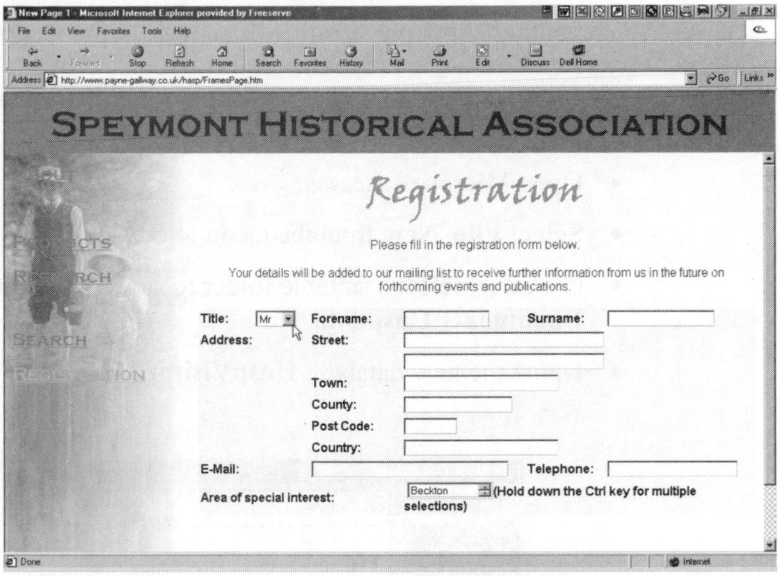

Figure 11: The Registration page

Once the visitor has completed the form, they must submit the data to the site using the Submit button. They will then get a confirmation message of the data sent.

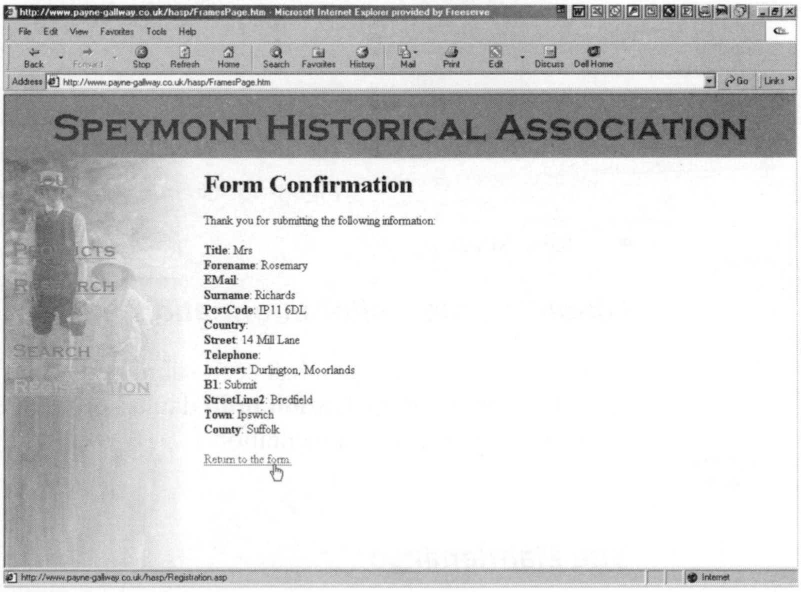

Figure 12: Form Confirmation

Creating a database to hold visitor registrations

The data that people submit will be kept in the **Registration** database on the web server. You will need to export this data, held in a table called **Results**, to a blank database on your computer. Before doing this for the first time, you must create a blank database on your hard disk. To do this:

- Open Microsoft Access.

- Select **File**, **New** from the menu to create the new database.

- Create or select a suitable folder to save the database in, e.g. **My Documents\Haspdata**.

- Name the new database **HaspVisitor.mdb**.

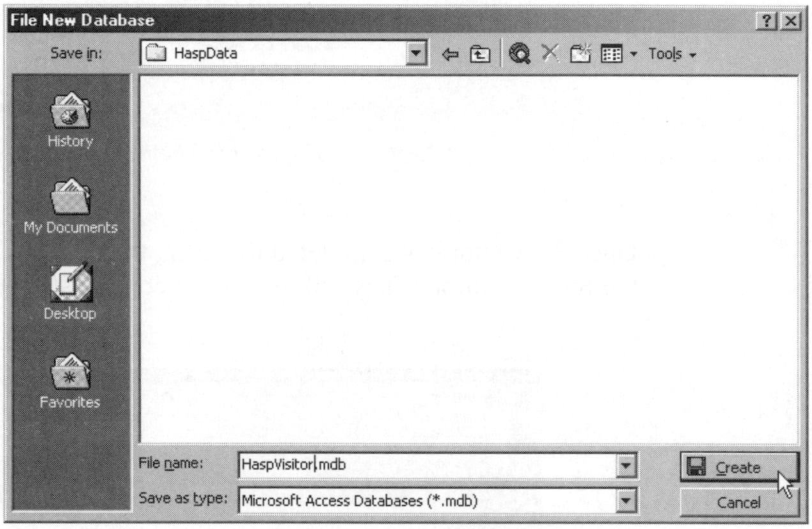

Figure 13: Creating a blank database

- Close Access.

Obtaining the visitor information

To get the information that has been submitted to the site, you will need to export the data from the **Registration.mdb** database stored on the Web server. (This does not form part of this documentation.)

If you are turning this into a major project, the database and mail merge will need to be documented. This project however, is only concerned with the development of the web site.

Site Maintenance

If you encounter any problems in maintaining this web site, please call A. Student on 01473 123456.

Appendix B
AQA Project Guidelines

19 Guidance for Setting Centre-Assessed Component

19.1 AS Module 3

Coursework: Task Solution   In the AS Module 3 project, emphasis will be on the full exploitation of particular generic application software and the advanced facilities available within them. The project will be a self-contained problem. The emphasis in the project will be on the candidate's ability to produce a high quality implementation to the problem.

It is anticipated that teachers will introduce candidates to problem-solving techniques involving the use of a range of generic software facilities. These will include relational databases, spreadsheets, document processing, desk top publishing, multi-media presentations and graphics packages. However, teachers may well wish to introduce other types of software or packages and are encouraged to do so.

For successful completion of this module, candidates will be expected to devise and test a solution to a task-related problem that provides them with adequate scope to employ appropriate and advanced package skills. **The criteria are so devised as to genuinely provide an opportunity for candidates to learn and progress throughout the duration of the project rather than only provide an assessment point at the end of the module.** The standards expected from this project are to be maintained but, the software tools for completion of the work are not restricted to a single package. Candidates should focus on the issue of "appropriate tools for the task" and if this requires the use of facilities from two or more generic packages then this is deemed to be wholly appropriate.

Great emphasis in the marking criteria has been placed on the issue of planning for testing, the methods of completing this testing and assessment of results, and, while the main focus remains on the acquisition and use of software skills, candidates are required to show an appreciation of whether their solution is appropriate in the context of the problem and for the IT solution as a whole.

In completing a project, the candidate will be required to undertake the following processes.

> The definition of a problem in information technology terms.

> The derivation or specification of information technology tasks.

> The completion of appropriate design work from which to implement the solution.

> The determination of a schedule of activities.

> The determination of a plan for testing, which should be clearly documented.

> The implementation and testing of a solution, which will involve the use of advanced functionalities of the package(s) in the most efficient way to achieve the desired results.

> Evaluation of the solution against the requirements of any potential user.

Candidates are required to provide a written commentary of these processes in document form.

Specification

The following comments on the method of assessment should be read with reference to the module specification and the assessment criteria.

From a clear statement of the problem to be solved, with background information, there should be an appropriate specification given. This specification, depending on the problem area, should reflect the end-user's requirements of the solution, the desired outcomes (as an implementation free specification) and any constraints or limitations on the development of the solution, e.g. human and physical resources.

The input, processing and output needs, which match the requirements specification, must be clearly stated, although the format of this section will vary according to the software solution available. For example, a database solution will need a database design from which to complete the project.

Before implementation, the candidate should produce an appropriate test strategy. This should address the elements which need to be completed as progress is made towards the solution, the type of test to be carried out and the desired outcome from which success or otherwise can be measured.

In addition, an effective and full testing plan should be devised. The testing plan should include, for each element, the test data to be used, the reasons why this data has been selected and the expected outcomes.

From this section, the candidate is expected to have a clear understanding of the exact nature of the problem to be solved and the steps that will be needed to achieve this solution. The candidate should be aware of the need for testing, to be able to select appropriate tests for the various stages and be clear on the success criteria for those stages.

Implementation and Testing

The ultimate goal of these sections is for the candidate to produce an effective solution to be problem stated. This is one which satisfies the requirements specification and specifically, can be operated in the proposed environment and the interface provided maps well to the skills of the intended end-user. It is expected that the candidate will make sensible and appropriate use of data capture and validation procedures, data organisation methods, output contents and formats and user interfaces. This will of course be dependent upon the software selected and/or available for the completion of the solution.

It is very much in the spirit of this specification that candidates will implement and test in a modular fashion and that the evidence for this aspect, and that of the Testing section, may well be presented together. Candidates are expected to consider the limitations of not just the whole solution but individual aspects and gain further credit by identifying improvements, designing new test criteria, implementing and testing again as the project develops.

For example, on completion of part of a project where data is input, it may become apparent that validation is needed where none was previously considered. Further credit is then available if the candidate corrects this, implementing an improved version and making appropriate tests.

This approach is designed to be more conductive to candidates learning throughout the duration of the coursework whilst still providing an appropriate form of assessment.

Documentation is expected on the implementation work completed, which will contribute to the assessment of whether the candidate fully employed their package specific skills in an effective and appropriate manner. Also, that the selections of the chosen hardware and software facilities have been fully justified in relation to the solution developed. The project log recommended in the specification for module 3 is expected to contribute towards the evidence for this aspect.

The results of any testing activities should be fully documented with hard copy evidence available, where practicable, this being cross-referenced to the original test plans.

Evaluation

A written evaluation is expected at the conclusion of the project. This should reflect the candidate's own awareness of the effectiveness of their solution in meeting the initial requirements specification. The candidate, regardless of success, is expected here to show an awareness of the criteria for a successful information technology solution and how well their solution maps to the selected criteria. This assessment should discuss any remaining limitations of the solution and the reasons for these constraints.

User Guide

The candidate is expected to produce extensive user documentation which is appropriate for the solution and also the hardware and software available. This may include on-line help in some format in addition to paper-based user guides and manuals. It should cover all aspects that are relevant to the solution but it is expected that this will always include normal operation of the software solution and common problems that have been found to occur along with the solutions. Regardless of the nature of the user guides or help provided, the material presented should always be appropriate to the needs of the end-user.

20   Assessment Criteria

20.1	Introduction	
	Assessment of project work	It is necessary to provide a structure for the assessment of project work so that all teachers are, in general, following a common procedure. Such a procedure will assist with the standardisation of assessment from centre to centre. Each project is therefore to be assessed in accordance with the criteria set out below. In assessing candidates, centres must ensure that comparable standards are observed between different teaching groups. Each centre must produce a single order of merit for the centre as a whole.
20.2	Criteria for the assessment of Unit 3	The following categories are to be used in the assessment of the project. The criteria for marking these categories are listed below. The project is marked out of a total of 60.

Specification	13 marks
Implementation	20 marks
User Testing	12 marks
Evaluation	6 marks
User Documentation	9 marks
Total	**60 marks**

Specification (13 marks)

11-13
A detailed requirements specification has been produced for the identified problem, which matches the needs of the stated end-user(s).
The input, processing and output needs, which match the requirements specification, are clearly stated.
Effective designs have been completed which would enable an independent third party implementation of the solution.
An appropriate test strategy has been determined. An effective test and full testing plan has been devised. The testing plan includes the test data and expected outcomes and directly relates to the requirements specification.

8-10
A detailed requirements specification has been produced for the identified problem, which matches the needs of the stated end-user(s).
The input, processing and output needs, which match the requirements specification, are stated.
Designs have been completed but lack detail so as not to allow an independent third part implementation of the solution or, are inefficient in relation to the problem stated.
A test strategy has been determined and testing plan have been devised but are limited in scope or do not relate to the requirements specification stated.

4-7
A requirements specification has been produced for the identified problem but does not fully match the needs of the stated end-user(s) or lacks detail and clarity.
The input, processing and output needs are stated but do not fully match the requirements' specification or are not sufficiently clear.
Design work has been attempted but is incomplete and does not reflect an efficient solution to the problem stated.
A test strategy has been determined but is either incomplete or does not relate to the requirements specification stated. The testing plan is either vague or missing.

1-3
The requirements specification is vague or missing.
The input, processing and output needs are only vaguely considered or are absent.
There is little or no design effort.
The test strategy and testing plan are vague or missing.

0
The candidate has produced no work.

Implementation (20 marks)

16-20   An effective solution has been developed which is operable in the proposed environment by the intended end-user.

Appropriate data capture and validation procedures, data organisation methods, output contents and formats and user interface(s) have been used.

Generic and package specific skills have been fully employed in an effective and appropriate manner.

The selection of the chosen hardware and software facilities has been fully justified in relation to the solution developed.

11-15   A solution has been developed which is operable in the proposed environment by the intended end-user but has some inefficiencies.

There is evidence of the use of some appropriate data capture and validation procedures, data organisation methods, output contents and formats and user interface(s).

Generic and package specific skills have been fully employed but not always in an effective and appropriate manner.

The selection of some of the chosen hardware and software facilities has been justified in relation to the solution developed.

6-10   A partial solution has been developed, but those aspects completed are useable by the intended end-user.

There is some evidence of the use of some data capture and validation procedures, data organisation methods, output contents and formats and user interface(s).

Generic and package specific skills have been employed but not always in an effective and appropriate manner.

The selection of some of the chosen hardware and software facilities has been only vaguely justified in relation to the solution developed.

1-5   A solution has been developed which is very limited and is not practically operable in the proposed environment by the intended end-user.

Few, if any, data capture and validation procedures, data organisation methods, output contents and formats and user interface(s) have been used.

The generic and package specific skills used are simplistic and/or were not always applied appropriately.

The selection of the chosen hardware and software facilities are not justified in relation to the solution developed.

0   The candidate has not implemented the system.

Testing (12 marks)

9-12   The test strategy and test plan previously devised have now been followed in a systematic manner using typical, erroneous and extreme (boundary) data.

The results of testing are fully documented with outputs cross-referenced to the original plan. Corrective action taken due to test results will be clearly documented.

5-8   The test strategy and plan devised have been followed in a systematic manner but using only normal data.

The results of testing are partially documented with some evidence of outputs cross-referenced to the original plan.

There is some evidence of corrective action taken due to test results.

1-4   The test strategy and plan devised have been followed in a limited manner using only normal data.

There is little or no documentation of the results of testing.

There is little or no indication of corrective action required due to test results.

0   There is no evidence of testing.

Evaluation (6 marks)

4-6   The effectiveness of the solution in meeting the detailed requirements specification has been fully assessed with the candidate showing full awareness of the criteria for a successful information technology solution.
The limitations of the solution have been clearly identified.

1-3   The effectiveness of the solution in meeting the original requirements specifications has only been partly assessed with the candidate showing only partial awareness of the criteria for a successful information technology solution.
The limitations of the solution are vague or missing.

0   There is no evidence of evaluation.

User Documentation (9 marks)

7-9   There is extensive user documentation for the solution which covers all relevant aspects including normal operation and common problems and is appropriate to the needs of the end-user.

4-6   A user guide is present which describes the functionality of the solution and is appropriate to the needs of the end-user.

1-3   A limited user guide is present which describes only the basic functionality of the solution.

0   There is no evidence of user documentation.

Index

'A' Level ICT (2nd Edition)

by P.M.Heathcote

March 2000   384 pp   ISBN 0 9532490 8 5

This text, updated for the 2001 syllabus, is suitable for a wide range of ICT courses including 'A' Level, Advanced VCE (GNVQ), HNC and first year degree courses in Information Technology and numerous other courses having an ICT element or module. It explains how and why computers are used, and how information systems can help people make decisions and solve problems. Computer hardware, software and applications are covered in a clear and interesting manner and over fifty case studies are used to illustrate the concepts covered.

This comprehensive yet concise textbook covers all the topics studied for the AQA 'A' Level course in ICT. Each chapter covers material that can comfortably be taught in one or two lessons, and the chapters are sequenced in such a way that practical sessions can be based around the theory covered in class. Exercises and questions from past exam papers are given at the end of each chapter. The answers and a complete set of OHP masters can be downloaded from our web site.

"An excellent, clearly written, comprehensive 'A' Level text, also useful for GNVQ and undergraduate IT."
Roger Taylor, PGCE IT Coordinator, Brunel University.

'AS' Level ICT

by P.M.Heathcote

March 2000   224pp   ISBN 0 9532490 9 3

This 'AS' Level ICT textbook comprises modules 1, 2 and 3 of **'A' Level ICT** described above.

Tackling Computer Projects in Access with Visual Basic for Applications (3rd edition)

by P.M.Heathcote

March 2000   200pp   ISBN 1 903112 22 2

This is the third edition of the text previously published by Letts. It will help students on a Computing course to complete a project in MS Access, using version 2, 7, or 2000. It covers database design, creating tables, forms and subforms, queries, importing and exporting data to other packages, analysing and processing data, reports, and programming in Visual Basic for Applications. It includes advice on choice of projects and a sample project.

Computing Projects in Visual Basic

by Derek Christopher

Aug 2000   224pp   ISBN 1 903112 33 8

This book has been written mainly for students of AS/A level Computing, 'A' level ICT and Advanced VCE ICT. It assumes no knowledge of programming and covers everything needed to write a large program. Students on other courses of a similar standard, such as BTEC National, and first year HND and degree courses, should also find the material useful.

Software:

Algorithms and Data Structures (2nd Edition)
by P.M.Heathcote and E.Morgan

Published March 1st 1998. Site Licence £90.00 (plus VAT)
ISBN 0 9532490 1 8

This highly popular interactive package can be loaded and run on a network and gives students approximately 10 hours of interactive tuition on how to tackle problems involving data structures. It contains 6 units covering Programming fundamentals, Sorting and Searching, Linked Lists, Queues, Stacks and Trees. A seventh unit tests students on the concepts they have learned.

A Level Computing Interactive Revision
by P.M.Heathcote and E.Morgan

Published March 1st 1998. Site Licence £70.00 (plus VAT)
ISBN 0 9532490 2 6

This popular interactive Revision Aid for A Level Computing contains 12 modules, each consisting of a quiz on one area of the syllabus. A full explanation is given to the student after each question is attempted. A random 10 questions from the bank of 30 questions on each topic are given each time a student attempts a quiz, and the score can be recorded each time on the student's own disk.

Hundreds of centres have already discovered the benefits of our two computer-aided learning packages, written especially for 'A' Level Computing students and unique in the market! The packages are straightforward to install and run, offer excellent value for money and keep students interested and motivated.

The software is supplied on 3½" disks for Windows 3.1, 95, 98, NT Server or 2000 / Me (not MacOS). Schools and colleges may order both the above packages for the special price of £140.00 plus VAT.

Consult our Web site www.payne-gallway.co.uk *for latest news on titles and prices.*

Inspection copies of books and a free disk containing a demonstration version of both 'Algorithms and Data Structures' and 'A Level Computing Interactive Revision' are available from our distributors:

BEBC Distribution
P.O. Box 3371
Poole, Dorset
BH12 3LL

Tel: 01202 712909   Fax: 01202 712913   E-mail: pg@bebc.co.uk